COMING SOON

To Scott and Kimberly Hahn
with profound gratitude and love

MICHAEL BARBER

COMING SOON

Unlocking the Book of Revelation

and Applying Its Lessons Today

Steubenville, Ohio
A Division of Catholics United for the Faith

Emmaus Road Publishing
827 North Fourth Street
Steubenville, Ohio 43952

Printed in the United States of America
15 14 13 8 9 10 11

Library of Congress Control Number: 2005929577
ISBN: 1-931018-26-X
ISBN: 978-1931018-26-5

Cover design and layout by
Beth Hart

Cover artwork:
Raphael, *The Disputa of the Sacrament*

Nihil Obstat: Rev. James Dunfee, *Censor Librorum*
Imprimatur: ✠ R. Daniel Conlon, D.D., J.C.D., Ph.D., Bishop of Steubenville
February 21, 2005

CONTENTS

Abbreviations

The Old Testament
Gen./Genesis
Ex./Exodus
Lev./Leviticus
Num./Numbers
Deut./Deuteronomy
Josh./Joshua
Judg./Judges
Ruth/Ruth
1 Sam./1 Samuel
2 Sam./2 Samuel
1 Kings/1 Kings
2 Kings/2 Kings
1 Chron./1 Chronicles
2 Chron./2 Chronicles
Ezra/Ezra
Neh./Nehemiah
Tob./Tobit
Jud./Judith
Esther/Esther
Job/Job
Ps./Psalms
Prov./Proverbs
Eccles./Ecclesiastes
Song/Song of Solomon
Wis./Wisdom
Sir./Sirach (Ecclesiasticus)
Is./Isaiah
Jer./Jeremiah
Lam./Lamentations
Bar./Baruch
Ezek./Ezekiel
Dan./Daniel
Hos./Hosea
Joel/Joel
Amos/Amos
Obad./Obadiah
Jon./Jonah
Mic./Micah
Nahum/Nahum
Hab./Habakkuk
Zeph./Zephaniah
Hag./Haggai
Zech./Zechariah
Mal./Malachi
1 Mac./1 Maccabees
2 Mac./2 Maccabees

The New Testament
Mt./Matthew
Mk./Mark
Lk./Luke
Jn./John
Acts/Acts of the Apostles
Rom./Romans
1 Cor./1 Corinthians
2 Cor./2 Corinthians
Gal./Galatians
Eph./Ephesians
Phil./Philippians
Col./Colossians
1 Thess./1 Thessalonians
2 Thess./2 Thessalonians
1 Tim./1 Timothy
2 Tim./2 Timothy
Tit./Titus
Philem./Philemon

Heb./Hebrews
Jas./James
1 Pet./1 Peter
2 Pet./2 Peter
1 Jn./1 John
2 Jn./2 John
3 Jn./3 John
Jude/Jude
Rev./Revelation (Apocalypse)

PREFACE

Of all the biblical books about which to write, why would anyone ever choose Revelation? After all, it's so complicated! Well, the need for this kind of book was made clear to me after I taught two Bible studies in southern California. Almost three hundred people came to the weekly studies to hear John's Apocalypse explained. It soon became clear that, while most people remain uninterested in Scripture in general, they are very curious about the Apocalypse.

Most people *ought* to begin their Scripture studies with a Gospel or the Book of Genesis. Unfortunately, many people unfamiliar with the Bible have a hard time getting excited about reading these books. Yet these same people are often fascinated with the Apocalypse. Whether this is your first Bible study or just one more in a long series, it's my prayer that once you see the glorious riches of the Book of Revelation, you will be eager to learn more about the rest of Scripture. And once you learn more, that you'll keep coming back to this wonderful book, as I do.

INTRODUCTION

It's Greek to Me

"Revelation" in Greek literally means "unveiling." But if the last book of the Bible is supposed to contain the unveiling of God's plan, we might be tempted to insist, "Put the veil back on!" Dragons, beasts, horsemen, a killer lamb—it's almost too much to bear. It's scary, it's frightening—and it's many people's favorite biblical book.

In fact, although Hollywood has virtually abandoned biblical movies (not to mention biblical morals!), our corner theaters display the names of "apocalyptic" movies week after week on their marquees. How many times have we seen it? The end of the world is coming because Kirk Cameron has discovered that he is among those "left behind" after the rapture. The world will end unless Arnold Schwarzenegger is able to prevent a woman from being impregnated with the seed of the Antichrist at the end of the millennium. Or (my personal favorite) an ancient Sumerian god is about to come to New York City in the form of a five hundred-foot Stay-Puft Marshmallow Man to destroy the world (starting with Bill Murray and Dan Akroyd).

All of these movies, as well as scores of others like them, show that our culture is fascinated with the end of the world. But somehow I'm skeptical that such films will point us in the right direction. Does the coming of a giant marshmallow man really have anything to do with the unveiling of God's plan?

Read the Book, Don't Wait for the Movie

What is the *real* message of Revelation? Who are the four horsemen, the twenty-four elders, and the 144,000? What are we to make of the thousand-year reign, the four living creatures, and the sea of glass? Well, that's what this book is for.

In this book, we will take an in-depth look at the Apocalypse. Chapter by chapter, verse by verse, we will move through this difficult and confusing book of the Bible. Along the way, we will steer clear of fanciful interpretations by faithfully following the criteria laid out by the *Catechism of the Catholic Church* and the Second Vatican Council for studying Scripture:

The content and unity of Scripture: We will look at the Book of Revelation in the context of the rest of the Bible, seeing how its message fits into God's fatherly plan (the *oikonomia*).

The Church's living Tradition: The Book of Revelation cannot be properly understood without seeing its relationship to the Church's Tradition, as passed on through her liturgy.

The analogy of faith: As we consider the concepts and images presented in this book, we will remain faithful to the teachings of the Church, using them to guide us to faithful interpretation.[1]

Rest assured: The Holy Spirit inspired the human authors of Scripture, and He helps us to understand Scripture as the Faith is passed on through the life of the Church, particularly in her liturgy and in her teaching authority.

Keeping It Simple

I have done my best to keep the main text of this book as free from academic jargon as possible. This book is intended for anyone who wants to learn what the Book of Revelation is all about. I have provided a little background knowledge in those instances where it is necessary.

Whenever anyone attempts to explain a book like Revelation, readers often wonder whether the interpretation that is laid out can be backed up by credible sources or whether it is simply the result of the creativity of the author. Recognizing that other Catholics who strive to be faithful to the Church might come up with different interpretations of Revelation, I have done my best to provide extensive support in the endnotes for the positions I have taken in this book. At any rate, the notes at the end of the book are available for those who wish to dig a little deeper and study John's Apocalypse more extensively. But don't get bogged down in the endnotes! Use them if you need them, but don't try to read them all. This book is not as complicated as it may look.

Chapter One

HOLY GHOST WRITER

Who Wrote the Apocalypse and When?

Will the Real John Please Stand Up?[1]

One of my father's favorite musical groups is a Christian vocal ensemble called "Acappella." I remember listening to their incredible harmonies as a teenager—fascinated by just how low their voices could go. The bass parts sounded as deep as any instrument I have ever heard. If you turned it up loud enough, everything would rumble. My favorite song was probably "John the Revelator."

But who is this John the Revelator, who authored the Book of Revelation? Some modern scholars challenge the notion that John was the "revelator." Others, while agreeing that John is the author, disagree as to the identity of this John. Was it John the Apostle, or was there another John who merely shared the same name?

The proponents of the "other John" theory of authorship point to several passages in the works of the early Church Fathers that appear to speak of another John. For example, Eusebius of Caesarea, the great historian of the early Church, quotes Papias (AD 60 or 70–*c.* 125): "And again, if anyone came who had been a follower of the Elders—what was said by Andrew, or by Peter, or by Philip, or by Thomas or James, or by John or by Matthew, or any other of the Lord's disciples, and what Aristion and the *Elder John* say . . ."[2] In this passage Papias seems to identify two separate Johns who were active in the leadership of the Church.[3]

Eusebius (*c.* 206–*c.* 339) accepts the existence of another John, but he bases his conclusions primarily on the writings of Papias. Saint Jerome also accepts the existence of the other John. However, he believes that John the Apostle is the author of the Apocalypse.[4]

Saint Dionysius of Alexandria (*c.* 190–*c.* 265) argues for authorship by a John other than the disciple.[5] Yet his conclusion is based not on history, but on his analysis of the style of the Gospel of John, in contrast with the Book of Revelation. This stylistic difference will be discussed in more detail later.

To say that this second John was the author of Revelation is problematic, however, for even many of those who knew of John the Elder still held that the Apostle John wrote the Apocalypse. Concluding that this second John wrote the Book of Revelation does not necessarily follow from the ancient evidence.

In fact, the earliest Christian sources tell us that John the Apostle wrote the Book of Revelation. These include authors such as Saint Justin (AD *c.* 100–*c.* 165), Saint Irenaeus (*c.* 140–*c.* 202), Saint Clement of Alexandria (*c.* 150–*c.* 215), Origen (*c.* 185–*c.* 254), Tertullian (*c.* 160–*c.* 220), Saint Hippolytus (*c.* 170–*c.* 236), Epiphanius of Salamis (*c.* 315–402), and Saint Jerome (*c.* 340–*c.* 420).[6]

A Johnny Come Lately?

Moreover, it seems highly unlikely that anyone other than an apostle could write with such authority to seven different churches in Asia Minor. This is especially true if John the Apostle had authority over the churches in this region at the time, as a well-attested ancient tradition suggests.[7] Indeed, who would dare write to John's churches, overstepping the apostle, to explain how things should be set in order?

The Book of Revelation is very different from the other writings of the New Testament. It is the only work of an apocalyptic genre that is in the New Testament. There were other apocalyptic writings, such as the Apocalypse of Peter, in circulation at the time. Yet, only the Apocalypse of John was widely accepted, because it was commonly seen as having apostolic authority. Other apocalyptic works, which were deemed not to have been written by an apostle, were discarded.

It is hard to believe, then, that the writer of Revelation, who assumes a position of authority over seven different churches, and who presents himself as one with special authority from the Lord, is not an apostle.[8]

A Matter of Style?

Many scholars argue that Revelation is significantly different from the Fourth Gospel; therefore, the same John could not have written it. The first scholar who made this case was the third-century theologian Dionysius. As we shall see below, this position is not sufficient to dismiss the book as authentically Johannine—that is, written by John the Apostle.

For one thing, authors often employ different styles when writing. Before Karol Wojtyla became Pope John Paul II, he wrote a story called *The Jeweler's Shop*. This work is absolutely nothing like *Fides et Ratio*, his encyclical on the relationship between faith and reason. Yet no one concludes that different men must have written these two works. Likewise, if a journalist, while out in the field, wrote a love letter to his wife, we would certainly hope it would not read like typical newspaper prose. Stylistic differences between the two works, then, are not sufficient to deny that they are written by the same author.

Furthermore, although the two books are very dissimilar stylistically, there are many interesting literary parallels. In fact, many concepts and ideas found in the Fourth Gospel are also found in the Apocalypse:

—Jesus as the Word (Jn. 1:1, 14; Rev. 19:13)
—Jesus as the Lamb (Jn. 1:29, 36; Rev. 5:6, 8, 12, etc.)
—Christian worship as something done "in the Spirit" (Jn. 4:23; Rev. 1:10)
—Salvation as the gift of "living water" (Jn. 4:14; Rev. 21:6)
—Jesus as the Giver of true manna (Jn. 6:48–50; Rev. 2:17)
—The Mother of Jesus as the Mother of all believers (Jn. 19:26–27; Rev. 12:17)
—The Bridegroom and the Bride (Jn. 3:29; Rev. 19:7, 21:2, 9)

—The call to love not our lives even unto death (Jn. 12:25; Rev. 12:11)
—Satan being "cast out" (Jn. 12:31; Rev. 12:9)
—The Mother of Jesus being called "Woman" (Jn. 2:4; Rev. 12:1, 5)
—Jesus as the true temple (Jn. 2:21; Rev. 21:22)
—Christ as Shepherd (Jn. 10:1–16; Rev. 7:17)[9]

One can understand, then, why those who lived closest to John knew him as not only "Saint John the Evangelist" (the Gospel writer) but also "Saint John the Revelator."

Double Dating

Determining the date of the writing of the Apocalypse is of critical importance to interpreting it. Today, most hold that the book was written in the 90s during the reign of the Emperor Domitian, who ruled from AD 81 to 96.[10] A growing number of scholars, however, have come to the conclusion that it was written decades earlier, sometime before the destruction of the Jerusalem temple in 70.

Those who espouse the view that the Apocalypse was written in the 60s, during the reign of Nero, also have ancient evidence to support their hypothesis. The Syriac version of the Book of Revelation begins by stating that it was "written in Patmos, to which John was sent by Nero Caesar." Also, another Syriac work, *The History of John, the Son of Zebedee,* asserts that Nero exiled John.[11]

Since proponents of the variant dates for the writing of the Apocalypse can point to early Church writings to champion their views, other factors must be examined to fix an accurate date.

Seizure by Caesar

While Revelation scholars disagree about the date the book was written, there is strong agreement that it was written in a time of persecution (see Rev. 1:9; 2:10; 12:11; 13:15). This is supported in the writings of the Church Fathers. For example, Clement of Alexandria says that John wrote the Apocalypse while on the island of Patmos, where he had been banished by a "tyrant."[12]

Although the political situation for Christians was difficult in the 90s under Domitian, some scholars believe that there is no evidence that any widespread imperial persecution took place under him.[13]

A Little Caesar Story

While there are questions concerning the extent of Domitian's persecutions, it is clear that Nero, who reigned from 54 to 68, was notable for his tyrannical persecutions. Numerous writers from the period document Nero's unquenchable thirst for blood. The Roman writer Pliny describes him as "the destroyer of the human race," "the poison of the world," and "the enemy of mankind."[14] According to Apollonius of Tyana, he was "commonly called a tyrant."[15] Tacitus relates that he "put to death so many innocent men."[16]

Death and destruction followed Nero from his rise to his fall. He came from a family known for its cruelty. Another Roman historian, Suetonius, tells us that Nero's father was "hateful in every walk of life."[17] At the age of twelve, Nero sought the prosecution and ruin of his own brother and aunt. His mother, Agrippina, schemed to advance him into high places of power, and she may have been the one who poisoned the previous emperor, Claudius.[18]

When he came to power at the age of seventeen, Nero poisoned his own brother. He later had his mother killed and was responsible for the deaths of his childhood tutors. He had his first wife exiled and then beheaded. While his second wife was pregnant with his son, he kicked her to death. His perverse sexual appetites are also well documented.[19]

In the year 68, a fire broke out in Rome; it was commonly believed that Nero himself set it. He blamed the Christians for the fire and launched the first major imperial persecution of the Church. Saints Peter and Paul were among those martyred during his persecution.[20] In a chilling description, Tacitus relates how Nero amused himself with the torture of early believers: "Mockery of every sort was added to their deaths. Covered with the skins of beasts, they were torn by dogs and perished, or were nailed to crosses, or were doomed to the flames and burnt, to serve as night-ly illumination, when day had expired. Nero offered his gardens for the spectacle, and was exhibiting a show in the circus. . . . [T]here arose a feeling of compassion; for it was not, as it seemed, for the public good that they were being destroyed."[21]

Nero eventually committed suicide, lamenting in self-pity, "What an artist the world is losing!"[22]

Although Domitian was a tyrant, he failed to reach the levels of cruelty set by Nero. Since scholars agree that Revelation was written during a time of persecution, and since there are questions about Domitian's actions, the evidence indicates that the book was likely written during the Neronic period.

Beast of Burden

Another source for determining which tyrant was responsible for banishing John is the very text of the Book of Revelation. Exploration of the internal data of the document helps us best set the date of Revelation during Nero's reign.

For example, in Revelation 17, we read about seven hills, which symbolize seven kings: "The seven heads are seven hills on which the woman is seated; they are also seven kings, five of whom have fallen, one is, the other has not yet come, and when he comes he must remain a little while" (Rev. 17:9–10). The seven hills clearly refer to Rome, which was built on seven hills. The seven kings likely refer to seven Roman emperors. Josephus, Suetonius, and other ancient historians list the first seven emperors as follows:

1. Julius Caesar	46–44 BC
2. Augustus	27 BC–AD 14
3. Tiberius I	AD 14–37
4. Gaius Caesar (Caligula)	37–41
5. Claudius I	41–54
6. Nero	54–68
7. Galba	68–69[23]

Interpreting the passage in the light of this list, I believe that Nero was reigning at the time Revelation was written. Galba, then, is the seventh king, the one whom John prophesied would reign for only "a little while" (Rev. 17:10).

Another possible indication that the Book of Revelation was written in Nero's time is the number of the beast, the infamous "666" (Rev. 13:18). Just as the Romans used letters for numbers (e.g., I = 1, V = 5, X = 10), the Israelites used the Hebrew alphabet for numbers. When the Greek form of the name "Nero Caesar" is transliterated into Hebrew and converted into numerals, it adds up to 666. Further evidence that the early Christians understood "666" to indicate Nero can be seen in the fact that some ancient manuscripts of Revelation have the variant numeral 616 instead of 666. This number also points to Nero because when the Latin form of the name "Nero Caesar" is transliterated into Hebrew and converted into numerals, it adds up to 616.[24]

Here Comes the Judge

There is another compelling argument for the early dating of the Book of Revelation that can be found in reading the text. The sacred writer conveys a sense of urgency, giving a clear message that Jesus is coming soon. Saint John writes:

—"The revelation of Jesus Christ, which God gave him to show to his servants *what must soon take place*" (Rev. 1:1).
—"[T]he time is *near*" (Rev. 1:3).
—"The Lord . . . has sent his angel to show his servants *what must soon take place.* And behold, *I am coming soon*" (Rev. 22:6–7).
—"Do not seal up the words of the prophecy of this book, *for the time is near*" (Rev. 22:10).
—"Behold, *I am coming soon*" (Rev. 22:12).

Yet we still await the Second Coming two thousand years later. Was Jesus wrong? The answer to this question is key to understanding Revelation and will help us understand when the book was written and why.

* * *

Multiple Choice

1. Scholars generally agree that the Book of Revelation was written during a time __________.
(a) of persecution
(b) of great famine
(c) of peace
(d) of a solar equinox

2. The Caesar who persecuted the Church with the most hatred was ___________.
(a) Julius
(b) Galba
(c) Domitian
(d) Nero

3. "666" is the numeric value of the Hebrew name of ____________.
(a) Satan
(b) Nero
(c) Magog
(d) it doesn't equal the value of any name

4. According to the way ancient historians counted the Caesars, Nero was the ________ Emperor.
(a) first
(b) second
(c) sixth
(d) last

5. The city of seven hills is __________.
(a) Jerusalem
(b) Ephesus
(c) Rome
(d) Egypt

Answers 1. a; 2. d; 3. b; 4. c; 5. c

Discussion/Study Questions

1. How does understanding the original situation of those who read the Book of Revelation help us better apply it to our lives? (See pages 1–2)

____

____

____

____

2. Name some of the similarities between John's Gospel and the Apocalypse. (See page 3)

____

____

____

____

3. Why do some scholars think that the Book of Revelation was written during the 90s, during the reign of Domitian? What reasons are there for dating the book to the reign of Nero (the 60s)? (See pages 4–6)

____

____

____

____

Chapter Two

THE END OF THE WORLD AS WE'VE KNOWN IT

The Importance of AD 70

Was Jesus Wrong about the End of the World?

As we saw at the end of the last chapter, the Apocalypse clearly teaches that Jesus is "coming soon" (Rev. 22:20). As a matter of fact, the imminent return of Jesus is a major theme not only of Revelation, but also of the entire New Testament. Yet the world keeps turning, and over twenty-one centuries later we keep praying, "Come, Lord Jesus!" This has led some scholars to speculate about the "delay" of Jesus' coming. They argue that perhaps Jesus simply got it wrong—maybe He wasn't coming back as soon as He thought.

Some have tried to get around this problem by pointing to 2 Peter 3:8, which reads, "[W]ith the Lord one day is as a thousand years, and a thousand years as one day." They try to explain that with this sense of "soon," Jesus was thinking "long term"—admittedly, very long term. Unfortunately, this explanation does not make sense of Jesus' words. He tells His own contemporaries, "[T]he sun will be darkened, and the moon will not give its light, and the stars will fall from heaven, and the powers of the heavens will be shaken; then will appear the sign of the Son of man in heaven, and then all the tribes of the earth will mourn, and they will see the Son of man coming on the clouds of heaven with power and great glory" (Mt. 24:29–30). Jesus then says, "Truly, I say to you, this generation will not pass away till all these things take place" (Mt. 24:34). *Gene*, the Greek word that means "generation," refers to a period of forty years.[1] Since Jesus died around the year 30, He predicted that "all these things [would] take place" by 70.

This prediction seems to pose a problem. The last time I checked, the stars were still securely tucked away in the sky, the moon was still giving forth light, and the sun had yet to burn out. Nearly twenty centuries later, the world is still here. So if Jesus said that the world would end in one generation, either He was wrong, or we are misunderstanding what He meant.

To understand these words of Jesus in Matthew 24:34, we must examine how this sermon began. If we turned to the beginning of Matthew 24, we would see that Jesus' teaching concerning the last days began as a response to the apostles, who were marveling at the splendor of the Jerusalem temple: "Jesus left the temple and was going away, when his disciples came to point out to him the buildings of the temple. But he answered them, 'You see all these, do you not? Truly, I say to you, there will not be left here one stone upon another, that will not be thrown down'" (Mt. 24:1–2).

Jesus' words about the last days, therefore, must be interpreted in this larger context. But what does the destruction of the temple have to do with the end of the world?

Using Common Senses

One of the reasons people have a hard time making sense of the Bible is that they do not realize that the Bible has several layers of meaning. These layers of meaning are known as the four senses of Scripture. By understanding how these four senses work, we can come to a much better appreciation of the Bible.

The *Catechism of the Catholic Church* identifies these four senses: "According to an ancient tradition, one can distinguish between two *senses* of Scripture: the literal and the spiritual, the latter being subdivided into the allegorical, moral and anagogical senses. The profound concordance of the four senses guarantees all its richness to the living reading of Scripture in the Church" (no. 115; emphasis in the original).

To help us understand the Book of Revelation, we shall examine these four senses.

Literally Confused

Let's start with the literal sense. Do we mean that everything in Scripture must be taken literally? Of course not. The literal sense refers to the literary or historical meaning intended by the authors. Our job in reading the Bible is to discover how the biblical writers intended their words to be understood. Sometimes, they intended to relate historical facts; other times, they intended to write poetry; and still at other times, they intended to recount a parable, a story with a deeper meaning. We can't interpret every passage in the same way. Making that mistake would have unfortunate consequences.

Take, as an example, the Song of Solomon. In this book, Solomon describes his beloved. Consider carefully his words in chapter 3. He says, "Behold, you are beautiful, my love, behold, you are beautiful!" (Song 3:1). Okay, so far so good. She's beautiful.

But is she really so wonderful? Listen to what he goes on to say. "Your navel is a rounded bowl that never lacks mixed wine. Your belly is a heap of wheat, encircled with lilies. Your two breasts are like two fawns, twins of a gazelle" (Song 7:2–3). Solomon also says that his beloved's eyes are "doves" (Song 4:1), that her hair looks like a "flock of goats" (Song 6:5), and that her teeth are like "shorn ewes that have come up from the washing, all of which bear twins, and not one among them is bereaved" (Song 6:6). If you ask me, this woman isn't beautiful—she's frightening!

Of course, I'm being facetious. Solomon didn't really mean to say that his beloved had sheep in her mouth. It's poetry. It wasn't meant to be taken "literally." We must try to understand these passages the way they were meant to be interpreted. Their literal sense, then, is the beloved's beauty—which is described poetically in metaphors.

Thus, the literal sense is not always the same as the "literal meaning." At the same time, we must affirm that the biblical authors often intend to relate actual historical events. The Second Vatican Council, for example, teaches that the Gospels recount what Jesus "really did and taught."[2] Just as we can wrongly interpret some passages too literally, we can also fall into the trap of "spiritualizing" other passages by saying that they do not describe real events.

The literal sense is the foundation of all the other senses. One cannot study the spiritual senses (the allegorical, the moral, and the anagogical) unless one begins with the literal. Pope Pius XII taught that when interpreting the Bible, the "foremost and greatest endeavor should be to discern and define clearly that sense of the biblical words which is called the literal."[3]

History as His Story

The Bible doesn't work like our modern history books do. It gives us theological history—history from God's point of view. The Bible's purpose isn't to tell us when the kings of every major dynasty lived (although it sometimes does list such dynasties), which years major battles occurred (although it often does record such battles), or intricate scientific details. Rather, the Bible tells the story of how God fathers His Family through history. The *Catechism of the Catholic Church* uses the word the early Church Fathers had for this fathering process: *oikonomia* (no. 236).[4]

God is the Author of all history, which He fashions for the salvation of the world. When humans write books, we use words to signify realities. "Book" refers to the thing you are now holding in your hand; "chair" refers to a thing in which you may be sitting at this moment. God "writes" the world as men write books—except, instead of using only words, He can use historical realities to signify other historical realities.

An example is the Passover. There was once a real Passover in Egypt that saved Israel from real bondage—a Passover at which a real lamb was really slaughtered and eaten. This historic event prefigures another moment in history—the sacrifice of Christ as the true Passover Lamb, who died to set us free from bondage to sin. As God makes historical events prefigure other events in salvation history, He reveals Himself as the Lord of history.

Sensing Something Spiritual

Now we come to the spiritual senses: the allegorical, the moral, and the anagogical. The *allegorical* sense refers to the way in which Christ fulfills the Old Testament in Himself, the *moral* sense, to the way Christ leads us to act justly, and the *anagogical* sense, to the way Christ brings all things to fulfillment in Himself and in heaven (*Catechism*, no. 117).

For example, the literal-historical sense of the temple is the building that stood in Jerusalem. Christ fulfilled the temple allegorically in Himself, since His body is the true temple (Jn. 2:21). Paul illustrates the moral sense of the "temple" when he writes: "Do you not know that your body is a temple of the Holy Spirit within you, which you have from God? You are not your own; you were bought with a price. So glorify God in your body" (1 Cor. 6:19–20). Because Christians are temples of the Holy Spirit (1 Cor. 3:16), we are called to act morally. Finally, the Book of Revelation tells us how the anagogical fulfillment of the earthly temple is "the Lord God the Almighty and the Lamb" (Rev. 21:22).

And so we can see how "temple" illustrates the four-fold sense of Scripture:

Literal sense
–the historical / literary meaning
–the temple structure

Allegorical sense
–referring to fulfillment in Christ
–Christ is the true Temple

Moral sense
–how Christ brings fulfillment in Himself through the Church
–the Church and its members are temples of the Holy Spirit

Anagogical sense
–how Christ brings fulfillment in Himself through bringing the Church into heavenly glory
–the Church in heaven dwells in the Heavenly Temple—God Himself

While it is important to distinguish the literal sense from the spiritual senses, one must be careful not to overlook the inner connections between them. In fact, the literal sense of many New Testament passages is also a spiritual reading of Old Testament passages. For instance, when Jesus "spoke of the temple of his body" (Jn. 2:21), the literal meaning encompasses the allegorical sense. There the literal sense is Christ's explanation of how He is the true Temple.

Why the Temple Meant the World to Israel

Now we are ready to look more closely at Jesus' words. Why did Jesus describe the end of the world when he predicted the destruction of the temple (Mt. 24:1–2)? The answer is connected to the way God "writes" the world.

To ancient Israel, the temple was a miniature model of the world. When Moses built the tabernacle (a mobile temple) and Solomon built the temple itself, they did so in "sevens"—seven days, seven months, seven years. Why? They imitated the way God created the world in seven days. In fact, the Book of Job describes creation in terms of temple building (Job 38:4–7). The temple is a scale model of the world, and the world is one giant temple.[5]

The temple meant the world to Israel—literally. The temple was the symbol of the world. For Jesus and the people of Israel in His day, then, the destruction of the temple symbolized the end of the world. That is why Jesus' sermons on the end of the world are always given in the context of a prediction of the destruction of Jerusalem and its temple.

And Jesus was true to His words. In AD 70, about forty years after He ascended back into heaven, Jerusalem and its temple were destroyed. With this event, the ritual order of the Old Testament came to a definitive end. The temple sacrifice and the Old Testament priesthood were no longer possible. Jesus was right—the end came within one "generation" (Mt. 24:34).

Furthermore, Christians heeded Jesus' warning: "Then let those who are in Judea flee to the mountains, and let those who are inside the city depart" (Lk. 21:21). The early Christians escaped from Jerusalem and fled to Pella just before the Roman legions arrived to besiege Jerusalem. Not a single Christian perished.

Moreover, Jesus' warning to flee Jerusalem can also be understood spiritually as an admonishment to abandon the obsolete temple sacrifices. Now that He has come and has offered Himself as our sacrifice, there is no longer the need for the Levitical system of priestly sacrifice. Jesus is saying: "Don't be attached to it, but flee!"[6]

Coming Soon?

Was Jesus mistaken? Of course not. But what of the image of the "sun being darkened," the "moon not giving light," and the "stars falling from heaven" (Mt. 24:29)? The sun is still shining brightly, and the moon is still giving light. The stars, too, are still in the sky. So how, in these instances, has Jesus' prophecy been fulfilled?

We have to understand what Jesus' prophecy meant to those who heard Him in the first century. The sun, moon, and stars were important for measuring days, months, and years; the ancients used them to tell time. To say that they would fall from the sky and be darkened was like saying, "Your time is up!" The same image is used in the Book of Isaiah, where God describes His coming judgment on Edom: its time was up (Is. 34:4, 10).

According to the Book of Revelation, Jesus is "*coming* soon" (Rev. 22:20). In the Old Testament, God's "coming" often entails His judgment. For example:

—"Behold, the LORD is riding on a swift cloud and *comes* to Egypt; and the idols of Egypt will tremble at his presence, and the heart of the Egyptians will melt within them" (Is. 19:1).

—"For behold, the LORD is *coming* forth out of his place to punish the inhabitants of the earth for their iniquity, and the earth will disclose the blood shed upon her, and will no more cover her slain" (Is. 26:21).

—"'Now it is I who speak in judgment upon them.' Behold, he *comes* up like clouds, his chariots like the whirlwind; his horses are swifter than eagles—woe to us, for we are ruined!" (Jer. 4:11–13).

The Jewish leaders and those who went along with them rejected Jesus and therefore would face God's judgment—His "coming." Jesus has strong words for them:

> Woe to you, scribes and Pharisees, hypocrites! for you build the tombs of the prophets and adorn the monuments of the righteous, saying, "If we had lived in the days of our fathers, we would not have taken part with them in shedding the blood of the prophets." Thus you witness against yourselves, that you are sons of those who murdered the prophets. Fill up, then, the measure of your fathers. You serpents, you brood of vipers, how are you to escape being sentenced to hell? Therefore I send you prophets and wise men and scribes, some of whom you will kill and crucify, and some you will scourge in your synagogues and persecute from town to town, that upon you may come all the righteous blood shed on earth, from the blood of innocent Abel to the blood of Zechariah the son of Barachiah, whom you murdered between the sanctuary and the altar. Truly, I say to you, all this will come upon this generation. O Jerusalem, Jerusalem, killing the prophets and stoning those who are sent to you! How often would I have gathered your children together as a hen gathers her brood under her wings, and you would not! Behold, your house is forsaken and desolate. (Mt. 23:29–38)

The year 70, then, was truly a kind of "second coming," wherein Jerusalem was judged.[7] It marked the end of the world as Jesus' hearers knew it.

Once we appreciate the significance of the year 70, we are in a much better position to understand the message of Revelation. As we have seen, it is reasonable to believe that the book was written sometime in the late 60s, during the reign of Nero, before the cataclysmic events of 70. So when John says that Jesus is "coming soon," he could well be prophesying the destruction of Jerusalem.

All Have Sinned

At this point a few important remarks about anti-Semitism must be made. John is not anti-Semitic; nor is he anti-Jewish. After all, Jesus was a Jew! Mary was a Jew! In fact, John tells us that "[m]any of the Jews . . . believed in Him" (Jn. 11:45). Even though some of the Jewish leaders persecuted the early Church, others were tolerant of the first Christians. Paul's teacher, the great Rabbi Gamaliel, urged the people to leave the Christians alone (Acts 5:33–40).

Anti-Semitism is despicable and thoroughly anti-Christian. After all, "we are all spiritual Semites."[8] The Fathers of Vatican II articulated the Church's clear condemnation of anti-Semitism: "Furthermore, in her rejection of every persecution against any man, the Church, mindful of the patrimony she shares with the Jews and moved not by political reasons but by the Gospel's spiritual love, decries hatred, persecutions, displays of anti-Semitism, directed against Jews at any time by anyone."[9] Whenever we speak, then, of the judgment of the year 70, we in no way condone anti-Semitism. We must affirm the Old Testament teaching that Israel is God's "first-born son" (Ex. 4:22).

Jerusalem's destruction is a warning to any city or nation that rejects God and persecutes His people. The lesson God wants to teach us is that all are subject to His judgment. If *even* the Chosen People can be judged, nobody is safe.

The biblical narratives again reveal that anti-Semitism is groundless. Israel sinned because it wanted to be "like the nations" (Ezek. 20:32; cf. Ezek. 25:8; 1 Sam. 8:20; 2 Kings 17:15). How much more sinful, then, are the nations—the Gentiles—than the Jews!

Come Again?

If these predictions of Jesus were fulfilled in the first century, does this mean there won't be an end of the world? Of course not. The year 70 is a dress rehearsal for the real thing. The destruction of Jerusalem symbolizes the end of the world and teaches us the lessons we need to prepare for it.

What relevance does Revelation have for us today? In the next chapter, we'll see how you and I, very soon, will witness the return of Jesus. He is coming—and soon.

* * *

Multiple Choice

1. After speaking of the sun being darkened, the moon not giving light, and the stars falling from heaven, Jesus said that His words would be fulfilled _________.
(a) in one generation
(b) in 2000 years
(c) at the end of time

2. The word for "generation" denotes __________.
(a) ten years
(b) thirty years
(c) forty years
(d) seventy years

3. Jesus' sermon on the end times in Matthew 24–25 begins when the apostles ask Him about ________.
(a) Herod
(b) the temple
(c) Caesar
(d) the Eucharist

4. Match the following sense of Scripture to its meaning: Literal___, Allegorical___, Moral/Tropological___, and Anagogical___
(a.) refers to how things are fulfilled in Christ
(b.) refers to how Christ leads us to act justly
(c.) the "literary"/ historical meaning
(d.) refers to the way Christ brings all things
to fulfillment in heaven

5. The temple was a model of _________.
(a) Solomon's palace
(b) the world
(c) nothing

Answers: 1. a; 2. c; 3. b; 4. c, a, b, d; 5. b.

* * *

Discussion/Study Questions

1. What is the connection between the end of the world and the destruction of the temple in AD 70? (See page 16)

____

____

____

____

2. What is the "*oikonomia*"? (See page 14)

____

____

____

____

3. Explain what "the stars falling from the sky" meant to the ancients? (See page 17)

____

____

____

____

4. Explain why the literal sense does not necessarily imply a "literal" interpretation. (See page 13)

____

____

____

____

5. Why is seeing the message of the Apocalypse as describing the destruction of the temple contrary to anti-Semitism? (See page 19)

____

____

____

____

REVELATION'S MASS APPEAL
The Liturgy of Heaven

"Altar-ier" Motifs

If Revelation is speaking about something that happened nearly two thousand years ago, what relevance does it have for us today? Is there really going to be a Second Coming? If so, when will it be?

Let's take things one at a time. While Jesus did prophesy about the destruction of Jerusalem,[1] its fall is not the end of the story. As stated before, the destruction of the temple is a symbol for the ultimate end of the world. The destruction of the temple points us forward to a time when Jesus will return. Paul tells us in 1 Thessalonians that the Lord is coming back to raise the dead and lead us into the heavenly kingdom: "For the Lord himself will descend from heaven with a cry of command, with the archangel's call, and with the sound of the trumpet of God. And the dead in Christ will rise first; then we who are alive, who are left, shall be caught up together with them in the clouds to meet the Lord in the air" (4:16–17).

Of course, this passage says nothing of people being "left behind" as a result of the rapture, a concept that is prevalent in some Protestant circles. The word "rapture" never even occurs here, nor does it occur anywhere else in the whole Bible. Although the Church does not accept this Protestant view of the rapture, she does teach that Christ will come again at the end of time, raise the dead, and take all the saints, body and soul, into heaven. As the *Catechism* says, "Though already present in His Church, Christ's reign is nevertheless yet to be fulfilled 'with power and great glory' by the king's return to earth [Lk. 21:27; cf. Mt. 25:31]" (no. 671).

Thus Christians have prayed from the earliest times, "From thence He will come again to judge the living and the dead." Yet there's also much more the Apocalypse shows us.[2]

The Book of Revelation is unique among all ancient "apocalyptic" books. While other apocalyptic books might mention an altar or the temple, none of them feature liturgical themes as prominently as Revelation.[3] Revelation is full of liturgical images: chalices, incense, hymns, altars, priests, etc. In fact, Cardinal Ratzinger calls the Apocalypse "the book of the heavenly liturgy, which is presented to the Church as the standard for her own liturgy."[4]

In his widely acclaimed book, *The Lamb's Supper*, Scott Hahn lists a number of things familiar to Catholics from the Mass that are also found in the Apocalypse:

Sunday worship *1:10*
A high priest *1:13*
An altar *8:3–4; 11:1; 14:18*
Priests (presbyteroi) *4:4; 11:15; 14:3; 19:4*
Vestments *1:13; 4:4; 6:11; 7:9; 15:6; 19:13–14*
Consecrated celibacy *14:4*
Lampstands (Menorah) *1:12; 2:5*
Penitence . . . . *ch. 2 and 3*
Incense *5:8; 8:3–5*
The book, or scroll *5:1*
The Eucharistic Host *2:17*
Chalices . . . . *15:7; ch. 16; 21:9*
The Sign of the Cross (The tau) *7:3; 14:1; 22:4*
The Gloria *15:3–4*
The Alleluia *19:1, 3, 4, 6*
Lift up your hearts *11:12*
The "Holy, Holy, Holy" *4:8*
The Amen *19:4; 22:21*
The Lamb of God . . . . *5:6 and throughout*
The prominence of the Virgin Mary *12:1–6; 13–17*
Intercession of angels and saints *5:8; 6:9–10; 8:3–4*
Devotion to St. Michael the Archangel *12:7*

Antiphonal chant *4:8–11; 5:9–14; 7:10–12; 18:1–8*
Readings from Scripture *2–3; 5; 8:2–11*
The priesthood of the faithful *1:6; 20:6*
Catholicity, or universality *7:9*
Silent contemplation *8:1*
The marriage supper of the Lamb . . . . *19:9, 17*[5]

We can also identify the Mass in the very structure of the Book of Revelation. Revelation can be divided into three parts. First, there are seven letters calling for repentance (Rev. 2–3). Next, there is a book with seven seals, which is opened, unleashing seven judgments (Rev. 4–11). Finally, seven chalices are poured out, climaxing with the marriage supper of the Lamb, where the Church is united to Christ (Rev. 12–22). Here we have something analogous to the Liturgy. First we have the Penitential Rite, in which we repent of our sins. After this, we celebrate the Liturgy of the Word, where the Scriptures are opened and read. Finally, we celebrate the Liturgy of the Eucharist, where the Church is united to Christ through the celebration of the Lamb's Supper.[6]

The Book of Revelation, then, shows us that the coming of the Lord is inseparable from the liturgy. It is in Eucharistic celebration that the Lord truly comes to the Church. In fact, the word used in the New Testament for the Lord's "coming" is *parousia.* Interestingly, the primary meaning of the word *parousia* is not "coming" but "presence." Truly the Lord's coming is found in the Real Presence of the Blessed Sacrament. Cardinal Ratzinger explains, "Every Eucharist is Parousia, the Lord's coming."[7]

Double Meaning

What would jokes be without "puns"? Take this one. A piece of string walks into a bar and says, "Give me a cold one." The bartender points to a picture of a string on the wall with a line crossed through it and says, "Sorry, we don't serve your kind here." The piece of string goes outside, gets all tangled up and tatters his ends by rolling around, and comes back in. The bartender says, "Didn't

I just tell you that we don't serve strings?" The string responds, "No, I'm a frayed knot."

Puns are important for understanding the Bible. John especially liked to use words with double meanings. For example, in John chapter 3, Jesus uses the word *pneuma*, which can mean either "spirit" or "wind." In speaking about the spiritual rebirth of Baptism, through which man is born of "water and Spirit," He uses the double meaning of this word to explain the invisible work of the Holy Spirit. "The wind [*pneuma*] blows where it wills, and you hear the sound of it, but you do not know whence it comes or whither it goes, so it is with everyone who is born of the Spirit [*pneuma*]" (Jn. 3:8).

John does something similar in the Apocalypse. In Revelation 1:10, he tells us on which day of the week he saw the visions contained in Revelation: "I was in the Spirit on the Lord's day." What is the "Lord's day"? On one hand it's the day that the Lord will come in judgment, foretold by the prophets and known as the "Day of the Lord." Consider some of the following prophecies:

—"Wail, for *the day of the LORD* is near; as destruction from the Almighty it will come! . . . Behold, the day of the LORD comes, cruel, with wrath and fierce anger, to make the earth a desolation and to destroy its sinners from it" (Is. 13:6, 9).

—"That day is *the day of the Lord* GOD of hosts, a day of vengeance, to avenge himself on his foes. The sword shall devour and be sated, and drink its fill of their blood" (Jer. 46:10).

—"Son of man, prophesy, and say, Thus says the Lord GOD: "Wail, 'Alas for the day!' For the day is near, *the day of the LORD* is near; it will be a day of clouds, a time of doom for the nations" (Ezek. 30:2–3).

—"Alas for the day! For *the day of the LORD* is near, and as destruction from the Almighty it comes"(Joel 1:15).

— "The great *day of the LORD is near*, near and hastening fast; the sound of the day of the LORD is bitter, the mighty man cries aloud there. A day of wrath is that day, a day of distress and anguish, a day of ruin and devastation, a day of darkness and gloom, a day of clouds and thick darkness" (Zeph. 1:14–15).

Yet John's reference to the Lord's day has another meaning as well. In the early Church, the "Lord's Day" was the word used for Sunday, the day the Lord rose from the dead. It was on this day that the Eucharist was celebrated (Acts 20:7). Following the New Testament, the first Christians recognized Sunday as the "Lord's Day."[8] Sunday, therefore, is the "day of the Lord" since it is in the Eucharist that Christ "comes again." This is why just before the consecration, the faithful pray, "Blessed is He who comes in the name of the Lord."

Things Are Looking Up

So why does John portray the coming of Jesus with liturgical symbols? The answer is simple: Christ is coming to the Church in the liturgy. Yet there are even deeper implications. When John speaks about the liturgy in the Book of Revelation, he doesn't speak of any earthly liturgy, but a liturgy in heaven.

We might have expected John to show the early Christians singing hymns on earth as Jesus returns in glory. Instead, John shows us that it is the angels and saints in heaven who sing "Holy, Holy, Holy." John shows us that the liturgy we celebrate is the same as the liturgy of the angels. We are worshipping *with* them. In other words, the Apocalypse shows us that when we celebrate the liturgy on earth, we join with the angels and saints in their liturgy in heaven.

Revelation teaches us that heaven touches down to earth on the altars of our parish churches every time we gather for Mass. The liturgy we celebrate is not our own. In the Mass, we are taken up into heaven and stand with the angels and saints, as they praise God forever in His presence.

This is the teaching of Vatican II: "In the earthly liturgy we take part in a foretaste of that heavenly liturgy which is celebrated in the holy city of Jerusalem toward which we journey as pilgrims, where Christ is sitting at the right hand of God, minister of the holies and of the true tabernacle; we sing a hymn to the Lord's glory with all the warriors of the heavenly army."[9]

When we are at Mass, we "lift up our hearts," and we are caught up in the Spirit, much like John was (Rev. 1:10). We stand next to our departed loved ones who have gone on to be with the Lord. We stand next to our patron saints and guardian angels. In a real way, we leave earth and are transported to the heavenly Jerusalem.

The Book of Revelation teaches the Church how to celebrate. That is why the early Church used the Apocalypse in designing churches and developing the liturgy. The great liturgical scholar Gregory Dix explains that from the earliest times the arrangement of the Christian assembly at Mass was modeled on what John saw in the Book of Revelation.[10]

Therefore, the altar was placed at the front of the congregation, just as in John's vision, where "everything centers upon 'the golden altar, which is before the throne of God.'" Likewise, images of angels and saints in a church remind the faithful that they are sharing in the heavenly liturgy. Similarly, the celebrant's chair symbolizes the Throne of God. Dix also points out how the early arrangement of smaller chairs in a semi-circle around the throne of the Bishop, was meant to image the seats of the twenty-four elders around the throne of the Lamb.[11] Cardinal Ratzinger calls Revelation, "the book of the heavenly liturgy, which is presented to the Church as the standard for her own liturgy."[12]

The Book of Revelation shows us, then, that Christ's coming is not just limited to the past event of AD 70, or to a future coming of Christ at the end of the world. It is past, present, and future. It tells us of Christ "who is and who was and who is to come" (Rev. 1:4). In other words, Christ is the One who was to come, who is coming, and who is to come on the last day.

Now, with all of this as background, we are ready to jump into the Apocalypse.

* * *

Multiple Choice

1. The word "rapture" occurs in Scripture how many times?
(a) once
(b) twice
(c) seven times
(d) never

2. The Book of Revelation is full of ____________ images.
(a) liturgical
(b) Egyptian
(c) pleasant
(d) undecodable

3. The word *parousia*, which is usually understood in terms of the "second coming," literally means __________.
(a) coming
(b) rain
(c) reign
(d) presence

4. In the early Church, "the Lord's Day" referred to the day of judgment and __________.
(a) the Last Supper
(b) the temple
(c) Sunday
(d) the Sabbath

5. Vatican II taught that the faithful take part in a ___________ of the heavenly liturgy in the Eucharist.
(a) imitation
(b) restoration
(c) foretaste
(d) dramatization

Answers: 1. d; 2.a; 3. d; 4. c; 5. c

* * *

Discussion/Study Questions

1. How does seeing the Mass in the Apocalypse affect the way we celebrate it? In what ways does it help us participate more deeply in the liturgy? (See pages 27–28)

2. Name some of the elements of the Mass found in the Apocalypse. (See page 24)

3. Why does John describe the coming of Christ in liturgical images? (See page 27)

4. How does the structure of the Book of Revelation parallel the structure of the Mass? (See page 25)

5. How was church architecture shaped by the Book of Revelation, according to Gregory Dix? (See page 28)

____

____

____

____

Chapter Four

IN ALL HIS GLORY AND SPLENDOR

John's Vision of the Son of Man (Rev. 1:1–20)

Introduction

Rev. 1:1–2. 1 The revelation of Jesus Christ, which God gave him to show to his servants what must soon take place; and he made it known by sending his angel to his servant John, 2 who bore witness to the word of God and to the testimony of Jesus Christ, even to all that he saw.

1:1–2. As we have seen, the Book of Revelation was written during a time of persecution and suffering. Because of this, John sets out from the very beginning to explain suffering. Thus, in the first verse, he speaks of himself as a "servant." The word "servant" evokes the image of the "suffering servant" in Isaiah 53. From the earliest times, this passage was understood as a prophecy about Jesus, the true suffering Servant, who "makes himself an offering for sin" (Is. 53:10). It speaks of our Savior, who "was wounded for our transgressions . . . bruised for our iniquities; upon him was the chastisement that made us whole, and with his stripes we are healed" (Is. 53:5).

Christians may also be called "suffering servants," since they have a share in the work of Christ. Paul explains, "Now I rejoice in my sufferings for your sake, and in my flesh I complete what is lacking in Christ's afflictions for the sake of his body, that is, the church" (Col. 1:24). Paul first began to understand this relationship between the suffering of the Church and the suffering of Christ when he encountered Jesus on the road to Damascus. Although Paul was persecuting the Church, Jesus explained to him, "I am Jesus, whom you are persecuting" (Acts 9:5).

Christians share in the work of Christ, the suffering Servant, when they join their own afflictions to His. John is Christ's servant because he has been exiled on account of his testimony to Him. Likewise, the Book of Revelation is written to those being persecuted for the Lord, John's fellow servants.

"How Do You Talk to an Angel?"

It is also important to note that the revelation from Jesus comes through "His angel." It might seem odd that Jesus doesn't simply give His message straight to John—odd, that is, until you read the Old Testament. In the Old Testament, God frequently deals with Israel through the "angel of the Lord." This angel acts and speaks on Yahweh's behalf. He is God's special messenger and is closely associated with God Himself.

We see this, for example, in the story of the burning bush. Exodus 3:2 explains that the "angel of the LORD appeared to [Moses]." Yet the author of Exodus also tells us that it was the Lord Himself who spoke through the bush: "And he said, 'I am the God of your father, the God of Abraham, the God of Isaac, and the God of Jacob'" (Ex. 3:6). We see, then, that the Lord Himself is truly present through the workings of His angel.

In Revelation, John frequently applies things traditionally associated with Yahweh to Jesus. In this, John shows that Jesus is truly God. Jesus acts as Yahweh by communicating in a similar way as God did in the Old Testament—through an angel. At the end of the book, the angel identifies himself to John as a "fellow servant" (Rev. 22:9). In this, John learns a profound truth: Christ is now present and working through humans in the same mysterious way He once worked only through angels. Just as God now raises humans to share in the heavenly liturgy, He also now works in and through them as He once did only through the angels.

Liturgical Blessing

Rev. 1:3. Blessed is he who reads aloud the words of the prophecy, and blessed are those who hear, and who keep what is written therein; for the time is near.

1:3. It is important to note that the blessings on those "who read" and those "who hear" imply a liturgical setting. In the first century, people didn't go out, buy their own copies of Revelation from a local bookstore, go home, and read it. Copies of books were expensive and were not usually kept for personal use. The proper place this book was read was in the Church's Eucharistic liturgy. This is why there is a blessing for the reader (the lector) and a blessing for the assembled congregation.

From the very outset, therefore, the Book of Revelation must be understood not only in its original historical setting, but also in the context of the liturgy. The Apocalypse can never be explained properly apart from Christ's coming to the Church in the Eucharistic celebration (cf. *Catechism,* no. 1137). It is there that the Church unites her suffering with Christ's and truly experiences Him coming to her.

Seven Spirits, Faithful Witness, Firstborn from the Dead, Kingdom of Priests

Rev. 1:4–6. 4 John to the seven churches that are in Asia: Grace to you and peace from him who is and who was and who is to come, and from the seven spirits who are before his throne, 5 and from Jesus Christ the faithful witness, the first-born of the dead, and the ruler of kings on earth. To him who loves us and has freed us from our sins by his blood 6 and made us a kingdom, priests to his God and Father, to him be glory and dominion for ever and ever. Amen.

1:4. Many times people become so caught up in trying to explain how Revelation describes events in our present day that they overlook the fact that John writes to seven, specific historical churches. The seven churches—Ephesus, Smyrna, Pergamum, etc.—were real Christian communities with their own particular needs. To understand John's message, then, we have to try to understand his historical situation.

At the same time, the book's teaching is for the whole Church, represented by these seven communities. The Fathers rightly pointed out that "seven" is the number of wholeness. Therefore, by writing to seven churches, John writes to the whole Church. This theme will be explored further in the next chapter.

And who are the "seven spirits" referred to in verse 4? Grace and peace come not only from God the Father and Jesus, but also from "the seven spirits." Since grace is given not by angels, but by God Himself, the phrase "seven spirits" appears to be a reference to the Holy Spirit. Seven, which is a number of wholeness and holiness, is used here to designate the most perfect Spirit of all.[1] This verse contains an implicit reference to the Trinity—God the Father, Jesus, and the Holy Spirit (the seven spirits).

1:5–6. In these verses, John employs several different, yet important, terms to describe Jesus as Priest-King. First, He is the "faithful witness." The word for "witness" in Greek is "martyr." Also, He is the "first-born of the dead." "First-born" has priestly implications since, before the sin of the golden calf, the first-born sons were the priests in Israel (Num. 3:44–45).[2] Jesus is Priest and Victim—First-born and Martyr. Finally, He is the "ruler of the kings on earth"—the King of the world. These concepts—martyr, first-born, priest, and king—all fit together to form a vitally important theme in the Book of Revelation. In this, we will learn how Christ fulfills, in Himself and His Church, the original calling of the first man, Adam. Let us look at this more closely.

Reading the Garden Properly

Adam was created with the life of grace in his soul and made to be a child of God. Luke, in fact, calls him the "son of God" (Lk. 3:38).[3] However, Adam had to undergo a test, so God put him in a garden, which he was directed to guard (cf. Gen. 2:15). Unfortunately for all of us, Adam failed. The serpent got in. But how?

The "serpent" of Genesis 3 is not your typical "garden variety" snake. The word "serpent" in Hebrew, *nahash*, is used elsewhere to describe the dragon known as the "Leviathan" (cf. Is. 27:1). Revelation 12 tells us this is exactly what this "ancient serpent" was: "And another portent appeared in heaven; behold, a great red dragon, with seven heads and ten horns" (Rev. 12:3).

Adam was to guard the garden, but because of his fear, he failed. The devil presented a life-or-death threat to Adam. He could either confront the devil and engage him in combat to defend his bride and the garden—a battle he never could have won on his own, given the immense power of this fallen angel—or he could go along with the devil's suggestion and eat the fruit. The devil promised: if you eat the fruit, you won't die (cf. Gen. 3:4). Adam didn't want to die, so he just ate the fruit.

Adam fell because he loved his earthly life more than supernatural life. He refused to be a martyr. He refused to give God his own life in love. Adam had a choice: he could have life in heaven or natural life on earth. Scott Hahn explains, "Like a riddle, the story of Adam and Eve operates on two levels. The drama describes, at once, the natural and supernatural stakes of the first couple's decisions. They had to choose between two kinds of life: natural and supernatural. They had to choose between two kinds of death: physical and spiritual."[4]

Out of fear of suffering, Adam chose the latter. This is what Hebrews 2:14–15 implies when it tells us that the devil brought us into bondage to sin "through fear of death."[5]

The Love of Your Life

But why was the price so high to get to heaven? Why death? Couldn't it have been a simple "taste test"? Not if you know what heaven is.

Heaven is not a place where little naked baby angels fly around all day. It is not a place with golden highways, nor is it an endless strip of harp dealerships. Heaven is entering into the very life of God. The *Catechism* explains: "This perfect life with the Most Holy Trinity—this communion of life and love with the Trinity, with the Virgin Mary, the angels and all the blessed—is called 'heaven'" (*Catechism*, no. 1024).

If Heaven is sharing in the life of the Trinity, it is fair to ask: What does the Trinity do? The answer: love. The life of the Trinity is eternal life-giving love. The Father, out of love, pours His life into the Son; the Son, the Image of the Father, gives Himself back to the Father in life-giving love; the love that the Father and Son share is the Spirit. This is why John tells us in one of his letters, "God is love" (1 Jn. 4:7). This is not because God is some kind of egomaniac, always telling Himself, "I am so good. I love me so much. Man, what a good God I am." No! God is love because God is Three Persons who share all that they have, holding nothing back.

Heaven is entering into the life of perfect love. There we will experience and share in true love. This is our fulfillment. All the let downs and broken hearts of this life create a yearning in us to experience perfect love, which we are unable to find on earth. Rest assured, it's waiting for us in heaven.

This is why Adam had to die—because that is what total life-giving love looks like when it is offered by a human being. This is why Jesus had to die. It is not because God likes to see blood and suffering; rather, Jesus simply did in His human nature what He does from all eternity as the Son—He pours out His life in love. Adam had to learn to embrace life-giving love because that was what he was called to embrace in heaven. The test of the garden was meant to teach man the one lesson he needed to learn to enter heaven—self-giving love.

Son-Kind of Priest

Offering his life in sacrificial love was Adam's calling. Therefore, it is not surprising that Genesis uses priestly terms to describe Adam's role in the garden. For example, when God tells Adam to "till" and "keep" the garden (Gen. 2:15), He is giving him priestly duties. These words in Hebrew, *'abad* (till) and *shamar* (keep), are used throughout the Old Testament to describe priestly service. The garden itself is described as a sanctuary, since it is there that Adam ministers.[6]

"Priesthood" and "sonship" are connected in the Old Testament. To be a son requires life-giving love. Instead of offering an animal, a son learns to offer his life.

Adam is also described as a "king," having "dominion." Adam, therefore, was a priest-king. We too are all called to be priest-kings, who give to God everything over which we have dominion—our lives, our possessions, all that we are—in sacrificial love.

The Book of Revelation combines these concepts. Revelation 1:5–6 states, "[Grace and peace] from Jesus Christ the faithful witness [martyr], the first-born of the dead, and the ruler of kings on earth. To him who loves us and has freed us from our sins by his blood and made us a kingdom, priests to his God and Father." Jesus is the "first-born," who makes Himself a sacrifice as a "martyr," freeing us by His blood, and making us a "kingdom of priests." Throughout the Book of Revelation, we will continue to find this link between martyrdom, being a child of God, priesthood, kingship, and sacrifice.

Coming on the Clouds

> **Rev. 1:7.** Behold, he is coming with the clouds, and every eye will see him, every one who pierced him; and all tribes of the earth will wail on account of him. Even so. Amen.

1:7. In verse 7, John alludes to two passages. First, Jesus' coming on the clouds evokes Daniel 7:13. In Daniel 7, the Son of Man comes in the clouds to receive the kingdom. He then turns and gives it to the saints who persevered through persecution. We will talk more about the importance of Daniel 7 in our discussion of Revelation 1:12–13.

The reference to those who "will wail" upon seeing Him whom they "pierced," comes from Zechariah 12:10: "And I will pour out on the house of David and the inhabitants of Jerusalem a spirit of compassion and supplication, so that, when they look on him whom they pierced, they shall mourn for him, as one mourns for an only child." In Zechariah 12, the people look upon the death of the Davidic king and mourn for him. Because of this, the people repent, and sin is cleansed from the land. God comforts the inhabitants of the Jerusalem and restores His people to Himself (Zech. 13:1–9).

John combines two passages that both speak about the Messiah's victory over evil and the coming messianic kingdom. As we will see, Christ is the Son of Man about whom Daniel prophesied. He brings about the restoration of God's kingdom. Likewise, Jesus is the Davidic King who is pierced in Zechariah. People from all nations will look upon Jesus, pierced for our sins, and they will "wail on account of Him" and repent.

The imagery here recalls a story I read about a man who, after seeing Mel Gibson's *The Passion of the Christ,* repented and confessed to an unsolved murder. We too need to confess and repent for, indeed, we are all responsible for Christ's death since He died for all of our sins. The more deeply we contemplate Christ's sacrifice, the more deeply we repent.

There is also a deeper Eucharistic meaning to this passage. Just as the Son of Man comes in the cloud, Christ comes to the Church in every Eucharist.[7] Since the Old Testament often depicts the Holy Spirit in terms of the cloud of presence (Ex. 40:34–38; Sir. 24), Jesus' "coming in the clouds" can also be understood as His coming "in the Spirit."[8] Moreover, the Greek word for "coming," *parousia,* also means "presence." Christ's coming, therefore, is found in His real presence in the Eucharist, where He comes to us "in the unity of the Holy Spirit."

Alpha and Omega

Rev. 1:8. "I am the Alpha and the Omega," says the Lord God, who is and who was and who is to come, the Almighty.

1:8. The description of Jesus as the One who "was and is and is to come" recalls the name God reveals to Moses, "Yahweh." Yahweh can be translated either "I am who I am" or "I will be what I will be." In his Gospel, John recounts how Jesus applied this name to Himself (cf. Jn. 8:58–59; 18:6). John is therefore again emphasizing that Jesus is God. He is not some lower "god," but the one true God Almighty.

Brother in Suffering

Rev. 1:9. I John, your brother, who share with you in Jesus the tribulation and the kingdom and the patient endurance, was on the island called Patmos on account of the word of God and the testimony of Jesus.

1:9. It is important to point out that John is sharing in the same persecution his readers are experiencing in Asia Minor. What persecution could this be? Since there is no evidence that Christians outside of Rome were persecuted by Nero, it is very unlikely that this implies some sort of Imperial assault on Christianity. Instead, it is probable that the general population throughout the Roman empire, following the example of Caesar and the policy of their capital city, began to persecute Christians at the local level. Likewise, certain Jews, who looked to the Jerusalem leaders for guidance, would have begun to persecute Christians in the Gentile territories where they lived. This kind of "trickle-down" persecution is probably what affected the early Church in Asia Minor.

John's mention that he shares in the "kingdom" is often overlooked. What is this "kingdom" that he shares with his readers? Let us look at this more closely.

The Kingdom, the Power, the Glory

What was the theme of Jesus' ministry? There is one clear answer—the kingdom. Jesus spoke more often about the "kingdom" than about anything else. It is so frequent in the Gospels that we might even overlook it. Consider the following examples:

—Picking up the theme of John the Baptist, Jesus begins His own ministry with the words, "Repent, for the *kingdom* of heaven is at hand" (Mt. 4:17).

—Matthew describes Jesus' message as "the gospel of the *kingdom*" (Mt. 4:23).
—Jesus declares, "Blessed are the poor in spirit, for theirs is the *kingdom* of heaven" (Mt. 5:3).
—The Lord's Prayer teaches us to pray, "Thy *kingdom* come" (Mt. 6:10).
—Many of the parables begin, "The *kingdom* of heaven may be compared . . ."
—Jesus leaves Peter the "keys to the *kingdom* of heaven" (Mt. 16:19).

The theme isn't limited to the Gospels. The Book of Acts begins by explaining that Jesus spent forty days after the Resurrection "speaking about the *kingdom* of God" (Acts 1:3). Then, throughout the Book of Acts the message of the kingdom is proclaimed.[9] The book concludes with Paul in Rome, "preaching the *kingdom* of God" (Acts 28:31).

But what exactly is the kingdom of God? It's the kingdom God swore to give to David. Indeed, the Old Testament calls the Davidic kingdom the "kingdom of the Lord" (2 Chron. 13:8). This kingdom would be an everlasting kingdom (2 Sam. 7:13). Through this kingdom, God would fulfill all His Old Testament promises, extending His covenant blessings to all mankind. However, after Solomon died, the kingdom was split in half, and eventually crushed in 586 BC. The prophets announced that the kingdom would be restored by the Messiah, the Son of David.

Of course, all of this is fulfilled in the coming of Jesus, who announced, "The kingdom of heaven is at hand." Jesus did not come to abolish the Old Covenant but to fulfill it (Mt. 5:17). This kingdom is not an earthly political power—it's God's covenant family. It is present in the Church, under the successor of Peter, who is given the "keys" of the kingdom. Through the Church's sacramental life, mankind is brought back into God's family. Moreover, the kingdom is especially present at the Eucharistic celebration, since it is there that the King is truly present.[10]

The Lord's Day

Rev. 1:10–11. 10 I was in the Spirit on the Lord's day, and I heard behind me a loud voice like a trumpet 11 saying, "Write what you see in a book and send it to the seven churches, to Ephesus and to Smyrna and to Pergamum and to Thyatira and to Sardis and to Philadelphia and to Laodicea."

1:10–11. We have already seen how the term "the Lord's Day" calls to mind both the day of judgment (the Day of the Lord) as well as the Eucharist, which the early Church celebrated on Sunday, the day of the Lord's Resurrection. The trumpet mentioned here brings both of these images together.

In the Old Testament, a trumpet is blown to warn the people that God's judgment is coming: "The great day of the LORD is near, near and hastening fast . . . a day of trumpet blast and battle cry against the fortified cities" (Zeph. 1:14, 16).[11] At the same time, the trumpet is a liturgical instrument. It was used in the temple by the priests as well as in sacred processions. Ezra 3:10 tells us how Ezra consecrated the second temple: "[T]he priests in their vestments came forward with trumpets, and the Levites, the sons of Asaph, with cymbals, to praise the LORD, according to the directions of David, king of Israel."[12] Later we will see how these two uses are connected with another occasion on which the trumpet was used—battle.

Jesus as the Son of Man

Rev. 1:12–13. 12 Then I turned to see the voice that was speaking to me, and on turning I saw seven golden lampstands, 13 and in the midst of the lampstands one like a son of man, clothed with a long robe and with a golden girdle round his breast;

1:12–13. At first it seems strange that John turns to "see" a "voice." However, John may be alluding to an ancient version of Daniel 7:11, in which Daniel says: "[T]hen I beheld the voice." After this Daniel sees "one like a son of man" (7:13).[13] This is similar to John, who turns to see a voice and then beholds "one like a son of man." As we shall see, Daniel 7 is one of the most important Old Testament passages for understanding Revelation. Images such as "the son of man," "beasts," and "kingdom," used throughout the Apocalypse, are all found in this important Old Testament passage.

The seven golden lampstands are seven Menorahs—the seven-branched candlestick. Most Americans are probably familiar with this symbol, since modern Jews frequently use it, especially around Chanukah. This lampstand stood in the Holy of Holies inside the Jerusalem temple. Thus, in seeing the seven golden lampstands John finds himself in the heavenly temple.[14]

John's vision of Christ in the midst of the seven lampstands is also echoed in the traditional arrangement of three candlesticks placed on either side of the crucifix on the high altar. Christ is the main candle—the light of the world—with three candles on either side.

Daniel-Son

The "Son of Man" is a term frequently used for Jesus in the New Testament. But what exactly does it mean? Some scholars have tried to argue that "Son of Man" is simply a title of humility—Jesus' way of saying, "I'm just a lowly son of man." However, once we examine the background of this term, we find that it has a deeper meaning.

Jesus used the phrase "Son of Man" to describe Himself more than any other term. Furthermore, *only Jesus* uses this special term to describe His identity. From this, we can see just how important it is to understand the term "Son of Man."

Although this term is used throughout the Old Testament, it is Daniel 7 that is the all-important source text for Jesus' use of it. For example, Daniel 7 links the "son of man" with a "coming in the clouds," as Jesus frequently did (cf. Mt. 24:30; 26:64; Mk. 13:26; 14:62). Moreover, the "son of man" in Daniel 7 is the one who brings the kingdom of God to the saints. This was another important theme of Jesus' ministry, as He states in passages like Luke 4:43: "I must preach the good news of the kingdom of God to the other cities also; for I was sent for this purpose."

Daniel's historical situation is also important. Daniel 7 tells of four beasts that are four kingdoms, which will persecute the Jews: Babylon, Medo-Persia, Greece, and Rome. The people in Christ's day recognized that they were living in the time of the fourth beast. Since Daniel prophesied that the "son of man" would come at the time of this beast, messianic hopes were at a fever pitch in Jesus' day.

For Daniel, the "son of man" does not simply describe a human Messiah; this "son" is a supernatural figure. He looks "like" a man, but he is much more than that.[15] The "son of man" receives from God (called "the Ancient of Days") the kingdom, which will then be given to the saints. In Jesus' day, this prophecy was well known, and its implications were clear: Rome would fall and the righteous would receive the kingdom.

This also has implications for the Church. Ever wonder why it's so important that we are not only "Catholic," but "Roman Catholic"? The early Christians knew why. Saints like Peter and Paul went to Rome hoping that, by the shedding of their blood, the fourth beast would convert, so that the kingdom of God would be made manifest through it. The term "Roman Catholic," then, reflects not some kind of implicit political alliance between the Church and Italy, or any other earthly power, but the fulfillment of God's plan, which He announced through Daniel.

Clothing Time

The vestments of Christ are also noteworthy. The vestments seem to be a reference to Christ's role as high priest.[16] The long robe was worn by the high priest (Ex. 28:4; 29:5; Wis. 18:24; Sir. 45:8) as well as the girdle (Ex. 28:4; 39:29; Lev. 16:4). This concurs with the testimony of the ancient historian Josephus: "[The high priest] puts on that which is called *Machanase*, which means [something] that is tied. It is a girdle. . . . Over this he wore a linen vestment, made of fine flax doubled. . . . This vestment reaches down to the feet."[17] Incidentally, from this we can see the similarities between the Jewish high priest and the celebrant at Mass who wears a stole covered with a chasuble.

John's vision of Christ, therefore, shows Him to be the heavenly High Priest. His priestly role is also highlighted by the fact that He stands in the midst of the lampstands, since tending to the Menorah was the high priest's duty.[18] Indeed, Christ's priestly role has already been implicitly mentioned in Revelation 1:5–6, where Christ is said to have freed us by His blood—a reference to His sacrifice, which makes us a "kingdom of priests."

Description of the Son of Man

> **Rev. 1:14–16.** 14 his head and his hair were white as white wool, white as snow; his eyes were like a flame of fire, 15 his feet were like burnished bronze, refined as in a furnace, and his voice was like the sound of many waters; 16 in his right hand he held seven stars, from his mouth issued a sharp two-edged sword, and his face was like the sun shining in full strength.

1:14–15. Much of the imagery here is taken, not only from Daniel 7, but also from Daniel 10: "I lifted up my eyes and looked, and behold, a man clothed in linen, whose loins were girded with gold of Uphaz. His body was like beryl, his face like the appearance of lightning, his eyes like flaming torches, his arms and legs like the gleam of burnished bronze, and the sound of his words like the noise of a multitude" (10:5–6).

Daniel's vision of the divine warrior is very similar to John's vision of Jesus: both are girded with gold, both have fiery eyes, both have the appearance of bronze, and both speak with a thundering voice. The voice in Daniel sounds like a multitude; the one John hears sounds like "many waters." Interestingly, John later says in Revelation 19:6 that the voice of the "multitude" sounds like "many waters."

1:16. The seven stars in Jesus' hands, we are later told, are the "seven angels of the seven churches" (Rev. 1:20). The link between God's people and the Menorah's seven lamps was already established in Jewish tradition. The seven lamps in Zechariah 4:2 were often linked with the saints of Daniel 12:3, who, it is said, will shine like the "seven stars." John is simply following a tradition of linking the lampstands with God's people.[19]

Another possible source for the imagery of the seven stars may be found on Imperial coins. Roman Emperors used the image of the seven stars on the coins that they minted as a symbol of their political power.[20] The fact that John sees Jesus holding the stars would thus imply that He is the true King of kings.

The "two edged" sword coming from the mouth of Christ calls to mind Isaiah 11. There we read the prophecy about the Messiah who will "smite the earth with the rod of his mouth" (Is. 11:4). It also recalls God's covenant judgment: "And I will bring a sword upon you, that shall execute vengeance for the covenant; and if you gather within your cities I will send pestilence among you, and you shall be delivered into the hand of the enemy" (Lev. 26:25). This covenant judgment came in the year 70.

John's vision of Jesus' face as "shining like the sun in full strength" echoes Daniel's description of the son of man's face as having "the appearance of lightning" (Dan. 10:6). However, the exact wording, "shining like the sun in full strength," comes from a Greek version of Judges 5:31, which describes a divine warrior.[21] In fact, this passage in Judges was often linked with the passages from Daniel 12 and Zechariah 4 mentioned above.[22]

This Means War!

Not only, then, is Jesus described in "priestly" terms, but also as the heavenly warrior of Daniel 10. John's vision also shares much in common with other visions of heavenly warriors in the Old Testament. In Joshua 5, Joshua "looked, and behold, a man stood before him with his drawn sword in hand" (v. 13). Joshua then falls at his feet (Josh. 5:14) as Daniel and John do (Dan. 10:9; Rev. 1:17).

Why is John connecting priesthood and battle? He is simply following the example of the Old Testament. One of the most dramatic examples of this connection is the defeat of Jericho in Joshua 5–6—a story in the backdrop of Revelation 8–11. Given the parallels between Joshua 5 listed above, it is not unlikely that John has this story in the back of his mind. Let's review it.

Tearing Down the Walls

Joshua, in leading the Israelites to the Promised Land, is directed by the Lord to the biggest Canaanite stronghold of them all—Jericho. This city was surrounded by huge walls. And yet God tells Joshua to go to this city and capture it. To Joshua it might have been almost humorous. How was little Israel, a wandering nation of nomads, supposed to win? Not to fear—God had a plan.

What is this plan? A supernatural missile? Lightning from heaven? Special swords on loan from the angels? No. God explains that Israel will defeat Jericho by marching around the city. Here's the plan: for six days all the people will march around the city with the ark of the covenant, led by seven priests who will blow seven trumpets. On the seventh day, they must walk around seven times, and when they are done, the priests will blow the trumpets and all the people will shout. By doing this, the walls will come down.

I'm sure the people of Jericho found this quite comical. They see little Israel marching around in circles. "Yeah," they may have scoffed sarcastically, "this is really intimidating." I'm sure Israel was getting pretty tired on the seventh day before they blew the trumpet the last time. The people of Jericho looked over their walls that day and saw Israel marching around and around, watching some of them struggle to keep the pace in that hot Middle Eastern sun. Yet, Israel got the last laugh, because—true to God's word—the walls tumbled down and Jericho was defeated.

The Power of Prayer

What is the moral of the lesson? Liturgy is war. By praying together with the priests and blowing the trumpets before the ark, Israel was much more powerful than any military, for they were seeking the Lord's help.

This lesson is taught over and over again throughout the Book of Revelation. All the events in John's vision—from the pestilence and famine to the final destruction of the city—begin with some liturgical prayer or action of the angels and saints in heaven. The saints worship God, and the consequences are earth-shattering.

There is something that needs to be learned from all of this. We won't win the world over for Christ or effect positive changes in our society primarily through City Hall or political activism. We conquer through the liturgy, through which history is affected and directed.

John Falls at Jesus' Feet

Rev. 1:17. When I saw him, I fell at his feet as though dead. But he laid his right hand upon me, saying, "Fear not, I am the first and the last,

1:17. This verse mirrors Daniel's account:

> And I, Daniel, alone saw the vision, for the men who were with me did not see the vision, but a great trembling fell upon them, and they fled to hide themselves. So I was left alone and saw this great vision, and no strength was left in me; my radiant appearance was fearfully changed, and I retained no strength. Then I heard the sound of his words; and when I heard the sound of his words, I fell on my face in a deep sleep with my face to the ground.
>
> And behold, a hand touched me and set me trembling on my hands and knees. And he said to me, "O Daniel, man greatly beloved, give heed to the words that I speak to you, and stand upright, for now I have been sent to you." While he was speaking this word to me, I stood up trembling. Then he said to me, "Fear not, Daniel, for from the first day that you set your mind to understand and humbled yourself before your God, your words have been heard, and I have come because of your words" (Dan. 10:7–12).

Both Daniel and John fall down to the ground and are told not to fear. Indeed, in the Gospel of John, the Apostle is called the "beloved disciple" much like Daniel is called "man greatly beloved."

Jesus' title, "the First and the Last," hints at His divinity. The Lord God calls Himself by this title in Isaiah (Is. 41:4; 44:6; 48:12). The use of the phrase, "I am," is also one that seems to denote divinity, as we noted earlier. The seven "I am" sayings are also one of the characteristic themes of John's Gospel:

1. "I am the bread of life" (Jn. 6:35, 48, cf. 6:51).
2. "I am the light of the world" (Jn. 8:12).
3. "I am the door" (Jn. 10:7, 9).
4. "I am the good shepherd" (Jn. 10:11, 14).
5. "I am the resurrection and the life" (Jn. 11:25).
6. "I am the way, the truth, and the life" (Jn. 14:6).
7. "I am the true vine" (Jn. 15:1, cf. 15:5).

Revelation seems to be framed by such sayings, which occur at the beginning and end of the book.

1. "I am the Alpha and the Omega" (Rev. 1:8).
2. "I am the First and the Last" (Rev. 1:17).
3. "I am the one who searches mind and heart" (Rev. 2:23).
4. "I am the Alpha and the Omega" (Rev. 21:6).
5. "I am the root and offspring of David, the bright morning star" (Rev. 22:16).

The Keys

Rev. 1:18–19. 18 and the living one; I died, and behold I am alive for evermore, and I have the keys of Death and Hades. 19 Now write what you see, what is and what is to take place hereafter.

1:18. Here is another instance where Jesus' divinity is subtly implied. The phrase "I am alive forever" is very close to the title, "the one who lives forever," which is used to describe God in the Greek version of Daniel 12:7.[23] 1 Enoch 5:1 also calls the Lord God, "Him who lives for ever."[24]

1:19. The command to write "what you see, what is, and what is to take place hereafter" should probably be understood in light of Revelation 4:2: "Come up hither and I will show you what must take place after this." Thus, John is to write about two things: something present ("what is"), and something in the future ("what is to take place hereafter"). Revelation chapters 2–3 give us a description of the present state of the churches in Asia Minor. Revelation chapters 4–22 describe the events that bring about the coming of the Lord.[25]

Seven Stars, Seven Lampstands, Seven Churches

> **Rev. 1:20.** As for the mystery of the seven stars which you saw in my right hand, and the seven golden lampstands, the seven stars are the angels of the seven churches and the seven lampstands are the seven churches.

1:20. Daniel is the only Old Testament book where the theme of the "mystery" is found (Dan. 2:18–19, 27, 30, 47; 4:9). Again, in this verse, we see the dominance of references to Daniel in the Apocalypse. Also, as in the Book of Daniel, the messenger who appears to John explains the meaning of the symbols in the vision.

It is apparent from this verse that Revelation must not be interpreted too literally. John tells us in Revelation 1:17 that Jesus touches him with His right hand; however, in Revelation 1:20, Jesus is holding the seven stars in His hands. The symbols are thereby meant to convey a spiritual meaning and should not be interpreted in an overly literal fashion.

Commentators often debate about the meaning of the "angels" of the seven churches. Since the seven letters in chapters 2 and 3 are written to these angels, some have argued that the "angels" are really bishops. It should be noted, however, that everywhere else this word is used in the Apocalypse, it denotes "angels." John gives no indication that this word means something different here.[26]

Nonetheless, the association of the angels with the churches is striking, and implies that the Church is not merely an earthly reality. As mentioned above, a Jewish tradition, which linked Zechariah 4 to Daniel 12, saw the lampstands as representing the righteous. Taken together, the lampstands and the angels may serve as reminders that the Church is both an earthly and heavenly reality. As one Protestant scholar writes, when John is taken up in the Spirit on that remarkable Sunday, he learns that "one of the purposes of the church meeting on earth in its weekly gatherings (e.g., 1:2, 9) is to be reminded of its heavenly existence and identity by modeling its worship and liturgy on the angels' and heavenly church's worship."[27]

Applying the Lessons of Revelation 1 Today

While it is true that Jesus loves us as our Brother and true Friend, we often emphasize Jesus' gentleness and humanity to the neglect of His glory and divinity. A modern American Catholic would probably have expected something much different than what we read in Revelation 1. Instead of the vision of the Son of Man having a sword coming out of His mouth and fiery eyes, a modern version of Revelation might have envisioned Christ calling John on the phone and asking if he could spend the day fishing with Him.

Our secular society tends to pervert ideas of God's nature. Some people treat God as if He were a kind of butler or genie. They expect Him to bring us whatever we need, whenever we ask. Others treat Jesus as though He was nothing more than a fishing buddy, who just wants everyone to have a nice time. Still others dismiss God the Father as a kind of senile old man who has forgotten how to work in the marvelous ways He "used to." These are all perverted attitudes towards God. Revelation 1 corrects these distortions.

When Jesus' glory is revealed, even John, the beloved disciple, the apostle who rested His head on Jesus at the Last Supper, falls down at His feet as though dead. John doesn't audaciously slap Jesus on the back and say, "Wow, good to see you! How was that Ascension thing? It looked fun. Can I do that?" Saint John recognizes his own unworthiness, and falls down and worships. How can we do anything different?

Revelation 1 unveils the awesome glory of Jesus. It teaches us that we can't put God in a box of our choosing. We can't simply construct a frame for a picture of God that makes us feel comfortable. Yes, God can be scary: He shatters all our preconceptions and assumptions. Thankfully, He is also a Father who loves us and doesn't want us to be fearful. But we can't simply forget with whom we are dealing. We must put our pride away and come before the Lord with humility, acknowledging our own unworthiness. Only when we do this, will we truly appreciate His awesome love.

* * *

Multiple Choice

1. By speaking through a special angel, John implies that Jesus is ________.

(a) in heaven
(b) God
(c) the Son of Man
(d) High Priest

2. The major theme of Jesus' ministry was ________.
(a) My yoke is easy
(b) condemnation
(c) miracle working
(d) the kingdom

3. The image of the Son of Man, the beasts, and the coming of the kingdom evoke the visions seen by the prophet ________.
(a) Isaiah
(b) Daniel
(c) Elijah
(d) Ezekiel

4. Like Revelation, the Gospel of __________ contains several "I am" sayings.
(a) Matthew
(b) Mark
(c) Luke
(d) John

5. The theme of the "mystery" is found in the prophet ________.
(a) Isaiah
(b) Jeremiah
(c) Daniel
(d) Zechariah

Answers) 1. b; 2. d; 3. b; 4. d; 5. c.

* * *

Discussion/Study Questions

1. What lessons can we learn from John's response to seeing Jesus in His glory? (See pages 52–53)

____

____

____

____

2. How is Jesus depicted as a priest in Revelation 1? (See pages 45–46)

____

____

____

____

3. Who is the "son of man"? What significance does that term have? (See page 43–45)

____

____

____

____

4. The visions of the Apocalypse were seen "on the Lord's day." How is that important for understanding the book's message? (See page 43)

____

____

____

____

5. Why is Jesus depicted as both a warrior and a priest? What does this teach us about liturgy? (See pages 47–49)

____

____

____

____

P. S.: REPENT!

The Seven Letters (Rev. 2:1–3:22)

Revelation chapters 2–3 contain letters to the seven churches: (1) Ephesus, (2) Smyrna, (3) Pergamum, (4) Thyatira, (5) Sardis, (6) Philadelphia, and (7) Laodicea. What is important here is the number "seven." As stated earlier, we must see these letters in terms of real churches, who struggled with their own particular problems. However, since "seven" is a number indicating "wholeness," the letters should also be understood as being written to the "whole church." Thus, an ancient compilation of New Testament books, the Muratorian Canon, states: "John too, indeed, in the Apocalypse, although he writes only to seven churches, yet addresses all."[1]

Because of this, the message of each letter contains important lessons that are as true for Christians today as they were two thousand years ago. Indeed, many people are often surprised to find just how similar the struggles of the early believers in Asia Minor are to those Christians face today. Nonetheless, these lessons will only be understood properly after we have first considered the original historical conditions of the churches in John's day.

While the reasons these particular seven churches were chosen is not entirely clear, their selection may have had to do with their location. Geographically, the seven churches form a kind of circle. A missionary could very easily walk from one to the next. The order in which the churches are named—Ephesus first, Smyrna second, etc.—lends credence to this view, since this is the order in which they would have been visited by someone walking this route.

Promises Kept

Many of the promises made by Christ to the Churches in these letters are fulfilled at the end of Revelation.

—a share in the fruit of the Tree of Life (2:7; 22:2)
—the New Jerusalem, which comes down from heaven (3:12; 21:2, 10)
—dwelling in the temple of the New Jerusalem (3:12; 21:22)
—God's name is written on the saints (3:12; 22:4)
—being written in the book of life (3:5; 21:27)
—the morning star (2:28; 22:16)
—a share in Christ's kingship (2:26–27; 3:21; 22:5)
—deliverance from the second death (2:11; 21:7–8)[2]

John shows us that Jesus is faithful to His words.

A Perfect Fit

But how do these letters fit into the main theme of the book? The answer is more pastoral than theological. If you were a Gentile Christian living outside of Jerusalem, the prediction of the fall of Jerusalem may have led you to pride. Jesus wants to make something very clear: if God won't spare His beloved city of Jerusalem, no one is above God's judgment.

In fact, *all of these churches*, from Ephesus to Laodicea, eventually fell away from the Gospel. They have been overrun by Muslim forces and are under their control to this day. This is a stern warning for Christians of all locations and times!

The Letter to Ephesus

Rev. 2:1–7. 1 To the angel of the church in Ephesus write: 'The words of him who holds the seven stars in his right hand, who walks among the seven golden lampstands.

2 "I know your works, your toil and your patient endurance, and how you cannot bear evil men but have tested those who call themselves apostles but are not, and found them to be false; 3 I know you are enduring patiently and bearing up for my name's sake, and you have not grown weary. 4 But I have this against you, that you have abandoned the love you had at first. 5 Remember then from what you have fallen, repent and do the works you did at first. If not, I will come to you and remove your lampstand from its place, unless you repent. 6 Yet this you have, you hate the works of the Nicolaitans, which I also hate. 7 He who has an ear, let him hear what the Spirit says to the churches. To him who conquers I will grant to eat of the tree of life, which is in the paradise of God."

2:1–6. Ephesus was the largest city of its province, probably because it was the best port of entry in the region.[3] It was well known as a religious city, having numerous temples. The most prominent of these temples was the one to Artemis. It was one of the seven wonders of the ancient world.[4] In fact, Ephesus was nicknamed "the temple warden."[5] Occult mysticism seemed to flourish there (cf. Acts 19:13–15, 18–19).

The church at Ephesus was also prominent in the days of the apostles. Saint Paul spent more time there—three years (Acts 20:31)—than anywhere else. Saint John lived and was buried there.[6] The Blessed Virgin Mary was another member of this church.[7] Other members included the great early Christian apologist, Apollos (cf. 1 Cor. 1:12), three daughters of the Apostle Saint Philip, Paul's disciple Timothy, and, according to some, Mary Magdalene.

Applying the Letter to Ephesus Today

Some have pointed out that the "toil and patient endurance" of the Ephesians might be linked to their ongoing struggle to maintain their harbor. River sediment would often fill in the port with silt. This was a major threat to the port, and thus a threat to the very heart of the life and economy of Ephesus. Losing the port would be tantamount to the city of Hollywood losing the entertainment business! Ephesus and the Ephesians were truly in danger of being "moved out of its place," as Christ warns in Revelation 2:5. In fact, over the years the silting has continued without any dredging, and, as a result, the city is six miles away from the sea today.[8]

God takes natural virtues—natural talents, if you will—and helps us use them for His glory. The Ephesians, applying their hard work ethic to understanding theology, became extremely knowledgeable about their faith. No wonder Paul stayed so long teaching them, taking them deeper than any other church into his rich knowledge of Scripture. They were good students. Paul's Letter to the Ephesians contains some of the most profound theology found in any of his Epistles. Why? Because these Christians were his best students.

The Ephesians—heeding Paul's warning to them, "Let no one deceive you with empty words" (Eph. 5:6)—prided themselves in their knowledge of the faith and their rejection of unorthodox teaching. Christ Himself commends them for rejecting the teaching of the Nicolaitans. The Nicolaitans were followers of the heretic Nicolas, who had been one of the deacons chosen by the apostles in the Book of Acts (Acts 6:5; for more about the Nicolaitans, see the note on Rev. 2:14-15).[9] It is interesting that Christ tells the Ephesians that they must "overcome" (conquer) these heretics, since their name derives from the word "overcome," *nikao*.[10]

Nevertheless, orthodoxy is not enough. Catholics can pride themselves on being orthodox in such a way that they become uncharitable to their brothers and sisters in Christ. They chronicle the false teachings of others and spread sensational stories of unfaithful Catholics, causing further division within the Church. Orthodoxy is not an option; it is a pre-requisite. But when we spend our time deploring the sins of others more than our own, we are not following Christ at all and must repent.

2:7. The call to "eat the fruit of the tree of life" was understood by the Fathers as a reference to the Eucharist. The Syrian Father Aphrahat writes: "So the fruit of the tree of life is given as food to the faithful and to virgins, and to those that do the will of God has the door been opened and the way made plain. And the fountain flows and gives drink to the thirsty. The table is laid and the supper prepared. The fatted ox is slain and the cup of redemption mixed. The feast is prepared and the Bridegroom at hand, soon to take his place."[11]

The Letter to Smyrna

Rev. 2:8–11. 8 And to the angel of the church in Smyrna write: "The words of the first and the last, who died and came to life.
9 "I know your tribulation and your poverty (but you are rich) and the slander of those who say that they are Jews and are not, but are a synagogue of Satan. 10 Do not fear what you are about to suffer. Behold, the devil is about to throw some of you into prison, that you may be tested, and for ten days you will have tribulation. Be faithful unto death, and I will give you the crown of life. 11 He who has an ear, let him hear what the Spirit says to the churches. He who conquers shall not be hurt by the second death."

2:8–9. There were some very anti-Christian Jews in Smyrna who became enraged that so many people in the city were converting to Christianity. These Jews persuaded the people of the city to persecute Christians.[12]

This is what Jesus is referring to when He speaks of "the slander of those who say they are Jews and are not, but are a synagogue of Satan." The point is simple: anyone who persecutes the Church is not a "true Jew."[13]

2:10. The reference to "ten days" is taken from a book already alluded to, Daniel. There we read how Daniel, Hananiah, Mishael and Azariah are tested for "ten days" (Dan. 1:12). Their captors marvel at their faithfulness and at the way God blesses them, and therefore allow them to continue to practice their faith.

Christ applies this lesson to Christian suffering. Christians are warned that persecution is coming, but comforted in knowing that the period of suffering is short compared to the eternal reward awaiting them on the other side of it. In the end, those who persevere will receive something much greater than earthly comfort—the crown of life.[14]

Applying the Letter to Smyrna Today

I was once told by a wise teacher, "If you can't see yourself committing the sins you come across in the Bible, it's because you haven't understood them properly." So what would test the early Christians so severely? Well, it helps to know that, at the time of the Book of Revelation, the Jews received a favored status in the Roman Empire. Christians could therefore avoid suffering if they compromised their faith a little to appease those Jews who opposed them. Yet, Jesus makes it clear that a compromise of faith is nothing less than a rejection of Him.

This is a lesson for all of us who are tempted to compromise or hide our faith, in an effort to make our lives easier. After all, no one wants to be labeled "rigid," a "radical," etc. Christ's words to the Smyrneans are as relevant today as they ever have been—don't be ashamed of Him!

2:11. In verse 11, we find the term "the second death" used. This term refers to the destruction of the soul in hell (cf. Rev. 20:13–15)—a fate far worse than physical death.

In times of persecution, this is an especially important lesson. Each Christian is given a choice, much like Adam was given: "What do you want, earthly life or supernatural life?" To choose earthly life means a death worse than physical death, the second death, which takes place in the lake of fire, where the wicked "shall be tormented with fire and brimstone . . . and the smoke of their torment goes up for ever and ever; and they have no rest, day or night" (Rev. 14:10, 11). (For more on "the second death," see the commentary on Rev. 20 in chapter 13.)

This passage is not simply relevant in times of persecution. At all times Christians must remain detached from this earthly life, keeping in mind that this is not their ultimate home. This is simply a test. We should not make worldly things and comfort our priority, but rather, hold them with a very loose grip.

The Letter to Pergamum

Rev. 2:12–17. And to the angel of the church in Pergamum write: "The words of him who has the sharp two-edged sword.

13 "I know where you dwell, where Satan's throne is; you hold fast my name and you did not deny my faith even in the days of Antipas my witness, my faithful one, who was killed among you, where Satan dwells. 14 But I have a few things against you: you have some there who hold the teaching of Balaam, who taught Balak to put a stumbling block before the sons of Israel, that they might eat food sacrificed to idols and practice immorality. 15 So you also have some who hold the teaching of the Nicolaitans. 16 Repent then. If not, I will come to you soon and war against them with the sword of my mouth. 17 He who has an ear, let him hear what the Spirit says to the churches. To him who conquers I will give some of the hidden manna, and I will give him a white stone, with a new name written on the stone which no one knows except him who receives it."

2:12–13. The ancient Roman writer, Pliny, said that Pergamum was "the most famous place of Asia."[15] Like the other seven cities mentioned in Revelation chapters 2–3, Pergamum was a place where the Roman religion thrived. In fact, it was a historical center, since it was there that the first temple was erected for Emperor worship. Here the Emperor Augustus was worshipped as a god.[16] Refusal to worship Caesar was a crime of "high treason." The early martyr Antipas may have been killed because, as a Christian, he could not obey this law.[17]

Other pagan temples were located in Pergamum as well. For example, the city had a famous temple dedicated to Zeus.[18]

Christ's description of the city as the place where "Satan's throne is," and where "Satan dwells," may be related to the fact that so many gods were worshipped there.

Christ's declaration that "Satan dwells" in this city may also be illuminated by another interesting fact about Pergamum. The city was the center for the worship of a snake-god, called Asclepius. In fact, the serpent became a symbol for the city itself.[19] Is it any wonder Christ saw something satanic about this city?[20]

2:14–16. The Nicolaitans are also mentioned in the letter to the church at Ephesus. They are compared to those who follow Balaam and Balak, who enticed the Israelites to sexual sins in the Book of Numbers (Num. 31:15–16; 25:1–5). This is probably because the Nicolaitans ignored the teaching of the Council of Jerusalem, which prohibited the eating of foods offered to idols and sexual immorality, which was part and parcel of pagan temple services (Acts 15:19–20, 29).

The name "Nicolaitans" is also similar to "Balaam," in that both mean "Conqueror [or Destroyer] of the people."[21] This passage also alludes to Balaam's fate. Those who fail to heed Christ's words will be destroyed with the "sword of His mouth," as Balaam himself was killed by the sword (Num. 31:8).

Jesus is warning the Christians of Pergamum, then, not to be like the generation of Israelites who fell into sin just before they entered into the Promised Land. These Christians are at the threshold of the "new heavens and the new earth," which John is about to see come down from heaven. Christ is urging them to hold fast to their faith in order to "conquer," so that, unlike the Israelites, they may enter the true Promised Land without falling into sin.

Applying the Letter to Pergamum Today

Like Christ's words to the other churches, the temptations to which the Nicolaitans fell are ones to which we often succumb, though not in the same way. The people of Pergamum lived in a time and place where pagan idolatry and immorality dominated the culture. The temples were not easy to avoid. Most of the economy of this city had to do with these pagan temples.[22] The city's life revolved around them. The Nicolaitans said, "It's okay. You can compromise. You have to live here after all. Jesus understands."

How often today do Christians justify their involvement in sin because it is culturally acceptable? It's all around us and hard to avoid. Renunciation of sin is usually viewed as "weird" or "outdated." Christ's words are an important reminder to us that we must be "set apart." "Everyone else is doing it" has never been an acceptable excuse.

2:17. The "hidden manna" is most likely a reference to the Eucharist. In the fourth Gospel, John records the famous "Bread of Life" discourse, in which Jesus says He is the true manna: "I am the bread of life. Your fathers ate the manna in the wilderness, and they died. This is the bread which comes down from heaven, that a man may eat of it and not die. I am the living bread which came down from heaven; if any one eats of this bread, he will live for ever; and the bread which I shall give for the life of the world is my flesh" (Jn. 6:48–51). The "manna" was a symbol in the New Testament and in the writings of the early Fathers of the Eucharist.[23] In fact, Eucharistic imagery permeates many of the seven letters. For example, in Revelation 3:20, Christ says "[I]f anyone hears my voice and opens the door, I will come in to him and eat with him, and he with me." The "hidden" manna is Christ, therefore, who is hidden in the Real Presence of the Eucharist.

The "white stone" can be linked with the "bdellium," a stone connected to the appearance of the manna in the Old Testament (Num. 11:7; Ex. 16:31). In fact, a tradition in rabbinic literature stated that these stones fell from heaven with the manna.[24] The "bdellium" was also found in the Garden of Eden (Gen. 2:12). The manna, therefore, represented Israel's calling to reverse the disobedience of Adam. Furthermore, the reference to it here, like the reference to the tree of life, may point to the new creation that Christ inaugurates at the end of Revelation.

The writing on the "white stone" may be an allusion to the stones worn by the high priest, which had the names of Israel written on them (Ex. 28:9–12).[25] As for the reference to a "new name," John borrows his imagery from Isaiah 62:2, which speaks of the restoration of Israel in terms of the New Exodus: "And you will be called by a new name."[26] Jesus is the New Moses. Through Him, God's people will be restored.

The Letter to Thyatira

> **Rev. 2:18–23.** And to the angel of the church in Thyatira write: "The words of the Son of God, who has eyes like a flame of fire, and whose feet are like burnished bronze.
>
> 19 "I know your works, your love and faith and service and patient endurance, and that your latter works exceed the first. 20 But I have this against you, that you tolerate the woman Jezebel, who calls herself a prophetess and is teaching and beguiling my servants to practice immorality and to eat food sacrificed to idols. 21 I gave her time to repent, but she refuses to repent of her immorality. 22 Behold, I will throw her on a sickbed, and those who commit adultery with her I will throw into great tribulation, unless they repent of her doings; 23 and I will strike her children dead. And all the churches shall know that I am he who searches mind and heart, and I will give to each of you as your works deserve."

2:18–23. Thyatira was one of the leading centers for trade in Asia Minor. Because of this it had an extraordinary number of trade guilds.[27] Each guild had a god whom all the members were required to worship.[28] This worship often included immoral sexual conduct and the eating of food offered to idols—practices condemned by the apostles at the Council of Jerusalem (Acts 15:19, 29). This situation posed a difficult dilemma for converts, who supported their families by working for these guilds.

Jesus recognizes that the church at Thyatira is continuing to grow and to do "better" works. However, apparently, someone in the community there was leading Christians into the sins of immorality and the eating of unclean food, quite possibly in the worship of the guild gods mentioned above. This person is compared to "Jezebel," the wife of Ahab, the king of Israel (1 Kings

21). There's a play on words here in Jesus' warning to these Christians. As one interpreter explains, "With grim humor, Jesus is saying, Do you want to 'get in bed' (i.e., commit fornication)? Very well—here's a death bed for you!"[29]

Jesus' self-description as the "one who searches the mind and heart" and who will "give to each of you as your works deserve" evokes what the Lord says in Jeremiah: "I the LORD search the mind and try the heart, to give to every man according to his ways, according to the fruit of his doings" (Jer. 17:10). Once again John implicitly underscores the fact that Jesus is the Lord. Jesus knows our inner self and sees through all of our "good deeds," knowing the state of our heart.[30]

Applying the Letter to Thyatira Today

The warning of Jesus remains applicable today. Sometimes we refuse to detach ourselves from certain sins, and so we try to justify ourselves by multiplying our good deeds. We try to bargain with God, thinking we can continue to sin as long as we "pay God His due." This is a perversion of the Gospel and a distorted vision of love. Jesus says, "If you love me, you will keep my commandments" (Jn. 14:15). We must give ourselves *totally* to Him, holding nothing back. Others may see our works and marvel, but Jesus sees our hearts.

> **Rev. 2:24.** 24 But to the rest of you in Thyatira, who do not hold this teaching, who have not learned what some call the deep things of Satan, to you I say, I do not lay upon you any other burden;

2:24. Ancient pagan religions claimed to be able to teach their members "profound truths" or "secret knowledge" often referred to as "mysteries." It is probably in reference to this that Jesus speaks of some in Thyatira as receiving knowledge of the "deep things of Satan." Christians at Thyatira therefore are warned not to join cults like Mithraism, which was associated with Roman soldiers and involved seven levels of secret initiation.[31]

Rev. 2:25–27. 25 "only hold fast what you have, until I come. 26 He who conquers and who keeps my works until the end, I will give him power over the nations, 27 and he shall rule them with a rod of iron, as when earthen pots are broken in pieces, even as I myself have received power from my Father;

2:25–27. Jesus tells believers that those who continue in His "works" will be allowed to share in His rule. The reference to the "iron rod" and "earthen pots" is no doubt an allusion to Psalm 2, which was typically understood as a prophecy concerning the Messiah. There the Davidic king conquers the rulers of the earth who have broken their covenant relationship with the king and tried to defeat him.[32] Jesus is thus comforting those who are struggling with fellow Christians who have fallen, and encouraging them not to reject Him.

Rev. 2:28–29. 28 and I will give him the morning star. 29 He who has an ear, let him hear what the Spirit says to the churches."

2:28–29. Christ's promise to give the faithful "the morning star" might be a reference to life in the new creation, which is about to dawn. Later, John learns that Christ is the morning star (Rev. 22:16). Those who endure, then, are promised that they will enter into Christ's presence forever in heaven. Of course, the Eucharist is a foretaste of this, where Christians are given a share in "the morning star."

The "morning star" might also refer to Numbers 24:17, where Balaam delivers to Balak a prophecy concerning the Messiah: "[A] star shall come forth out of Jacob, and a scepter shall rise out of Israel." Given the fact that Balaam has been mentioned already, it would not be surprising to find a reference here to a prophecy he had delivered.

The reference to "he who has an ear, let him hear" recalls the prophets' warnings to Israel to repent in the face of coming judgment. Isaiah was told to go to Jerusalem, ripe and ready for judgment, and say, "Hear and hear, but do not understand; see and see, but do not perceive" (Is. 6:9). Likewise, Jesus uses this expression after the Jewish leaders reject Him in Matthew 12, when He preaches in parables to them, saying, "He who has ears, let him hear" (Mt. 13:9). The implication in the Book of Revelation is, unless Christians in Thyatira repent, they will be judged.

The Letter to Sardis

Rev. 3:1–6. 1 And to the angel of the church in Sardis write: "The words of him who has the seven spirits of God and the seven stars.
"I know your works; you have the name of being alive, and
you are dead. 2 Awake, and strengthen what remains and is on the
point of death, for I have not found your works perfect in the sight
of my God. 3 Remember then what you received and heard; keep
that, and repent. If you will not awake, I will come like a thief, and
you will not know at what hour I will come upon you. 4 Yet you
have still a few names in Sardis, people who have not soiled their
garments; and they shall walk with me in white, for they are worthy. 5 He who conquers shall be clad thus in white garments, and
I will not blot his name out of the book of life; I will confess his
name before my Father and before his angels. 6 He who has an ear,
let him hear what the Spirit says to the churches."

3:1–3. Sardis was known for being the Beverly Hills of Asia Minor; it was an extremely wealthy city. The city was known throughout the ancient world as the place to shop for luxury goods. Carpets from Sardis were used in palaces as far away as Persia. Likewise, Sardis' perfumes were world renown.[33]

The church in Sardis apparently had a good reputation: "you have the name of being alive." However, the goodness of the church is only skin deep, for Jesus adds, "and you are dead." Jesus tells the church to "awake." He commands them to repent of sinfulness so they can live in Him.

Applying the Letter to Sardis Today

Sometimes parishes have incredibly busy calendars: dances, bingo nights, plays, pancake breakfasts, recycling drives, trips to sporting events, youth trips to amusement parks, etc. Yet, although the parish may have the reputation for "being alive," spiritually it may be dead. More people might go to bingo nights than to Mass. More people might stand in line for the pancake breakfast than for Confession.

Christ wants to teach us a different kind of "active" parish. We must always keep in mind that what really makes a parish "alive" isn't the social activities, but the sacramental life, which animates the Church. Likewise, a parish's liturgy is not "alive" because it has great singing, exciting guitars, or lively bongos—it's alive in as much as it centers itself on the Eucharist.

3:4–6. Those who have not fallen away from Christ are referred to as the ones who "have not soiled their garments." Revelation 19:8 tells us that the bright white linen garments are "the righteous deeds of the saints." Clean garments, therefore, imply continued Christian faithfulness. The early Christians adopted the use of white garments as a symbol for holiness by giving the newly baptized "white garments."[34] This is still practiced in some churches today.

The Letter to Philadelphia

Rev. 3:7–13. 7 And to the angel of the church in Philadelphia
write: "The words of the holy one, the true one, who has the key
of David, who opens and no one shall shut, who shuts and no one
opens.

8 "I know your works. Behold, I have set before you an open
door, which no one is able to shut; I know that you have but little
power, and yet you have kept my word and have not denied my
name. 9 Behold, I will make those of the synagogue of Satan who
say that they are Jews and are not, but lie—behold, I will make
them come and bow down before your feet, and learn that I have
loved you. 10 Because you have kept my word of patient
endurance, I will keep you from the hour of trial which is coming
on the whole world, to try those who dwell upon the earth. 11
I am coming soon; hold fast what you have, so that no one may
seize your crown. 12 He who conquers, I will make him a pillar in
the temple of my God; never shall he go out of it, and I will write
on him the name of my God, and the name of the city of my God,
the new Jerusalem which comes down from my God out of heav-

en, and my own new name. 13 He who has an ear, let him hear what the Spirit says to the churches."

3:7–13. Philadelphia suffered a devastating earthquake in AD 17. Several smaller ones rocked the city afterwards. It was rebuilt thanks to imperial funds.[35]

Jesus offers words of comfort and stability to the citizens of this city that was constantly shaken by earthquakes. The imagery of a "pillar" and a lasting temple assures these Christians a home in a city that will never need Imperial funds to rebuild—the city of the New Jerusalem.

Like Smyrna, a large number of anti-Christian Jews lived in Philadelphia who incited a persecution of the Christians.[36] This is most likely the background for the reference in 3:9 to the "synagogue of Satan" (see commentary on Rev. 2:9). True Judaism doesn't persecute Christianity.

Key Concepts

Jesus is pictured as the one who holds the "key of David," which is earlier referred to as "the keys of Death and Hades" (Rev. 1:18). This "key of David" is mentioned in Isaiah 22:22, where Eliakim replaces Shebna as the prime minister of the Davidic kingdom. There the "key" of the kingdom is a symbol of the authority of the Davidic king given to the prime minister, who acts with the authority of the king: "[H]e shall open, and none shall shut; he shall shut, and none shall open" (Is. 22:22). Jesus makes further reference to this in referring to Himself as the one "who opens and no one shall shut, who shuts and no one opens." Jesus holds the key because He is the Davidic king.

Moreover, Jesus, as the Davidic king, gives this authority to Peter, making him the "prime minister" of His kingdom. "I will give you the keys of the kingdom of heaven, and whatever you bind on earth shall be bound in heaven, and whatever you loose on earth shall be loosed in heaven" (Mt. 16:19). Peter, therefore, acts with the authority of Jesus, who is the true holder of the keys (Rev. 3:7). Furthermore, since the keys were meant to be passed on, as they are in Isaiah, Jesus intends Peter's authority to be transferred to a successor.[37] This authority has been handed on down through the centuries to Peter's successors, the popes.[38]

This was the understanding of the early Fathers. Tertullian stated that "Clement was ordained by Peter."[39] Irenaeus traces the authority of the bishop of Rome of his time:

> To this Clement there succeeded Evaristus. Alexander followed Evaristus; then, sixth from the apostles, Sixtus was appointed; after him, Telephorus, who was gloriously martyred; then Hyginus; after him, Pius; then after him, Anicetus. Sorer having succeeded Anicetus, Eleutherius does now, in the twelfth place from the apostles, hold the inheritance of the episcopate. In this order, and by this succession, the ecclesiastical tradition from the apostles, and the preaching of the truth, have come down to us. And this is most abundant proof that there is one and the same vivifying faith, which has been preserved in the Church from the apostles until now, and handed down in truth.[40]

Applying the Letter to Philadelphia Today

The Philadelphians are warned about those who called themselves Jews, but aren't. In other words, the church is to be careful of false teachers. For a Gentile convert, a Jew, having grown up with the Scriptures, would be seen as an authority on them. Nonetheless, Jews who persecute the Church have perverted Judaism and therefore may lead Christians astray.

In the same way, Christians need to watch out for those who say they teach true doctrines, but don't. Just as people like the Nicolaitans taught false doctrine to the churches in John's day, so too there are those who pose as teachers today, yet only lead the faithful astray. So how are we to know what the faith really says about various issues? We must remember the keys given to Peter and to his successors, the popes.

But some may object, "Doesn't obeying the Church mean giving up our freedom to think for ourselves?" Not any more than learning the laws of aerodynamics constricts airplane designers from coming up with "creative" ideas about flying. You can't fly if you don't know the laws of aerodynamics. So too, you cannot truly be free unless you seek to know Jesus' teachings, transmitted through the Church.

Contrary to popular opinion, ignorance is not bliss. God made us, so He knows what we are made for. He knows what's good for us, better than we do, since He designed us. Jesus has made God's teachings for our lives knowable through the Church. You may not like them at first. You may not understand them at first. But you must keep in mind—the Church isn't right because she is really old, but because Christ speaks in her through the Spirit.

When in doubt, then, Christians can always turn to the Holy Father and the Church's Magisterium. God has given the Church the authority to teach His message faithfully so we never need to be confused. We should, therefore, be well acquainted with the teachings of the Church. A practical way to do this would be to pick up the *Catechism of the Catholic Church*—a compendium of all the Church's teachings.

The Letter to Laodicea

Rev. 3:14–19. 14 And to the angel of the church in Laodicea write: " The words of the Amen, the faithful and true witness, the beginning of God's creation.

15 "I know your works: you are neither cold nor hot. Would that you were cold or hot! 16 So, because you are lukewarm, and neither cold nor hot, I will spew you out of my mouth. 17 For you say, I am rich, I have prospered, and I need nothing; not knowing that you are wretched, pitiable, poor, blind, and naked. 18 Therefore I counsel you to buy from me gold refined by fire, that you may be rich, and white garments to clothe you and to keep the shame of your nakedness from being seen, and salve to anoint your eyes, that you may see. 19 Those whom I love, I reprove and chasten; so be zealous and repent.

3:14–19. Laodicea was located between Hierapolis and Colossae. Colossae was situated at the foot of the mountains and received cold, refreshing drinking water. Hierapolis, on the other hand, was the source of hot, mineral pools, which were used for healing baths. The water in Laodicea was neither hot nor cold. Christ apparently uses this geographical data as an illustration of the spiritual state of the Church in Laodicea: "[B]ecause you are lukewarm, neither cold nor hot, I will spew you out of my mouth" (3:16).[41]

Like Philadelphia, Laodicea had been hit by an earthquake in the first century. However, unlike the Philadelphians, they were so rich they refused imperial help and rebuilt on their own.[42] This would explain why Christ warns the Church against boasting, "I am rich, I have prospered, and I need nothing." The Lord knows that, despite their earthly wealth, they are spiritually bankrupt: "[Y]ou are wretched, pitiable, poor, blind, and naked."

Just What the Doctor Ordered

Jesus' three-fold prescription, (1) "gold refined by fire," (2) "white garments," and (3) "salve to anoint your eyes," roughly corresponds to the needs of the Laodicean Church that must be met. "Gold refined by fire" is given to them for their "wretched, pitiable and poor" state. "White garments" are provided to clothe their "nakedness." Finally, eye "salve" is meant to cure their "blindness." These cures must be bought *from Jesus.* In other words, the Laodiceans must admit that they can't buy these kinds of cures on their own—they need Jesus.

The Laodiceans' state	**Jesus prescriptions**
"wretched, pitiable, poor"	"gold refined by fire"
"naked"	"white garments to cloth you"
"blind"	"salve to anoint your eyes"

The first cure is the most costly. "Gold refined with fire" is a symbol for purification through suffering (cf. Job 23:10; Mal. 3:2–3; Zech. 13:9; 1 Pet. 1:6–9). But does Jesus actually expect these Christians to desire a test of suffering? Yes, for only through trials will they learn how to love Christ unselfishly. Only in this will they learn life-giving love. Persecution, therefore, isn't necessarily a sign of God's rejection of His people, but rather a sign of His love for them. As Jesus states a little later, "Those whom I love, I reprove and chasten; so be zealous and repent" (Rev. 3:19).

The second prescription, "white garments" to cover their "nakedness," is an image rooted in the Old Testament. The "uncovering of nakedness" is often used in connection with sexual sins, especially those committed as part of idol worship.[43] Perhaps there is a veiled reference here to some kind of sexual immorality committed as part of pagan religious rituals. In any event, the "white garments" that the Laodiceans are to receive from the Lord are "the righteous deeds of the saints" (Rev. 19:8).

The charge of blindness is used in John's Gospel to describe those who refuse to acknowledge guilt and repent (Jn 9:39–41). The third prescription, which is meant to cure this, is the "salve." Eye salve was something the Laodiceans were well acquainted with. In fact, there was a famous Laodicean medical school that was known for its use of eye salve, derived from a Phyrgian powder.[44] However, the eye salve used by Laodicean doctors is inadequate to cure spiritual blindness, so "salve" must be bought from Jesus, the true Physician. This rich and proud community must acknowledge its weakness in humility and repent.

> **Rev: 3:20–22.** 20 Behold, I stand at the door and knock; if any one hears my voice and opens the door, I will come in to him and eat with him, and he with me. 21 He who conquers, I will grant him to sit with me on my throne, as I myself conquered and sat down with my Father on his throne. 22 He who has an ear, let him hear what the Spirit says to the churches."

3:20. The words of Christ concerning dining with the faithful is undoubtedly a Eucharistic reference. A non-Catholic, David Chilton, makes the following comment on this passage: "We must take seriously the Biblical doctrine of the Real Presence of Christ in the sacrament of the Eucharist. We must return to the Biblical pattern of worship centered on *Jesus Christ*, which means the weekly celebration of the Lord's Supper, as well as instruction about its true meaning. . . . In Holy Communion we are genuinely having dinner with Jesus, lifted up into His heavenly presence; and, moreover, we are feasting on Him."[45] Again, we see that the Eucharist is the context in which the Book of Revelation must be understood.

3:21–22. This appears to settle an ancient debate in Rabbinic Judaism as to how many thrones there are in heaven. Some said there was one, others said the Messiah would sit on a separate one. Here John shows us that there is only one. This is because the Messiah is God Himself.

Applying the Letter to the Laodiceans Today

For years, I did youth ministry in a parish near the Los Angeles harbor. Even when they come from broken homes or abusive families, teenagers are generally good at heart and have an instinct about right and wrong. Yet, when they start coming to Church and learning their faith, they quickly learn to ask one question: "Is that a mortal sin or a venial sin?" In other words, "I need to know whether that is a mortal sin or not, because if it's not then I'm going to do it." In this way, they would push the limits. I don't think these young people are much different than many adults.

This is the attitude Jesus warns against when He says, "Because you are neither cold nor hot, I will spew you out of my mouth." This is harsh language. Jesus is warning against a real and serious problem—spiritual indifference and complacency. Indeed, this is the most dangerous problem Catholics face today.

What a perversion of love this is! A man who loves a woman doesn't simply say, "Okay, tell me the things you don't like, and then tell me the things that would cause you to leave me. I need to know what I can get away with." Yet, this is exactly how we often treat the Lord. Love doesn't do the bare minimum. It goes all the way. Jesus wants total life-giving love—not token prayers every night.

In this we are reminded of the rich young man who came to Jesus asking, "[W]hat must I do to inherit eternal life?" Jesus tells him to keep the commandments, "You know the commandments:

Do not kill, Do not commit adultery . . ." The man replies, "All these I have observed from my youth" (Mk. 10:17, 19, 20).

Notice this: the man says he's kept all these commandments from his youth—a feat anyone would be hard pressed to follow. At this point we might expect Jesus to say, "No you haven't." But Jesus doesn't contradict the man, which tells us something amazing about him. Yet Jesus is about to give him one further command.

Mark tells us that Jesus, "looking upon him loved him," and then said, "You lack one thing: go, sell what you have and give to the poor and you will have treasure in heaven; and come follow me" (10:21). This is too much for the man. At this "his face fell," and he walks away. He kept the commandments perfectly, but loved his possessions more than Jesus.

Following Christ means more than simply stopping short of mortal sin, dangling our toes off the edge, and patting ourselves on the back for not yet falling off. Indeed, that pat of pride may be just enough to push us over. We need to look at the Cross and remember that Jesus, the sinless, innocent Son of God, gave everything He had in love, holding nothing back. What do we give Him? Indeed, if we aren't growing closer to Him, we are falling away.

* * *

Multiple Choice

1) Many prominent members of the early Church lived in __________.

(a) Ephesus
(b) Smyrna
(c) Philadelphia
(d) Corinth

2) The early heretics, the ______________, sought to relax the requirements of faith, allowing for immorality and idolatry.
(a) Gnostics
(b) Nicolaitans

(c) Idolatrinites
(d) Marcionites

3) The early Fathers understood the ____________ as the fruit of the Tree of Life.
(a) Eucharist
(b) true faith
(c) works of the faithful
(d) manna

4) The church condemned for lukewarmness is ____________.
(a) Ephesus
(b) Philadelphia
(c) Sardis
(d) Laodicea

Answer) 1. a; 2. b; 3. a; 4. d.

* * *

Discussion/Study Questions

1. Why does Jesus send a warning to the seven churches before He shows John the vision of the destruction of Jerusalem? (See page 58)

____

____

____

____

2. How does understanding the particular situations of the seven churches help us better understand the Book of Revelation and apply it today? (See page 58)

____

____

____

____

3. What is the main lesson of the letter to Ephesus? Smyrna? Pergamum? Thyatira? Sardis? Philadelphia? Laodicea? (See pages 59–77)

4. Which church's situation can you most identify with?

5. In Matthew's Gospel, Jesus gives Peter the keys. However, in Revelation, Jesus says He holds the keys. What can we learn from this? (See pages 71–72)

6. The Church of Ephesus was the home to many famous saints. Name some. (See page 59)

ON EARTH AS IT IS IN HEAVEN

The Seven Seals (Rev. 4:1–6:17)

Ever wonder what heaven would look like if you could see it? Well, John gets that chance in Revelation 4, and what he finds might surprise you. He doesn't encounter what we might expect. There are no houses in the clouds or naked baby angels flying around. What John sees is much greater than baby angels.

John Is Invited to "Come Up"

Rev. 4:1. After this I looked, and lo, in heaven an open door! And the first voice, which I had heard speaking to me like a trumpet, said, "Come up hither, and I will show you what must take place after this."

4:1. With the words, "Come up hither," John is taken up into heaven. The voice tells John that he is about to see "what must take place after this." John has now moved from seeing "what is"—that is, the situation of the seven churches—to "what will take place hereafter"—the future events that will lead up to fall of the harlot city (Rev. 1:19).

Many Protestants interpret this in terms of the "rapture" during which, they believe, Christians will be taken up into heaven. However, the word "rapture" never occurs. Instead, John is about to see how Daniel's prophecy concerning the Son of Man is fulfilled in Christ.

Prophet Hearing

There are, in fact, striking parallels between Daniel 7 and Revelation 4–5. Here are just a few of them:

1. introductory vision phraseology (Dan. 7:9 [cf. Dan. 7:2, 6–7]; Rev. 4:1)
2. a throne(s) set in heaven (Dan. 7:9a; Rev. 4:2a, *[9]* [cf. 4:4a])
3. God sitting on a throne (Dan. 7:9b; Rev. 4:2b)
4. God's appearance on the throne (Dan. 7:9c; Rev. 4:3a)
5. fire before the throne (Dan. 7:9d–10a; Rev. 4:5)
6. heavenly servants surrounding the throne (Dan. 7:10b; Rev. 4:4b; 6b–10; 5:8, 11, 14)
7. *[the image of a sea (Dan. 7:2–3; Rev. 4:6)]*
8. book(s) before the throne (Dan. 7:10; Rev. 5:1ff)
9. the book(s) opened (Dan. 7:10c; Rev. 5:2–5, 9)
10. a divine (messianic) figure approaching God's throne to receive authority to reign forever over a kingdom (Dan. 7:13–14a; Rev. 5:5b–7, 9a, 12–13)
11. the kingdom's scope: "all peoples, nations, and tongues" (Dan. 7:14a [MT]; Rev. 5:9b)
12. the seer's emotional distress on account of the vision (Dan 7:15; Rev. 5:4)
13. the seer's reception of heavenly counsel concerning the vision from one of the heavenly throne servants (Dan. 7:16; Rev. 5:5a)
14. the saints given divine authority to reign over a kingdom (Dan. 7:18, 22, 27a; Rev. 5:10)
15. concluding mention of God's eternal reign (Dan. 7:27b; Rev. 5:13–14).[1]

In all of this, John portrays Christ as the One who, in fulfillment of Daniel's prophecy, receives the kingdom and gives it to the saints. As we will see, John shows how all of this occurs in the liturgy.

In addition to Daniel, John's experience is foreshadowed by the visions of other prophets. Isaiah and Ezekiel were also given a vision of God's throne room in heaven (Is. 6; Ezek. 1–2). Isaiah and Ezekiel both saw God's glory when they were commissioned to prophesy about the coming destruction of the Jerusalem temple in 586 BC. God allowed these prophets to see His glory in heaven so that they would know that the temple on earth was only penultimate. The true temple is in the heavenly city above. As we shall see, John's vision is meant to reveal this to us.

In fact, the Book of Revelation closely follows the pattern in the Book of Ezekiel. David Chilton points out the following similarities:

1. The Throne-Vision (Rev. 4 / Ezek. 1)
2. The Book (Rev. 5 / Ezek. 2–3)
3. The Flour Plagues (Rev. 6:1–8 / Ezek. 5)
4. The Slain under the Altar (Rev. 6:9–11 / Ezek. 6)
5. The Wrath of God (Rev. 6:12–17 / Ezek. 7)
6. The Seal on the Saint's Foreheads (Rev. 7 / Ezek. 9)
7. The Coals from the Altar (Rev. 8 / Ezek. 10)
8. No More Delay (Rev. 10:1–7 / Ezek. 12)
9. The Eating of the Book (Rev. 10:8–11 / Ezek. 2)
10. The Measuring of the Temple (Rev. 11:1–2 / Ezek. 40–43)
11. Jerusalem and Sodom (Rev. 11:8 / Ezek. 16)
12. The Cup of Wrath (Rev. 14 / Ezek. 23)
13. The Vine of the Land (Rev. 14:18–20 / Ezek. 15)
14. The Great Harlot (Rev. 17–18 / Ezek. 16, 23)
15. The Lament over the City (Rev. 18 / Ezek. 27)
16. The Scavengers' Feast (Rev. 19 / Ezek. 39)
17. The First Resurrection (Rev. 20:4–6 / Ezek. 37)
18. The Battle with Gog and Magog (Rev. 20:7–9 / Ezek 38–39)
19. The New Jerusalem (Rev. 21 / Ezek. 40–48)
20. The River of Life (Rev. 22 / Ezek. 47)[2]

Ezekiel, like John, had foreseen the fall of Jerusalem and the establishment of the "new" Jerusalem. It makes sense, then, that John would draw on the Book of Ezekiel so heavily, since John also prophesies concerning the destruction of the temple and the coming of the heavenly city.

The Throne of God

Rev. 4:2–3. 2 At once I was in the Spirit, and lo, a throne stood in heaven, with one seated on the throne! 3 And he who sat there appeared like jasper and carnelian, and round the throne was a rainbow that looked like an emerald.

4:2–3. John sees God's throne similarly to how Ezekiel had seen it in his day (Ezek. 1:26–28). The stones of "jasper" and "carnelian," which John sees, are also significant. First of all, they were found in the Garden of Eden, the original earthly sanctuary (Ezek. 28:13). Furthermore, the Greek Old Testament tells us that these stones were worn by the high priest, when he ministered in Israel's sanctuary (Ex. 28:17–20, LXX). The rainbow, seen by both John and Ezekiel (1:28), signifies "new creation" imagery in its connection with the Flood of Noah (Gen. 9:13).[3]

The Twenty-Four Elders

> **Rev. 4:4–5.** 4 Round the throne were twenty-four thrones, and seated on the thrones were twenty-four elders, clad in white garments, with golden crowns upon their heads. 5 From the throne issue flashes of lightning, and voices and peals of thunder, and before the throne burn seven torches of fire, which are the seven spirits of God;

4:4. *Presbyteroi*, the Greek word for "elder," is the word from which we get the English word "priest." The number "twenty four," evokes 1 Chronicles 24–25, where David set up twenty-four divisions of priests to serve and sing in the temple. This is exactly what John's twenty-four elders do—sing and worship God.

These elders are also described in royal terms, since they sit on "thrones" and wear "golden crowns." Who are these elders? It is very unlikely that they are angels, since the term "elder" is usually used in the Old Testament in reference to humans.[4] It would seem that these elders represent the faithful, whom Christ has made "a kingdom, priests to His God" (Rev. 1:6).

These twenty-four elders, then, represent the saints, who have passed the test, by offering their lives in priestly sacrifice and who now have received the "crown of life" (Rev. 2:10). Their white garments are their righteous deeds (Rev. 19:8). Through their life-giving love, they have realized that which Adam had failed to obtain (see commentary on 1:5–6).

4:5. The image of "flashes of lightning, and voices and peals of thunder" calls to mind God's presence on Mount Sinai (cf. Ex. 19:16). At Sinai we can also see a connection between the use of the term "elder" and the use of the term "priest." There, after God has told Moses that He wants to make Israel a "kingdom of priests," Moses calls together "the elders of the people" (Ex. 19:6, 7). Here we see many parallels with Revelation 4:5. John is seeing the fulfillment not only of Adam's calling, but Israel's as well.

This passage contains other references to the Old Testament as well. The description of "lightning" coming from God's throne, which John sees in his vision, is also found in Ezekiel's vision (Ezek. 1:13).

John also draws here from Zechariah 4, describing the "seven spirits" in terms of "seven torches." We have already seen that the phrase "seven spirits" refers to the Holy Spirit. There also seems to be a connection between the seven torches and the seven lampstands. We know from chapter 1 that the seven lampstands are a symbol of the seven churches (cf. Rev. 1:20). It would seem that the seven torches rest on the seven lampstands—in other words, the Spirit dwells in the Church. The Apocalypse paints this picture to show us that the Spirit is present in and through the Church.[5]

The Sea of Glass

> **Rev. 4:6a.** and before the throne there is as it were a sea of glass, like crystal.

4:6a. The image of the sea of glass before the throne of God was prefigured in Solomon's temple by a bronze laver before the Holy of Holies (cf. Ex. 30:17–21; 1 Kings 7:23–26). Ancient Jews understood that their temple was only a copy of a heavenly one (cf. Wis. 9:8). When Moses built the tent, the proto-type for the temple, he did so according to a heavenly vision he saw on Sinai (cf. Ex. 25:9).[6] This view was taken up later by the author of Hebrews, who states: "For Christ has entered, not into a sanctuary made with hands, a copy of the true one, but into heaven itself, now to appear in the presence of God on our behalf" (Heb. 9:24).

The Four Living Creatures

Rev. 4:6b–7. And round the throne, on each side of the throne, are four living creatures, full of eyes in front and behind: 7 the first living creature like a lion, the second living creature like an ox, the third living creature with the face of a man, and the fourth living creature like a flying eagle.

4:6b–7. Many Catholic churches have a depiction of the four living creatures somewhere on a stained glassed window or altar rail—the man, the lion, the ox, and the eagle. The Fathers of the Church associate the four living creatures with the four Evangelists. Matthew is represented by the Man, since his Gospel begins with Jesus' human genealogy. The Lion stands for Mark, whose account begins with a voice in the wilderness, where lions live and roam. Luke is symbolized by the Ox, since his Gospel begins and ends with the temple, where oxen are slaughtered. Finally, the Eagle denotes John, whose Gospel "soars" to the heights in contemplation of Christ's divinity.[7]

The four living creatures in Revelation were also seen by Ezekiel, although somewhat differently (Ezek. 1:5–14). These living creatures, Ezekiel tells us, are angels, "cherubim," upon whom God "rides" (Ezek. 10:14–22). The earthly temple had a "copy" of this in the images of the two cherubim who were on top of the ark. Just as God's glory rested on the four living creatures, so too God's presence appeared over the cherubim on the ark in the temple, supplying the image of God riding on the cherubim.[8]

Looking Up

Some have pointed out that the imagery of the four living creatures comes from the Zodiac. For the ancients, the Zodiac symbolized all the stars in the heavens. The Zodiac divided the heavens into four parts. The signs in the middle of these four parts are the Lion (Leo), the Man (Aquarius, the Waterer), the Bull (Taurus), and the Eagle.[9] Scholars, therefore, believe that the four living creatures symbolize all of creation worshipping God.

Moreover, the twelve tribes of Israel seemed to be associated with the twelve signs of the Zodiac. In the wilderness, the twelve tribes of Israel were stationed around the sanctuary, with Judah, Reuben, Ephraim, and Dan leading Israel on each of the Tabernacle's four sides. These four tribes were associated with the Zodiac signs: Judah as the Lion, Reuben as the Man, Ephraim as the Bull, and Dan as the Eagle.[10] In their worship, therefore, Israel followed the pattern in heaven. Yet, whereas ancient Israel copied the worship of heaven—the Church actually participates in the heavenly liturgy.[11]

Holy, Holy, Holy

Rev. 4:8–10. 8 And the four living creatures, each of them with six wings, are full of eyes all round and within, and day and night they never cease to sing, "Holy, holy, holy, is the Lord God Almighty, who was and is and is to come!" 9 And whenever the living creatures give glory and honor and thanks to him who is seated on the throne, who lives for ever and ever, 10 the twenty-four elders fall down before him who is seated on the throne and worship him who lives for ever and ever; they cast their crowns before the throne, singing,

4:8–10. John sees the the four living creatures (cherubim) "covered with eyes." This imagery is used to show us that they are all-knowing. They work as God's agents, seeing all things and reporting them to Him.[12] Their description calls to mind the "seraphim" seen by Isaiah, who also have "six wings" (Is. 6:2). Like the seraphim in Isaiah's vision, the cherubim sing, "Holy, Holy, Holy" (Is. 6:3).

The twenty-four elders, that is, the saints, take their cue from the cherubim, for they fall down and worship whenever the angels do. Through all eternity, they continue to offer God their lives in love, which is symbolized in the way they "cast their crowns before the throne." Furthermore, the saints on earth participate in this liturgy. This is seen in 5:1, which tells us that the angels and twenty-four elders offer incense, which are the prayers of God's people.[13] At Mass then, the Church enters into this heavenly liturgy, as she sings with the angels and saints, "Holy, Holy, Holy."

The Praise of the Saints

Rev. 4:11. "Worthy art thou, our Lord and God, to receive glory and honor and power, for thou didst create all things, and by thy will they existed and were created."

4:11. The prayers offered in heaven to God harken back to David's prayer in 1 Chronicles 29:10: "Blessed art thou, O LORD, the God of Israel our Father, for ever and ever. Thine, O LORD, is the greatness, and the power, and the glory, and the victory, and the majesty; for all that is in the heavens and in the earth is thine; thine is the kingdom, O LORD, and thou art exalted as head above all." This prayer also seems to evoke the Greek version of Daniel 3.[14]

The Scroll with Seven Seals

Rev. 5:1–4. 1 And I saw in the right hand of him who was seated on the throne a scroll written within and on the back, sealed with seven seals; 2 and I saw a strong angel proclaiming with a loud voice, "Who is worthy to open the scroll and break its seals?" 3 And no one in heaven or on earth or under the earth was able to open the scroll or to look into it, 4 and I wept much that no one was found worthy to open the scroll or to look into it.

5:1–4. This scroll seems to be a covenant document. It is sealed with "seven" seals, the number associated with covenant making. It is also important to note that it is "written within and on the back"—like the tablets of the Ten Commandments (Ex. 32:15), another covenant document. But what exactly is a covenant?

Sworn In

Some think that a "covenant" is basically the same thing as a "contract." Nothing could be further from the truth. The difference between a covenant and a mere contract is that a contract involves the exchange of goods and services, while a covenant demands the giving of self.[15] Because of this, the difference between a covenant and a contract is like the difference between marriage and prostitution.[16]

Covenants, therefore, involve the forging of a bond that is so strong that it forms family ties, making sons and daughters, husbands and wives. Because of this, the great covenant scholar D. J. McCarthy noted that the father-son relationship is the basis for all ancient covenants.[17] In this we see that *what* God does reflects *who* God is.

Pope John Paul II explains, "God in His deepest mystery is not a solitude, but a family, since He has within Himself fatherhood, sonship, and the essence of the family which is love."[18] God is the primordial Family, of which all families are simply an image. God is the essence of family. God's work through the covenants of salvation history reflects who He is, bringing us into life of the divine Family. Since God is Family, He seeks to make us family.

One Big Happy Family

Adam was originally created to be in a covenant relationship with God—to enter into the divine family life of the Trinity—but he fell. Salvation history is the story of God seeking to bring all mankind back into that covenant family. The reversal of Adam's sin starts with Abraham, through whom God will "bless" all nations (cf. Gen. 22:18). God will work through Abraham's descendants, the people of Israel, to extend His covenant to all men. The Davidic covenant is an earthly blueprint of how God planned to fulfill His promises of old, as the nations come to know Yahweh through the son of David.

Christ brings all the covenants to fulfillment in Himself as the Lion of the Tribe of Judah—the conquering Davidic Messiah (see note on Revelation 5:5). The book that is sealed here in Revelation 5 represents God's covenant promises, from Adam to the time of Christ, which no man was worthy to fulfill.[19] Because Christ restores God's covenant relationship to all men, He is able to break open the seals.

The Lion and the Lamb

Rev. 5:5–6. 5 Then one of the elders said to me, "Weep not; lo, the Lion of the tribe of Judah, the Root of David, has conquered, so that he can open the scroll and its seven seals."

6 And between the throne and the four living creatures and among the elders, I saw a Lamb standing, as though it had been slain, with seven horns and with seven eyes, which are the seven spirits of God sent out into all the earth;

5:5. Jesus' ability to "open the scroll," that is, to fulfill God's covenant promises, depends on His Davidic lineage, which is implied by the phrase, "the lion from the tribe of Judah, the root of Jesse." David was from the tribe of Judah, and Jesse was his father. The covenants in the Old Testament reach their climax in God's covenant promise to David to establish an everlasting kingdom through his son (2 Sam. 7:8–16). The Davidic covenant restores:

—man's original calling to divine sonship (Lk. 3:38; 2 Sam. 7:14)
—Adam's vocation to be a priest-king (Gen. 2:15, see my chapter 4, "Son-Kind of Priest"; Ps. 110:4)
—God's promise to Abraham to extend covenant blessing to all people through his descendants (Gen. 22:18; Ps. 72:17)
—Israel's calling to be God's firstborn priestly nation (Ex. 4:22, 19:6; Ps. 89:27, 110:4)

As Jesus fulfills the Davidic covenant, He fulfills all God's promises in the Old Testament.[20] One cannot, therefore, overlook the importance of the Davidic covenant for Jesus' mission. As we go on, this will become more and more clear.

Looking Sheepish

5:6. John expects to see the mighty conqueror, the Lion of the tribe of Judah—instead, he finds a "slain lamb." The image is almost absurd. The very last animal we would probably associate with "triumph" is what we find—a little lamb. Even more, this lamb has been slain. It's obviously a miracle that this lamb is even "standing" at all. Indeed, it is a miracle, and we call it the Resurrection.

Jesus turns our idea of victory upside down. He conquers by suffering. He offers His life, and triumphs, giving an example to us, who must learn, "Be faithful unto death, and I will give you the crown of life" (Rev. 2:10). In fact, Isaiah prophesied that the coming Messiah would make himself "an offering for sin" as "a lamb that is led to the slaughter" (Is. 53:10, 7).

It's important to notice that even in heaven—after the Resurrection—Jesus still appears "as though slain." He still bears the wounds in His body, just as He showed the apostles the nail marks on Easter Sunday. Standing before the throne of God as the Lamb who had been slain, He continues to re-present His offering to the Father for all time. He died "once and for all," but continues to present Himself as Priest and Victim in heaven.

Yet, don't let the lamb's humility fool you. The seven horns of the Lamb symbolize that He is almighty, since "horns" were a symbol in the Old Testament for "power" (Deut. 33:17; 1 Kings 22:11; Ps. 89:17; Dan. 7:7–8, 24). Likewise, His "seven eyes" indicate that He sees all, as one who is all knowing. It may also be possible to connect this imagery to Daniel 7, where the fourth beast is described with horns and eyes. Christ, therefore, shows that He is the one who truly has authority and power.[21]

The Lamb Takes the Scroll

Rev. 5:7. and he went and took the scroll from the right hand of him who was seated on the throne.

5:7. How exactly would a lamb take a scroll from the hand of God? Hoofs, which lack opposable thumbs, aren't usually good for holding things. Here we see, once again, that we can't interpret the Book of Revelation in an overly literal fashion. The deeper meanings of the symbols are what are important here, such as the image of Christ as the Lamb—a sacrificial offering. Revelation must be interpreted as it was meant to be. It must be understood in terms of the symbols taken from the Old Testament. Thus, when people see things like "Red China" in the red dragon of Revelation 12, or "666" as a reference to the pope, they violate the original meaning of John.

The New Song

Rev. 5:8–13. 8 And when he had taken the scroll, the four living creatures and the twenty-four elders fell down before the Lamb, each holding a harp, and with golden bowls full of incense, which are the prayers of the saints; 9 and they sang a new song, saying, "Worthy art thou to take the scroll and to open its seals, for thou wast slain and by thy blood didst ransom men for God from every tribe and tongue and people and nation, 10 and hast made them a kingdom and priests to our God, and they shall reign on earth." 11 Then I looked, and I heard around the throne and the living creatures and the elders the voice of many angels, numbering myriads of myriads and thousands of thousands, 12 saying with a loud voice, "Worthy is the Lamb who was slain, to receive power and wealth and wisdom and might and honor and glory and blessing!" 13 And I heard every creature in heaven and on earth and under the earth and in the sea, and all therein, saying, "To him who sits upon the throne and to the Lamb be blessing and honor and glory and might for ever and ever!"

5:8–13. The heavenly congregation sings a "new song." The phrase "new song" may be associated with the hope for the New Exodus, in which Israel would be returned from the exile by the Messiah, who would restore the kingdom of David. In the first Exodus, Moses sang a song as Israel passed onto the other side of the Red Sea (Ex. 15:1–18). In the Book of Psalms, Moses reappears at the beginning of Psalms 90–100, which speak of the New Exodus and the singing of a "new song" (Ps. 96:1; 98:1).[22] Here in Revelation, the elders stand next to the "sea" (Rev. 4:6) and sing the "new song" of the New Exodus.[23]

The Lamb who takes the scroll from the right hand of God, has many echoes of Daniel's vision of the "son of man" receiving the kingdom from the "Ancient of Days." Like the authority given to the "son of man" in Daniel, the kingdom over which the Lamb rules includes "all peoples, nations, and languages" (Dan. 7:14; cf.

Rev. 5:9). Similarly, like the Lamb, Daniel's "son of man" receives "glory" (Dan. 7:13, 14; Rev. 5:12), and in the Greek version, "honor" (Dan. 7:14, LXX; Rev. 5:12).

Jesus fulfills this vision of the son of man through the liturgy. The twenty-four elders hold "harps," as the Levites did in the earthly temple (cf. 1 Chron. 25:6–31). Likewise, they offer up the prayers of the saints as "incense." Thus, it is in the Liturgy of the Eucharist that Christ bestows the kingdom to the Church. This is why, at the first Mass, the Last Supper, Jesus told the apostles: "[A]s my Father appointed a kingdom for me, so do I appoint for you that you may eat and drink at my table in my kingdom, and sit on thrones judging the twelve tribes of Israel" (Lk. 22:29–30). In the liturgical prayers of the Mass, therefore, we sing the "new song," as the kingdom comes with the King.

The Great Amen

Rev. 5:14. And the four living creatures said, "Amen!" and the elders fell down and worshiped.

5:14. The twenty-four elders follow the lead of the cherubim (the four living creatures). The angels teach the saints to worship God in heaven. When the cherubim say, "Amen," the elders fall down.

A Horse of a Different Color

In Revelation 6, we learn that what happens in the liturgy of heaven has earth-shaking consequences. Throughout the book, the events on earth are affected and even effected by the actions of Jesus with the angels and saints in the heavenly liturgy. Therefore, as Jesus opens the seven scrolls, things begin to unravel on earth.

The four horsemen, also mentioned in Zechariah 6:1–8, should probably be identified as four angels (cf. Rev. 6:1). The havoc they wreak seems to summarize the curses that Moses warned Israel would be triggered if they broke the covenant and were unfaithful to the Lord God (Lev. 26:18–28; Deut. 28:15–68). Just as Jesus warned, by rejecting Him, all the covenant curses came upon His generation when Jerusalem was destroyed:

> "Woe to you, scribes and Pharisees, hypocrites! for you build the tombs of the prophets and adorn the monuments of the righteous, saying, 'If we had lived in the days of our fathers, we would not have taken part with them in shedding the blood of the prophets.' Thus you witness against yourselves, that you are sons of those who murdered the prophets. Fill up, then, the measure of your fathers. . . . Therefore I send you prophets and wise men and scribes, some of whom you will kill and crucify, and some you will scourge in your synagogues and persecute from town to town, that upon you may come all the righteous blood shed on earth, from the blood of innocent Abel to the blood of Zechariah the son of Barachiah, whom you murdered between the sanctuary and the altar. Truly, I say to you, all this will come upon this generation (Mt. 23:29–36).

The horsemen, therefore, bring about God's covenant judgment on Jerusalem, which occurred in the destruction of the temple.

The Gospel Truth

It should be no surprise, then, that the judgments brought about by the opening of the first six seals correspond strikingly to Jesus' description of the fall of Jerusalem in the Gospels. This can be seen by the chart below, from Chilton:

Revelation 6	Matthew 24
1. War (v. 1–2)	1. Wars (v. 6)
2. International strife (v. 3–4)	2. International strife (v. 7a)
3. Famine v. (5–6)	3. Famines (v. 7b)
4. Pestilence (v. 7–8)	4. Earthquakes (v. 7c)
5. Persecution (v. 9–11)	5. Persecutions (v. 9–13)
6. Earthquake; De-creation (v. 12–17)	6. De-creation (v. 15–31)

Mark 13	**Luke 21**
1. Wars (v. 7)	1. Wars (v. 9)
2. International strife (v. 8a)	2. International strife (v. 10)
3. Earthquakes (v. 8b)	3. Earthquakes (v. 11a)
4. Famines (v. 8c)	4. Plagues and famines (v. 11b)
5. Persecutions (v. 9–13)	5. Persecution (v. 12–19)
6. De-creation (v. 14–27)	6. De-creation (v. 20–27)[24]

Although there are a few differences, given the enormous amount of similarity, it is impossible to think that it is the result of coincidence. In fact, the only Gospel without an apocalyptic discourse is John's—perhaps because he had already covered that ground in Revelation.

Wrath with Horsepower

The prophecy of the four horsemen may have actually found a fulfillment in a vision seen by many right before the destruction of Jerusalem. Josephus records signs that occurred in the city, which seemed to signal the coming of the end: "[A] certain prodigious and incredible phenomenon appeared; I suppose the account of it would seem to be a fable, were it not related by those that saw it, and were not the events that followed it so considerable a nature as to deserve such signals; for, before sunsetting, chariots and troops of soldiers in their armor were seen running about among the clouds." After narrating this, Josephus goes on to tell about a prophet who warned of "a voice from the four winds," which corresponds to what John sees at the beginning of the next chapter (Rev. 7:1).[25]

First Seal: The First Horseman

Rev. 6:1–2. 1 Now I saw when the Lamb opened one of the seven seals, and I heard one of the four living creatures say, as with a voice of thunder, "Come!" 2 And I saw, and behold, a white horse, and its rider had a bow; and a crown was given to him, and he went out conquering and to conquer.

6:1–2. It may be possible to see the first rider as Jesus Himself. Jesus comes riding on a "white horse" in Revelation 19:11. He is also said to "conquer," as this horseman does (cf. 3:21; 5:5; 17:14). Yet there are problems with this interpretation, since this horseman appears to share the same nature as the other horsemen (11:7; 13:7). There is nothing especially remarkable about him. He is simply one of the four. Therefore, this should probably be understood in terms of a "false Messiah," who comes before Christ and leads people astray.

Second Seal: The Second Horseman

Rev. 6:3–4. 3 When he opened the second seal, I heard the second living creature say, "Come!" 4 And out came another horse, bright red; its rider was permitted to take peace from the earth, so that men should slay one another; and he was given a great sword.

6:3–4. The second horse brings persecution and civil unrest. Given the parallels to the synoptic accounts, it may also denote international strife. Of course, this was exactly what occurred before the destruction of Jerusalem in the year 70. Josephus recounts how civil unrest abounded at this time in Palestine, as Romans, Jews, Syrians, and others broke out in violence against each other.[26] Likewise, Roman historians report that civil unrest in Rome was so great, it was thought that Rome itself would collapse and be conquered.[27]

Third Seal: The Third Horseman

Rev. 6:5–6. 5 When he opened the third seal, I heard the third living creature say, "Come!" And I saw, and behold, a black horse, and its rider had a balance in his hand; 6 and I heard what seemed to be a voice in the midst of the four living creatures saying, "A quart of wheat for a denarius, and three quarts of barley for a denarius; but do not harm oil and wine!"

6:5–6. The symbol of "a balance," or scales, is used as a symbol for "famine," since it is then that food needs to be carefully weighed and measured out, as the price of it skyrockets (cf. Ezek. 4:10). "A quart of wheat for a denarius, and three quarts of barley for a denarius," represents this kind of superinflation. These prices translate to mean that a whole day's work would only earn enough bread to last one man for one day.[28] Man is just living day to day, barely surviving.

It is also interesting that oil and wine are not to be harmed. Wheat is harvested during Pentecost, during the spring harvest. Yet, oil and wine are not affected indicating that the later harvest, associated with the Feast of Booths, has not been hurt. Thus, the famine is severe but does not last the whole year. The judgments of the seven seals, therefore, are escalating, but have not climaxed yet.[29] Perhaps it is significant that the sacramental elements are to be left untouched: bread, wine and oil.

Fourth Seal: The Fourth Horseman

> **Rev. 6:7–8.** 7 When he opened the fourth seal, I heard the voice of the fourth living creature say, "Come!" 8 And I saw, and behold, a pale horse, and its rider's name was Death, and Hades followed him; and they were given power over a fourth of the earth, to kill with sword and with famine and with pestilence and by wild beasts of the earth.

6:7–8. The color of this horse, usually translated "pale," is *chloros* in Greek. From this word, we get the English "chlorophyll," which gives leaves their green color. It is better translated "green" and should probably be understood in terms of a sickly color.

The rider's name, "Death and Hades," seems to demonstrate that he is the worst of the four. In fact, it seems that the fourth horseman is a combination of the other riders that came before.

The meaning of power over "a fourth of the earth" is unclear. It may be seen as part of the overall destruction narratives on the whole; the trumpets bring about the destruction of one third of the land (8:7–12), while the Chalices destroy all that's left.

The final horseman's judgment of famine and violence may find a first century fulfillment in the situation of Jerusalem before the judgment of the year 70. Josephus described the state of Jerusalem before it fell: "The madness of the seditious did also increase together with their famine, and both those miseries were every day inflamed more and more; for there was no corn which anywhere appeared publicly, but the robbers came running into, and searched men's private houses; and then, if they found any, they tormented them, because they had denied they had any; and if they found none, they tormented them worse, because they supposed they had more carefully concealed it. . . . [A] table was nowhere laid for a distinct meal, but they snatched the bread out of the fire, half-baked, and ate it very hastily."[30]

Hence, violence and famine afflicted Jerusalem, just as John foresaw.

Fifth Seal: The Souls under the Altar

Rev. 6:9–11. 9 When he opened the fifth seal, I saw under the altar the souls of those who had been slain for the word of God and for the witness they had borne; 10 they cried out with a loud voice, "O Sovereign Lord, holy and true, how long before thou wilt judge and avenge our blood on those who dwell upon the earth?" 11 Then they were each given a white robe and told to rest a little longer, until the number of their fellow servants and their brethren should be complete, who were to be killed as they themselves had been.

6:9–11. The image of disembodied souls under the altar, crying out for the judgment of their murderers, calls to mind Old Testament stories such as Abel's, whose blood cried out to God for vengeance on his brother Cain (Gen. 4:10). Of course, here in Revelation 6, the "souls" of the saints, not the "blood," cry out. However, since the Bible often closely associates "soul" and "blood" (cf. Lev. 17:11), the image is to be taken in the same way.

Human Sacrifices

The description of these saints as "under the altar" is probably meant to illustrate their deaths as sacrificial. When animals were sacrificed in the temple, the blood from the offering would actually run down to the base of the altar (Lev. 9:9) ending up "under the altar." The "blood," and hence, the "souls," of these martyrs are "under the altar," because they offered their lives in sacrifice to God.

John learns that these saints must wait until "the full number" of martyrs is killed, illustrating that God is holding back His judgment, which will eventually be poured out all at once. This evokes Jesus' words to the Pharisees, cited above: "Fill up, then, the measure of your fathers . . . that upon you may come all the righteous blood shed on earth, from the blood of innocent Abel to the blood of Zechariah the son of Barachiah, whom you murdered between the sanctuary and the altar. Truly, I say to you, all this will come upon this generation" (Mt. 23:32, 35).

The white garments symbolize the "righteous deeds" (Rev. 19:8) of these saints and thereby connects them with the twenty-four elders (Rev. 4:4), who have also offered their lives as priestly sacrifices.

Sixth Seal: The Wrath of the Lamb

Rev. 6:12–17. 12 When he opened the sixth seal, I looked, and behold, there was a great earthquake; and the sun became black as sackcloth, the full moon became like blood, 13 and the stars of the sky fell to the earth as the fig tree sheds its winter fruit when shaken by a gale; 14 the sky vanished like a scroll that is rolled up, and every mountain and island was removed from its place. 15 Then the kings of the earth and the great men and the generals and the rich and the strong, and every one, slave and free, hid in the caves and among the rocks of the mountains, 16 calling to the mountains and rocks, "Fall on us and hide us from the face of him who is seated on the throne, and from the wrath of the Lamb; 17 for the great day of their wrath has come, and who can stand before it?"

6:12–17. As we saw in chapter 2, since the sun, moon, and stars were the way the ancients told time, the image of their destruction is another way of telling Jerusalem, "Your time is up!" Similarly, the image of the barren fig tree was used by Jesus as a symbol for the "fruitlessness" of Jerusalem, ripe for judgement (Mt. 21:18–19; 24:32). In fact, the wording of this passage is taken almost verbatim from Isaiah 34, where Edom is told of God's coming judgment: "The host of heaven shall rot away, and the skies roll up like a scroll. All their host shall fall as leaves fall from the vine, like leaves falling from the fig tree" (Is. 34:4). The message is this: Jerusalem is about to experience the same judgment God leveled against the enemies of His people in the past, because Jerusalem has become like them.

"Mountains" and "islands" were places of refuge during troubled times. In saying that these places will be removed, John is telling his audience that there will be no place left to hide. Therefore those who "hid in the caves and among the rocks of the mountains" will also be judged. The wording here recalls Jesus' warning to the women who stood by weeping for Him as He carried His Cross: "But Jesus turning to them said, 'Daughters of Jerusalem, do not weep for me, but weep for yourselves and for your children. For behold, the days are coming when they will say, 'Blessed are the barren, and the wombs that never bore, and the breasts that never gave suck!' Then they will begin to say to the mountains, 'Fall on us'; and to the hills, 'Cover us.' For if they do this when the wood is green, what will happen when it is dry?" (Lk. 23:28–31).[31]

The reference to the green wood is best understood as a warning that the wickedness of the Jewish leaders who killed Him is nothing compared to the evil state of Jerusalem at the time of the destruction in the year 70.

Applying the Lessons of Revelation 4–6 Today

When I was a young boy, I used to visualize things during Mass. I used to wonder what I would do if attackers suddenly crashed through the stain glass windows and barred the doors. I would plan my escape—under the pews, unnoticed, right out through the back doors. I've found a number of other Catholic males who used to do this too. We like those action-packed scenarios.

But the Book of Revelation shows us that my "action-packed" fantasy is a snooze compared to what really happens at Mass. In the Mass, heaven itself touches down to earth. We participate in the very same heavenly liturgy the angels and saints celebrate. Whoever your patron saint is—Saint Patrick, Saint Theresa, Saint Joseph, etc.—in the Mass, he or she stands next to you.

No matter how bland or off-key the singing is—when we sing "Holy, Holy, Holy," we are joining in the heavenly chorus. No matter how boring the homily, Christ truly comes to speak with His Church. No matter how much the children in front of you goof off, you are really standing with the angels.

And this worship is powerful and effective. For just as the opening of the seals causes the coming of the horsemen who ravage the earth, the liturgy affects history. Ultimately, the Mass is the answer to all the world's problems—not politics, not government programs, not social action. In the Mass, we truly go to battle. As we reverse the sin of Adam and offer ourselves in life-giving love with the Lamb who was slain, we defeat the devil, who seeks to enslave us through selfishness and sin.

* * *

Multiple Choice

1. The twenty-four elders recall the twenty-four divisions of __________ installed by David.

(a) administers

(b) prophets

(c) priests

(d) soldiers

2. The precious stones around the throne of God evoke imagery from _________.

(a) the garden of Eden

(b) Egypt

(c) Palestine
(d) Galilee

3. The sea of glass found in the heavenly temple was symbolized in the earthly temple by ________.
(a) a fountain
(b) an icon
(c) a river
(d) a laver

4. The four living creatures are __________.
(a) saints
(b) martyrs
(c) cherubim
(d) seraphim

5. The scroll with seven seals symbolizes ____________.
(a) God's covenant
(b) the Torah
(c) the book of life
(d) the map of the world

The song sung by the saints recalls the song sung by __________.
(a) Moses
(b) David
(c) Hannah
(d) Solomon

Answers) 1. c; 2. a; 3. d; 4. c; 5. a; 6. a.

* * *

Discussion/Study Questions

1. What parallels are there between Revelation 4–5 and Daniel 7? (See pages 81–82)

2. How does the Book of Revelation mirror the Book of Ezekiel? (See page 83)

3. Revelation 4–5 teaches us the true heavenly nature of the Mass. How? (See page 101)

4. Why does Jesus appear as a Lion and Lamb? (See page 90)

5. What is the significance of the fact that the four living creatures represent the middle signs of the Zodiac? (See pages 86–87)

6. Why does the Triune God work through covenants? (See pages 88–89)

____

____

____

____

7. To what does "the souls under the altar" refer? (See pages 98–99)

____

____

____

____

RANSOM CAPTIVE ISRAEL

The Restoration of Israel with the Nations (Rev. 7:1–17)

"O Come, O Come Emmanuel," one of my favorite songs, contains the line: "Ransom captive Israel." This line surely refers to slavery to sin. We shall see that there is something very profound in all of this: God's actions throughout salvation history often reflect a deeper spiritual reality. In the Old Testament, God dramatizes His people's deliverance from sin by delivering them from slavery.

When Israel went into exile, it was the result of their rejection of God's covenant. Deliverance from the exile, therefore, was closely connected with God's coming to set them free from sin. For this reason, turning from sin is frequently explained by the prophets in terms of "returning" to the Lord. Likewise, Deuteronomy explains that the exile will end when Israel "returns" to the Lord (Deut. 30:2, 8). Renowned scholar N. T. Wright explains, "Forgiveness of sins is another way of saying 'return from exile.'"[1]

This forgiveness, for a Christian, is given through the sacrament of Baptism. Because of this, John's vision depicts the restoration of Israel from exile in terms of baptismal imagery. Let us look at this more closely.

The Four Angels Are Restrained

Rev. 7:1–3. 1 After this I saw four angels standing at the four corners of the earth, holding back the four winds of the earth, that no wind might blow on earth or sea or against any tree. 2 Then I saw another angel ascend from the rising of the sun, with the seal of the living God, and he called with a loud voice to the four angels who had been given power to harm earth and sea, 3 saying, "Do not harm the earth or the sea or the trees, till we have sealed the servants of our God upon their foreheads."

7:1. Contrary to popular opinion, the reason people in the ancient world spoke of the "four corners" of the earth was not because they simply pictured a flat world with four actual sides. Indeed, a "flat" earth theory could just as easily involve a triangular, octagonal, or almost any other multi-sided shape. Rather, the reason they spoke in terms of the "four-corners" was because they saw the earth as a giant temple. In the Book of Revelation, the earth is the altar upon which the faithful pour out their lives in sacrificial love.[2]

7:2–3. That the angel ascends with the sun in the east may be an allusion to Malachi 4:2: "But for you who fear my name the sun of righteousness shall rise, with healing in its wings." Another possibility is that the "rising of the sun" is a symbol for the Resurrection. In this way, the angel comes with the saving power of the resurrected Christ.

The Heir-Tight Seal

If you're considering how you can receive this seal of the saints, mentioned in Revelation 7:3, don't worry—if you've been baptized, you've already been sealed. Let me explain.

The "sealing of the saints" is taken from Ezekiel 9: "And the LORD said to him, 'Go through the city, through Jerusalem, and put a mark upon the foreheads of the men who sigh and groan over all the abominations that are committed in it.' And to the others he said in my hearing, 'Pass through the city after him, and smite; your eye shall not spare, and you shall show no pity; slay old men outright, young men and maidens, little children and women, but touch no one upon whom is the mark. And begin at my sanctuary'" (Ezek. 9:4–6). The word for "mark" in Hebrew is simply a Hebrew letter, a *taw*, which in paleo-Hebrew script looks like an x or +. The early Church Fathers saw this as the sign of the Cross, made on the forehead of believers. One of the earliest Christian writers, Tertullian, explained, "Now the Greek letter Tau and our own letter T is the very form of the cross, which He predicted would be the sign on our foreheads in the true Catholic Jerusalem."[3]

Furthermore, the Greek word for "seal" was frequently understood as a baptismal image. One of the most important non-biblical books read by Christians in the first century, the Shepherd of Hermas, states: "The seal, then, is the water: they descend into the water dead, and they arise alive."[4] The early writer Tertullian, in fact, sees Christ's baptism as His "sealing."[5] The *Catechism of the Catholic Church* explains that Baptism confers, "a sacramental *character* or 'seal' by which the Christian shares in Christ's priesthood and is made a member of the Church according to different states and functions" (no. 1121, emphasis in original).

The image in Revelation 7 depicts God's protection of His people from evil. These people are "sealed" by His power through Baptism. They become His people, His family, His sons and daughters.

In Revelation 7, John sees that God has protected His children. They are not, however, necessarily protected from physical harm. In fact, they are called to "love not their lives even unto death" (Rev. 12:11). Rather, God protects His Church from a greater threat. As Jesus said: "[D]o not fear those who kill the body but cannot kill the soul; rather fear him who can destroy both soul and body in hell" (Mt. 10:28).

The Hundred and Forty-Four Thousand

Rev. 7:4–8. 4 And I heard the number of the sealed, a hundred
and forty-four thousand sealed, out of every tribe of the sons of
Israel, 5 twelve thousand sealed out of the tribe of Judah, twelve
thousand of the tribe of Reuben, twelve thousand of the tribe of
Gad, 6 twelve thousand of the tribe of Asher, twelve thousand of
the tribe of Naphtali, twelve thousand of the tribe of Manasseh,
7 twelve thousand of the tribe of Simeon, twelve thousand of the
tribe of Levi, twelve thousand of the tribe of Issachar, 8 twelve
thousand of the tribe of Zebulun, twelve thousand of the tribe of
Joseph, twelve thousand sealed out of the tribe of Benjamin.

7:4–8. Jehovah Witnesses say that the 144,000 are special individuals who will make it to heaven. According to them, the rest, "the great multitude" spoken of in 7:9, will live on earth. The problem with this is that John later says that a "great multitude" is in heaven (Rev. 19:1).

So who are the 144,000? Well, John tells us. They are those who are from the twelve tribes of Israel. Why 144,000? Because this number represents the "full number" of Israelites saved. 144,000 is a symbolic number: 12 x 12 x 1,000. John seems to show that the twelve tribes are those restored in the Church, under the twelve apostles. One thousand is a number symbolizing completeness.

But is it Israel that is portrayed here? Could this be symbolic too? In other words, does John see *actual* Israelites, or does he see the Church as the replacement of Israel? Perhaps "Israel" is merely a symbol for the Church, God's people. To better understand what is going on here, we have to remember God's Old Testament promises.

And After This Our Exile

At this point, it will be helpful to briefly consider the major events in Israel's history, from David onward.

—1000 BC King David reigns over all twelve tribes.

—930 BC The northern tribes break away and form their own kingdom, called the House of "Israel" or "Ephraim." The southern kingdom becomes known as the House of "Judah."

—722 BC The Assyrians carry the northern tribes off into exile and scatter them to the nations. They are never heard from again.

—586 BC The Babylonians carry the southern tribes off into exile.

—538 BC The southern tribes, the Judahites, also called, "the Jews," return from their exile and start rebuilding.

Notice two things about the history of Israel summarized above: Not all Israelites are "Jews." Jews are only those from the southern kingdom of "Judah." Those who belonged to the northern kingdom were "non-Jewish" Israelites. This is important. Secondly, only the Jews from the southern house returned from exile. Those from the northern tribes who were carried away were *never* heard from again. This is also important.

Hey, Judah and Israel

So what happened to those northern tribes? Today they are spoken of as "the Lost Tribes of Israel." Although Mormons believe these tribes came to America and settled here, there is no biblical or archeological evidence to support this view. Indeed, the northern tribes were truly lost. Even the rabbis debated whether or not they would ever return.

The Old Testament, though, seems to be pretty clear on the matter. According to Isaiah, Jeremiah, and the rest of the prophets, God promised to bring them back. He promised a restoration of "all Israel." This restoration would not include every single Israelite—some would reject Him—but rather a restoration of all the tribes, the northern and the southern kingdoms. The famous prophecy that tells of the "new covenant" explicitly states this: "Behold, the days are coming, says the LORD, when I will make a new covenant with the house of Israel and the house of Judah" (Jer. 31:31). This idea of a reunited Israel is found throughout the Old Testament. Here are some examples:

—"In that day the Lord will extend his hand yet a second time to recover the remnant which is left of his people, from Assyria, from Egypt, from Pathros, from Ethiopia, from Elam, from Shinar, from Hamath, and from the coastlands of the sea. He will raise an ensign for the nations, and will assemble the outcasts of Israel, and gather the dispersed of Judah from the four corners of the earth. The jealousy of Ephraim shall depart, and those who harass Judah shall be cut off; Ephraim shall not be jealous of Judah, and Judah shall not harass Ephraim" (Is. 11:11–13).

—"For behold the days are coming, says the LORD, when I will restore the fortunes of my people, Israel and Judah, says the LORD, and I will bring them back to the land which I gave to their fathers" (Jer. 30:3).

> —"How can I give you up, O Ephraim! How can I hand you over, O Israel! . . . They shall go after the LORD, he will roar like a lion; yea, he will roar, and his sons shall come trembling from the west; they shall come trembling like birds from Egypt, and like doves from the land of Assyria; and I will return them to their homes, says the LORD" (Hos. 11:8, 10–11).

In fact, it's hard to find a prophet who doesn't express this hope!

And this hope isn't confined to biblical books. Other books written in and around the time of the first century express the hope for the New Exodus, wherein God will bring His people out of the nations to which they've been scattered—even the lost northern tribes. The Testament of Simeon recorded in the apocryphal book "The Testament of the Twelve Patriarchs" states: "And now, my children, obey Levi, and in Judah shall ye be redeemed: and be not lifted up against these two tribes, for from them shall arise to you the salvation of God. For the Lord shall raise up from Levi as it were a Priest, and from Judah as it were a King, God and man. So shall He save all the Gentiles and the race of Israel."[6] Similarly, the book called 2 Baruch speaks of the restoration of the twelve tribes, saying, "[God] with much mercy will gather together again those who were dispersed."[7] This idea was common in John's day.

Paul's Scatter-Brained Ministry

This is God's promise, but it seemed impossible to fulfill. After all, the northern tribes were scattered to the nations. They assimilated into them, intermarried, and became one with them. How could they ever return?

Paul explains how. Paul was the missionary to the Gentiles, but not to the Gentiles alone (Acts 9:15). Paul explained that he held fast to the promises "to which *our twelve tribes* hope to attain" (Acts 26:7). So why did Paul go to the Gentiles? Because that's where the descendants of Israel were! His hearers might not have known that, somewhere way back in their family tree, Israelites had intermarried with their ancestors, but God did.

In this respect, Paul compares his situation to Elijah's. Elijah worried that there were no righteous Israelites left in his day. God said, "I will leave seven thousand in Israel" (1 Kings 19:18). Elijah didn't know who they were. God just said, "Don't worry, I know where they are." So just like Elijah, Paul didn't know exactly who the remnant of Israel was. But that's okay. God was keeping track.

Paul's mission, then, was to preach to the Gentiles. However, Paul explains to the Romans how all of Israel would be saved: "A hardening has come upon part of Israel, until the full number of Gentiles come in, and so all Israel will be saved" (Rom. 11:25–26).[8] The restoration of the tribes represents the fulfillment of God's covenant promise to Israel.

Restoration in Revelation

The vision of the salvation of the 144,000 reveals that God has kept His promise. A righteous remnant from all the twelve tribes has been saved. This concern for the salvation of all the twelve tribes of Israel was also found in other writings from the early Church. The *Epistula Apostolorum,* dated to the middle of the second century, tells the command of the Lord: "Go and preach to the twelve tribes of Israel and to the Gentiles . . . and to the land of Israel towards east and west, north and south, and many will believe in me, the Son of God."[9]

The Great Multitude

Rev. 7:9–12. 9 After this I looked, and behold, a great multitude which no man could number, from every nation, from all tribes and peoples and tongues, standing before the throne and before the Lamb, clothed in white robes, with palm branches in their hands, 10 and crying out with a loud voice, "Salvation belongs to our God who sits upon the throne, and to the Lamb!" 11 And all the angels stood round the throne and round the elders and the four living creatures, and they fell on their faces before the throne and worshiped God, 12 saying, "Amen! Blessing and glory and wisdom and thanksgiving and honor and power and might be to our God for ever and ever! Amen."

7:9–12. Whereas in 7:4–8 John saw the 144,000 saved from Israel, in verses 9–12, he sees a group "from every nation, from all tribes." God saves Israel and the Gentiles. This was an important part of the New Exodus hope. In the first Exodus, God saved Israel by delivering them from the Egyptians. In the New Exodus, Israel will return to God, but this time the nations are coming with them.

Those in this vision hold palm branches in their hands. Palm branches were often used in the Old Testament to celebrate the restoration of the temple (Neh. 8:15; 1 Mac. 13:51). Here in the Book of Revelation the saints are celebrating their admittance into the true temple of heaven. In just a couple of verses, we read about how these saints are depicted as serving in the temple of God in heaven (Rev. 7:15).

Saints Alive!

There are also several parallels between Revelation 7 and the vision of the Lamb in Revelation 5.

Revelation 5	**Revelation 7**
"The Lion of the tribe of *Judah*" (v. 5)	Tribes beginning with "*Judah*" (v. 5)
"The Lamb *standing*" (v. 6)	The great multitude "*standing*" before the Lamb (v. 9)
from "every *tribe*, and *tongue*, and *people* and *nation*" (v. 9)	"from every *nation*, from all *tribes* and *peoples* and *tongues*" (v. 9)
"*power* and wealth and *wisdom* and *might* and *honor* and *glory* and *blessing*" (v. 12)	*Blessing* and *glory* and *wisdom* and thanksgiving and *honor* and *power* and *might*" (v. 12)

This shows that the saints in both chapters share in the same communion.

Those Dressed in White Robes

Rev. 7:13–14. 13 Then one of the elders addressed me, saying, "Who are these, clothed in white robes, and whence have they come?" 14 I said to him, "Sir, you know." And he said to me, "These are they who have come out of the great tribulation; they have washed their robes and made them white in the blood of the Lamb.

7:13–14. Washing robes and making them white is probably an allusion to Daniel 12:10. There the image is meant to portray those who have been delivered. The saints John sees are those who have been delivered as well.

The Reward of the Saints

Rev. 7:15–17. 15 Therefore are they before the throne of God, and serve him day and night within his temple; and he who sits upon the throne will shelter them with his presence. 16 They shall hunger no more, neither thirst any more; the sun shall not strike them, nor any scorching heat. 17 For the Lamb in the midst of the throne will be their shepherd, and he will guide them to springs of living water; and God will wipe away every tear from their eyes."

7:15–17. Here God is pictured as one who is the shelter for His people. Later on we are told that God and the Lamb actually *are* the temple of heaven. Those who enter heaven actually enter the life of God. Indeed, the "living waters" here, as we shall see in Revelation 22, can be understood as the Holy Spirit.

Prophet-ing the Messiah

There are also several allusions here to Isaiah's vision of the New Exodus. Look at the parallels:

Isaiah 49 The twelve tribes will be restored (v. 6)	**Revelation 7** The twelve tribes are restored (v. 4–8)
The nations will be saved (v. 6)	The nations are saved (v. 9–12)
"[T]hey shall not hunger or thirst" (v. 10)	"They shall hunger no more; neither thirst anymore" (v. 16)
"[N]either scorching wind nor sun shall smite them" (v. 10)	"The sun shall not strike them, nor any scorching heat" (v. 16)
"by springs of water [the Lord] will guide them" (v. 10)	"He shall guide them to springs of living water" (v. 17)
"For the LORD has comforted His people" (v. 13)	"God will wipe away every tear from their eyes" (v. 17)

Of course, all of this occurs through the Davidic Messiah. John evokes Ezekiel 34, another prophecy concerning the restoration of Israel. In this passage, the Lord explains that Israel is His sheep and that He will "bring them out from the peoples, and gather them from the countries, and will bring them into their own land" (Ezek. 34:13). This will happen through the Messiah. "And I will set up over them one shepherd, my servant David, and he shall feed them" (Ezek. 34:23). The Lamb, Jesus, is the True Shepherd, who restores Israel. The Lamb is placed in opposition to the false shepherds in Ezekiel 34, who drink "clear water" themselves as they mislead the sheep (Ezek. 34:18). In Revelation, Christ is the True Shepherd, who guides His people to "living water" (Baptism) and feeds them (the Eucharist).

Applying the Lessons of Revelation 7 Today

Revelation 7 shows us God's faithfulness to His promise to restore Israel. As impossible as it seemed, God knew where the tribes of Israel were and was able to restore them. Moreover, God transformed the horror of exile into hope for the nations. Through their captivity, God was able to extend His mercy to the nations who had taken the tribes of Israel away.

And there is an even deeper lesson here. As we mentioned at the beginning of the chapter, return from the exile symbolizes deliverance from sin. Therefore, just as God was able to save Israel, which seemed to be lost and forsaken, never to return again, so too God is able to save any sinner—no matter how far he wanders away.

The parable of the prodigal son is an example of this. The father has two sons, one who remains and one who goes off to "a far country" and ends up eating with the unclean swine (Lk. 15:13). The son finally returns, and the father slaughters the fatted calf. Here we have the story of God the Father's forgiveness for sinners, painted in terms of Israel's exile. For just as one son, representing Judah, remained at home, (after the exile and Ezra and Nehemiah), the other son went off to the nations like northern Israel. Yet Israel returns when the calf is slain—when they reject their sin of idolatry.

God spares no expense to find His lost children. We can run, but we can't hide. No matter how far we go away from Him, He can always bring us back home.

Moreover, just as God transformed the effects of the exile into salvation for the nations, God can redeem our sinful lives. For example, a convert's story can speak to those who have abandoned God in a way that a person who has never fallen can't. Likewise, Thomas Aquinas explained that just as God uses "matter" in all the sacraments to give grace—bread, wine, oil, etc.—in the sacrament of Confession, God transforms our very sins into vehicles of grace. Our sins teach us that we are weak and needful of grace and also show us God's great mercy. Our sins, now forgiven, teach us to hate sin even more, and they bring us closer to God.[10]

* * *

Multiple Choice

1. The 144,000 are a symbol of those restored from _________.
(a) the nations
(b) Israel
(c) Egypt
(d) Jerusalem

2. The "seal" placed on the foreheads of the righteous symbolizes _________.
(a) slavery
(b) Baptism
(c) the Eucharist
(d) the beast

3. The ten northern tribes were sent into the exile and -_________.
(a) returned from Babylon
(b) never returned
(c) migrated to North America

4. In order to bring back the lost tribes of Israel, Paul preached the Gospel to __________.
(a) the Jews
(b) the Gentiles
(c) the Samaritans
(d) those in the Far East

5. Palm branches were used for celebrations of the __________.
(a) Passover
(b) restoration of the temple
(c) *todah*
(d) Day of Atonement

Answers) 1. b; 2. b; 3. b; 4. b; 5. b.

* * *

Discussion/Study Questions

1. Why did Paul go out to the Gentiles to preach the Gospel? (See pages 110–111)

____

____

____

____

2. Read Ezekiel 34. What parallels are found there with this chapter in the Apocalypse? (See page 114)

____

____

____

____

3. How is the story of the prodigal son reminiscent of the story of the northern and southern houses of Israel? (See page 115)

____

____

____

____

4. What lessons can we learn from the way God deals with Israel? (See page 105)

____

____

____

____

TRUMPETING GOD'S VICTORY

The Seven Trumpets (Rev. 8:1–11:19)

Finally, we've reached the seventh seal. After six seals have released horsemen who bring earthquakes, falling stars, wars, and destruction, John reveals the terrible events that follow the opening of the seventh seal. We almost brace ourselves for what comes next. Is it the big boom of an explosion? A mushroom cloud? Once again, the answer may be surprising.

The Seventh Seal: Silence

Rev. 8:1. 1 When the Lamb opened the seventh seal, there was silence in heaven for about half an hour.

8:1. We've finally arrived at the seventh seal, and what does John hear? Silence. This seems so anti-climactic that we're almost let down. And yet this silence is truly thunderous.

So what is this half-hour of silence? The half-hour represents the Jewish rite of the offering of incense. The next few verses describe the angels in heaven performing the same ritual that the Levitical priests carried out in the earthly temple.[1] Here at the seventh and final seal, we see the liturgy as the great climax. The liturgical prayer of God's people is more earthshaking than any earthquake, more dramatic than the stars being darkened. You might not realize it standing among tone-deaf Catholics at Mass, but what we do in the church building every Sunday is the most powerful thing imaginable. Its effects are far more profound than we could ever imagine.

The Seven Trumpets

Rev. 8:2–5. 2 Then I saw the seven angels who stand before God, and seven trumpets were given to them. 3 And another angel came and stood at the altar with a golden censer; and he was given much

> incense to mingle with the prayers of all the saints upon the golden altar before the throne; 4 and the smoke of the incense rose with the prayers of the saints from the hand of the angel before God. 5 Then the angel took the censer and filled it with fire from the altar and threw it on the earth; and there were peals of thunder, loud noises, flashes of lightning, and an earthquake.

8:2–4. The "seven angels" may refer to an ancient Jewish tradition, which depicted seven angels standing in the presence of God. In the Book of Tobit, Raphael explains that he is "one of the seven holy angels who present the prayers of the saints and enter into the presence of God" (Tob. 12:15). The names of the other six are not mentioned by Scripture, although it appears that Gabriel might be one of them (cf. Lk. 1:19).[2]

Pray for Us!

The incense offered symbolizes the prayers of the saints. In the larger context of the rest of the book, it is closely linked with Revelation 5:8, where the prayers of the saints rising to God are also understood as incense.[3]

What does all this mean? It means that the angels offer our prayers to God in heaven. This is one of the reasons we Catholics offer prayers to Saint Michael and to guardian angels. It's not because we don't pray to God. Actually, we are not praying to angels at all, but asking them to pray *for us.*

Censoring Sin

8:5. The angel throwing the burning censor down onto the earth is an image of destruction. This is very similar to Ezekiel's vision of a "man clothed in linen" who takes heavenly coals out among the city as a sign of judgment (cf. Ezek. 10:2–7).[4] Therefore, when the censor is cast down to earth it comes down as fire, with lightning and thunder.

Most people know that fire coming down from heaven is often used in the Bible as a symbol of God's judgment (cf. Gen. 19:24; 2 Kings 1:10, 12, 14; Job 1:16; Ps. 11:6). A famous example of this is

Sodom and Gomorrah, which were destroyed by fire raining down from heaven (Gen. 19:24). Jerusalem is now about to be judged similarly. In fact, it's later called "Sodom" in Revelation 11:8.

Another interesting aspect of this image is that the cities destroyed by Israel were required to be burned with the fire from the altar used to light the coals of incense (cf. Deut. 13:16). This altar-fire originally came down from heaven itself (cf. Lev. 9:24; 2 Chron. 7:1). In Revelation 8, God's heavenly fire is now used to destroy Jerusalem.[5]

Some commentators have noticed that the last time the prayers of the saints were mentioned was in reference to the souls under the altar, crying out for vengeance (Rev. 6:9–11). The prayers of the saints may then specifically be understood as prayers for judgment. Hence, these prayers are mixed with fire and thrown down to earth, sending the justice for which they prayed.[6]

Trumpets that Blow the Wicked Away

Above I mentioned that the fire coming down from heaven evokes the memory of a wicked city of antiquity, Sodom. As I mentioned, this connection is made explicit in Revelation 11:8, where Jerusalem is called "Sodom." Jerusalem will therefore be judged in a similar way.

But Sodom isn't the only ancient city to which Revelation compares Jerusalem. The seven trumpets imply that Jerusalem is also like two other cities. First, it is compared to "Egypt" (Rev. 11:8). Thus, the trumpets bring about several "plagues" just like the ones Egypt experienced. The plagues recounted in Revelation 8–9 bear an uncanny resemblance to those described in Exodus (see Ex. 7–10 and "Plagued by Doubt" below).

Moreover, the seven trumpets that are blown in Revelation 8–9, leading to the defeat of the city, remind us of the fall of yet another ancient metropolis—Jericho.

—There's "silence in heaven" (Rev. 8:1), just as Joshua commanded Israel to be silent outside the walls of Jericho (Josh. 6:10).

—Seven trumpets are blown (Rev. 8–11; Josh. 6:13).
—God's people cry out in a loud voice (Rev. 11:15; Josh. 6:16).[7]

Jerusalem has become like Jericho, which persecuted God's people and attempted to keep them out of the Promised Land. Standing in the way of God's plan is not wise—don't try it.[8]

Horn Section

These trumpets also point to the end of the world. Paul explains in 1 Thessalonians 4:16, that the Lord will come on the last day "with the archangel's call, and with the sound of the trumpet of God." So, as we have seen, the destruction of Jerusalem points forward to the day of Christ's coming at the end of time.

The seven trumpets are also a liturgical symbol. Seven trumpets were used in the temple liturgy (cf. 1 Chron. 15:24; Neh. 12:41).[9] Thus, the trumpets blown by the angels can also be understood as part of the heavenly liturgy. Since the Mass is a share in that liturgy, we also see the judgment of the trumpets as an image of the Church's anticipation of Christ's coming in the liturgy—where we stand to be judged each Sunday (cf. 1 Cor. 11:28–29).

Plagued by Doubt

As noted earlier, the plagues in Revelation recall the plagues of Exodus. Moses sent ten plagues on Egypt while Revelation 8–9 only speaks of the blowing of seven trumpets. It is important to note, however, that the ten plagues were often summarized in lists that recounted them as only seven plagues. This is the case, for example, in Psalms 78:43–51 and 105:27–36. So John's summary of the ten plagues in a series of seven trumpets, is not without biblical precedent.

The first five trumpets bear a striking resemblance to passages in Exodus 7–10:

The Trumpets of Revelation 8–9	Plagues of Exodus
1. "[H]ail and fire," burn up a third of the "earth," "trees," and "all green grass" (8:7).	"[H]ail and fire" burn up "every plant" and "tree" (9:22–24).
2. "[A] third of the sea became blood, a third of the living creatures in the sea died" (8:8).	"[A]ll the water that was in the Nile turned to blood. And the fish in the Nile died" (7:20–21).
3. "A third of the waters became wormwood, and many men died of the water, because it was made bitter" (8:10–11).	"[T]he Nile became foul, so that the Egyptians could not drink water from the Nile" (7:21).
4. "[A] third of the sun was struck, and a third of the moon, and a third of the stars, so that a third of their light was darkened; a third of the day was kept from shining and likewise the night" (8:12).	"[T]here was thick darkness in all the land of Egypt three days; they did not see one another, nor did any rise from his place for three days" (10:22–23).
5. "[F]rom the smoke came locusts on the earth" (9:2).	"[T]he locusts came up over all the land of Egypt, and settled on the whole country of Egypt, such a dense swarm of locusts as had never been before, nor ever shall be again" (10:14).

Just as the Egyptians hardened their hearts against the Lord and doubted His mighty power, so also Jerusalem has hardened its heart by rejecting Christ. Now it will suffer similar judgment.

The First Trumpet: Hail and Fire

Rev. 8:6–7. 6 Now the seven angels who had the seven trumpets made ready to blow them.

> 7 The first angel blew his trumpet, and there followed hail and fire, mixed with blood, which fell on the earth; and a third of the earth was burnt up, and a third of the trees were burnt up, and all green grass was burnt up.

8:6–7. If the judgments of the seven trumpets refer to the destruction of Jerusalem, we might wonder whether or not it looked anything like what John described. "If only we could have seen it," you might say. Well, the first-century historian Josephus did. His accounts of the historical events that led up to the destruction of the city bear a striking resemblance to what John saw in the Apocalypse.

Of course, John is not trying to give us a blow-by-blow account, in exact chronological detail, of the Jewish war that led up to AD 70. He wants us to see the spiritual truths behind the historical events. For example, the judgments are described here in terms of the destruction of Jericho. Nonetheless, there are striking similarities between the imagery of the Apocalypse and Josephus' account.

Eyewitness Accounts

The description of the first trumpet corresponds to the many different natural disasters and social upheavals that occurred during the Jewish war that led up to the destruction of the city.[10] Thus, the first trumpet, which brings about the destruction of the land, the trees, and the grass, may refer to the utter destruction of vegetation that was caused by the Romans. Josephus explains:

> "[T]ruly, the very view itself of the country was a melancholy thing; for those places which were before adorned with trees and pleasant gardens were now become a desolate country in every way, and its trees were all cut down. Nor could any foreigner that had formerly seen Judea and the most beautiful suburbs of the city, and now saw it as a desert, but lament and mourn sadly at so great a change: . . . nor if anyone that had known the place before, had come on a sudden to it now, would he have known it again; but though he were standing at the city itself, yet would he have inquired for it notwithstanding."[11]

The Second Trumpet: A Mountain Cast into the Sea

Rev. 8:8–9. 8 The second angel blew his trumpet, and something like a great mountain, burning with fire, was thrown into the sea; 9 and a third of the sea became blood, a third of the living creatures in the sea died, and a third of the ships were destroyed.

8:8–9. The image of the mountain being cast into the sea is another image of the judgment of Jerusalem. The mountain is a reference to Jerusalem, which was built up on a mountain range. The sea is frequently used in the Old Testament to represent the nations. In Daniel 7, the Gentile nations are symbolized by the four beasts which arise out of the "sea" (Dan. 7:2–27). Another example of this is Psalm 65:7, where the "roaring of the Seas" is paralleled with "the tumult of the peoples." Thus, the image of a mountain thrown into the sea indicates that the nations will "swallow up" the city. Note especially the similarity of this image with that used in Jeremiah 51, where God foretells the fall of Babylon: "[A]nd [I will] make you a burnt out mountain. . . . The sea has come up over Babylon; she has been engulfed with its tumultuous waters" (Jer. 51:25, 42).[12]

In fact, Jeremiah 51 appears to be the background in which John places the seven trumpets. For just as the second trumpet has a reference to the burning mountain in Jeremiah 51, there is also a connection with the fifth trumpet in Revelation 9. Revelation 9 describes a plague of locusts that appears "like horses" (Rev. 9:7), as Jeremiah 51:27 describes "horses like bristling locusts." In addition, the judgment in Jeremiah 51 is linked with the blowing of a "trumpet" (51:27). John describes the fall of Jerusalem, the new Babylon, in terms of Jeremiah's vision of the fall of the first. Like the first Babylon, Jerusalem has turned against God's people.

It is important to point out that Jesus also used this image. As He and the apostles were walking toward Jerusalem, He told them, "[E]ven if you say to this mountain, 'Be taken up and cast into the sea,' it will be done" (Mt. 21:21).[13]

Thunder Mountain

The second trumpet foretells: "[A] great mountain, burning with fire, was thrown into the sea; and a third of the sea became blood, a third of the living creatures in the sea died, and a third of the ships were destroyed" (Rev. 8:8–9). Once again, Josephus writes about something similar that occurred during the destruction of the temple.

For example, Josephus explains how the Romans set fire to the city, causing Jerusalem to appear as one "blazing mountain." He explains, "[B]ecause this hill was high, and the works at the temple were very great, one would have thought the whole city had been on fire. . . . [F]or one would have thought that the hill itself, on which the temple stood, was seething-hot, as full of fire on every part of it, that the blood was larger in quantity than the fire."[14]

Likewise, Josephus tells about Jewish rebels, who tried unsuccessfully to fight against the Romans on the Gennesareth Lake. The Romans jumped on their ships and ran them through. Their ships were destroyed, and those who tried to swim away were killed by arrows and darts. Josephus explains, "[O]ne might then see the lake all bloody, and full of dead bodies." The shores were "full of shipwrecks and of dead bodies all swelled; and as the dead bodies were inflamed by the sun, and putrefied, they corrupted the air."[15]

The Third and Fourth Trumpets: The Fall of Wormwood and Darkness

Rev. 8:10–13. 10 The third angel blew his trumpet, and a great star fell from heaven, blazing like a torch, and it fell on a third of the rivers and on the fountains of water. 11 The name of the star is Wormwood. A third of the waters became wormwood, and many men died of the water, because it was made bitter.

12 The fourth angel blew his trumpet, and a third of the sun was struck, and a third of the moon, and a third of the stars, so that a third of their light was darkened; a third of the day was kept from shining, and likewise a third of the night.

13 Then I looked, and I heard an eagle crying with a loud voice, as it flew in midheaven, "Woe, woe, woe to those who dwell on the earth, at the blasts of the other trumpets which the three angels are about to blow!"

8:10–13. Just as the image of the burning mountain cast into the sea originally referred to the fall of Babylon, the fall of the "great star" from heaven echoes Isaiah's prophecy about Babylon's coming destruction: "How you have fallen from heaven, O Day Star, son of the Dawn!" (Is. 14:12). Also, "Wormwood" is another word with "judgment" overtones. It was frequently used in warnings to Israel (cf. Deut. 29:18; Jer. 9:15; 23:15; Lam. 3:15; Amos 5:7).

In addition, the eagle flying in mid-heaven evokes judgment prophecies. The image of a carrion bird was often used in contexts where Israel is told that it will be destroyed for breaking God's covenant (cf. Deut. 28:49; Jer. 4:13; Lam. 4:19; Hos. 8:1; Hab. 1:8). The point is clear—a reckoning is imminent. The angel warns that, with the last three trumpets, the final three "woes" shall come—a word which itself is a term usually associated with covenant judgment. Jesus, for example, pronounces a dreaded seven-fold woe on the Pharisees in Matthew 23, foretelling their judgment.

The Fifth Trumpet:
Locusts Unleashed from the Bottomless Pit

Rev. 9:1–5. 1 And the fifth angel blew his trumpet, and I saw a star fallen from heaven to earth, and he was given the key of the shaft of the bottomless pit; 2 he opened the shaft of the bottomless pit, and from the shaft rose smoke like the smoke of a great furnace, and the sun and the air were darkened with the smoke from the shaft. 3 Then from the smoke came locusts on the earth, and they were given power like the power of scorpions of the earth; 4 they were told not to harm the grass of the earth or any green growth or any tree, but only those of mankind who have not the seal of God upon their foreheads; 5 they were allowed to torture them for five months, but not to kill them, and their torture was like the torture of a scorpion, when it stings a man.

9:1–2. The image here of the "fallen star," should probably be understood as a "fallen angel." Stars, as we saw in Revelation 1:20, are used as symbols for angels. The image of fallen stars as fallen angels is also used in Revelation 12:4, 9–10, 13, and possibly in Jude 13.[16]

The "bottomless pit" also has deep roots in biblical and apocryphal writings. A certain tradition actually located the "bottomless pit" under the temple (see note on 20:1). This "pit" (the Greek word is *abussos*, meaning "abyss") is mentioned in Job as the dwelling place of Leviathan (Job 41:31),[17] which is interesting since Revelation describes Satan as the dragon (Rev. 12:3) and depicts him as cast into the "pit" (Rev. 20: 2–3). Revelation 9, therefore, is closely related to Revelation 12 and 20 (see commentary on these chapters).

9:3–5. As mentioned previously, the locusts are reminiscent of the plague that Moses sent on the Egyptians (cf. Ex. 10:14). In fact, John's description of the immense number of locusts as smoke, which darkens the sun and air, parallels Exodus 10:15, where we are told that the locusts "covered the face of the whole land, so that the land was darkened." Yet, the locusts John sees are far more dreadful than those seen by the Egyptians, since what he sees are not actual locusts, but demonic forces.

The "five months" of torture probably refer to the typical life span of locusts.[18] Locusts would hatch in the spring and die at the end of summer. The number "five" is also frequently used throughout the Bible as a number meaning "a few" (cf., Lev. 26:8; Jud. 7:30; 1 Cor. 14:19; Mt. 14:17; Mk. 6:38; Lk. 9:13; 12:6), so "five" could be used here to signify a short period of intense suffering.[19]

Furthermore, there is probably a connection between Revelation 9:1–5 and Luke 10. Like John's vision of a demon falling like a star, Jesus says, "I saw Satan fall like lightning from heaven" (Lk. 10:18). As the locusts are compared to scorpions, Jesus goes on to say, "I have given you authority to tread upon serpents and scorpions" (Lk. 10:19). Just as the locusts cannot harm those who have the seal, Jesus tells the apostles, "[N]othing shall hurt you" (Lk. 10:19). Luke also records the request of demons to Jesus that He not send them back into "the abyss" (Lk. 8:31).

The five months of the locusts may also have a certain first-century fulfillment in the persecution of Gessius Florus. Florus, the procurator of Judea, killed thousands of Jews for five months, beginning in May of AD 66. Josephus marked this persecution as the beginning of the war that destroyed Jerusalem.[20]

The Description of the Locusts

Rev. 9:6–10. 6 And in those days men will seek death and will not find it; they will long to die, and death will fly from them.

7 In appearance the locusts were like horses arrayed for battle; on their heads were what looked like crowns of gold; their faces were like human faces, 8 their hair like women's hair, and their teeth like lions' teeth; 9 they had scales like iron breastplates, and the noise of their wings was like the noise of many chariots with horses rushing into battle. 10 They have tails like scorpions, and stings, and their power of hurting men for five months lies in their tails.

9:6–10. The plague of locusts will be so harsh people will long for death. This is a common image used in the Bible to describe severe suffering.[21] There may also be a kind of pun here. John says death will "fly" from them, just as the locusts "fly away" leaving their victims in agony.

Revelation 9 "In appearance the locusts were like horses arrayed for battle" (7).	**Joel 1–2** "[The locusts'] appearance is like the appearance of horses, and like war horses they run" (2:4).
"their teeth like lion's teeth" (8).	"its teeth are lions' teeth, and it has the fangs of a lioness" (1:6).
"they had scales like iron breastplates, and the noise of their wings was like the noise of many chariots with horses rushing into battle" (9).	"As with the rumbling of chariots, they leap on tops of mountains . . . like a powerful army drawn up for battle . . . . Like warriors they charge, like soldiers they scale the wall" (Joel 2:5, 7).

Revelation 9:7–9 seem to be taken from Joel 1–2, which also describe the coming of an enemy nation as locusts descending on Israel. It is also interesting that, just as in Revelation 9, the locusts in Joel come at the blast of a trumpet.[22]

This prophecy of a demon-infested country seems to be confirmed in the accounts of Josephus. Josephus, who saw his own people plummet to the depths of wickedness in ways he could hardly imagine, described how the people of the city had an "insatiable inclination to plunder, and for the murdering of men, and abusing of the women, it was sport to them." They devoured whatever they found, even drinking blood. Like the locusts in Revelation, who had "hair like women" (9:8), the Zealots became transvestites. Josephus lists numerous wicked practices, which, out of decency, won't be repeated here.[23]

The King of the Bottomless Pit

> **Rev. 9:11–12.** 11 They have as king over them the angel of the bottomless pit; his name in Hebrew is Abaddon, and in Greek he is called Apollyon.
>
> 12 The first woe has passed; behold, two woes are still to come.

9:11–12. "Abaddon" is from the Hebrew word for "destruction," just as "Apollyon" is the Greek word for "destroyer." Here we see that the locusts are not simply annoying bugs, but minions of Satan. Some have also noted the close connection between "Apollyon" and the name of the god "Apollo." Roman Emperors frequently associated themselves with this god.[24] John, therefore, may also be revealing that demonic forces are the true power behind Rome's strength.

With the locusts, the "first" of the three woes mentioned at the end of Revelation 8 passes. John reminds his readers that two still remain. They are described in the following verses.

The Sixth Trumpet:
The Four Angels Are Released on the Earth

Rev. 9:13–16. 13 Then the sixth angel blew his trumpet, and I
heard a voice from the four horns of the golden altar before God,
14 saying to the sixth angel who had the trumpet, "Release the
four angels who are bound at the great river Euphrates." 15 So
the four angels were released, who had been held ready for the
hour, the day, the month, and the year, to kill a third of mankind.
16 The number of the troops of cavalry was twice ten thousand
times ten thousand; I heard their number.

9:13–16. Before the seventh seal was opened, John saw angels bringing the prayers of the saints to the golden altar (8:1–5). Here we have another reference to this altar. As we saw in Revelation 8, the prayers of the saints should probably be connected to the cries of the souls under the altar who pray for vengeance (see chapter 6, "The New Song"). Therefore, the reference to the golden altar here may imply that the events, which follow the sixth trumpet, represent God's response to the prayers of the saints.[25]

Invasion of a Nation

As in the other trumpet judgments, "a third" of men are killed. The "third" seems to indicate a "partial" number. The destruction is meant to lead those left to repent, though they do not (Rev. 9:20–21). The number of the troops as "ten thousand times ten thousand" is not meant to convey an actual number. The Greek Old Testament frequently uses this same construction to express a large group impossible to count.[26]

The coming of the army from the north of the Euphrates is also fulfilled by the Roman destruction of Jerusalem. The Roman legions came down from the north, through the Euphrates, on their way to Jerusalem.[27] In fact, Josephus tells us that the Tenth Legion, which helped in the destruction of the city, was stationed just beyond the Euphrates.[28]

The Evil Army

Rev. 9:17–19. 17 And this was how I saw the horses in my vision: the riders wore breastplates the color of fire and of sapphire and of sulphur, and the heads of the horses were like lions' heads, and fire and smoke and sulphur issued from their mouths. 18 By these three plagues a third of mankind was killed, by the fire and smoke and sulphur issuing from their mouths. 19 For the power of the horses is in their mouths and in their tails; their tails are like serpents, with heads, and by means of them they wound.

9:17–19. The description of the riders is similar to the locusts from the fifth trumpet judgment. They both wear "breastplates" (9:9, 17), are like horses (9:7, 17) and lions (9:8, 17), and have power to harm with their tails (9:10, 19). In other words, the two trumpets describe different waves of an attack by the same demonic forces. The association of these warriors with serpents also has obvious demonic implications.

That these warriors wound by their tails, which are like serpents, may be an allusion to the serpent of Genesis 3. That serpent didn't bring physical harm, but spiritual death. Perhaps this points to the real damage caused by this satanic army—they lead their victims off into sin.

That these warriors breathe "fire and smoke and sulfur" (Rev. 9:17) implies that the destruction they bring is connected with the final destruction of the Beast and the false prophet. The Beast and false prophet are cast into the lake of death, where their torment is associated with "fire" and "sulphur" (the Greek word can also be translated "brimstone") and "smoke" (Rev. 14:10; 19:20). This lake of fire is also mentioned as the destination of the wicked at the end of the world (Rev. 20:13–15).

We can see from this image the two-fold prophecy of the Book of Revelation. On one hand, the image points to Jerusalem, which will be destroyed by an army turned into a burning rubble of "fire and sulphur." Yet it also points to the end of the world, when the wicked will be cast into a "lake of fire" and be tormented in hell.

Those Who Survived the Plagues

Rev. 9:20–21. 20 The rest of mankind, who were not killed by these plagues, did not repent of the works of their hands nor give up worshiping demons and idols of gold and silver and bronze and stone and wood, which cannot either see or hear or walk; 21 nor did they repent of their murders or their sorceries or their immorality or their thefts.

9:20–21. The mention of those who did not give up their worship of "idols of gold and silver and bronze and stone and wood" is an allusion to Daniel, who warned the Babylonians to turn from idolatry and worship the true God, who otherwise will show Himself to them by bringing about their destruction. "[Y]ou have praised the gods of silver and gold, of bronze, iron, wood, and stone, which do not see or hear or know, but the God in whose hand is your breath, and whose are all your ways, you have not honored" (Dan. 5:23). Daniel then goes on to prophesy that the Medo-Persians will conquer Babylon.

In the same way, Jerusalem, the new Babylon, is about to be destroyed. In the Old Testament, the Babylonians came and destroyed the temple in Jerusalem. The corrupt leaders of Jerusalem, the new Babylon, destroyed the body of Christ, the true temple (cf. Jn. 2:19–22). They preferred an earthly temple, made of silver, gold, bronze, iron, wood, and stone, to the true temple, Christ.

The Angel with the Little Scroll

Rev. 10:1–4. 1 Then I saw another mighty angel coming down from heaven, wrapped in a cloud, with a rainbow over his head, and his face was like the sun, and his legs like pillars of fire. 2 He had a little scroll open in his hand. And he set his right foot on the sea, and his left foot on the land, 3 and called out with a loud voice, like a lion roaring; when he called out, the seven thunders sounded. 4 And when the seven thunders had sounded, I was about to write, but I heard a voice from heaven saying, "Seal up what the seven thunders have said, and do not write it down."

10:1–3. This figure is more than just a "mighty angel." This is Christ's own angel through whom His revelation is given (Rev. 1:1). He is so close to Christ that he radiates His glory and is therefore described in terms much like the Lord.

—He comes down on a cloud, as the Son of man depicted in Daniel 7 (Dan. 7:13).
—Over his head is a rainbow, just as there is a rainbow above the throne of God in Revelation 4:3.
—His face, is "like the sun," like Jesus' (Rev. 1:16).
—The figure here has a loud voice, "like a lion" (Rev. 10:3); Christ has already been identified as a "lion" (Rev. 5:5).
—His legs as "pillars of fire" recall the manifestation of God's presence in the wilderness as the fiery Glory-Cloud (Ex. 13:21–22; 14:19, 24).

What "On Earth" Is Going On?

The word "earth" here, in Greek, can also be translated "land." This seems to be a better translation. We have already seen how the "sea" is a symbol for the nations. Similarly, the "land" is a technical term. It refers to the "Promised Land" that God gave Israel. Israel, therefore, is often symbolized by "the land." The angel's stance on the "land" and on the "sea" refers to his authority over "Israel" (the land) and the nations (the sea) (cf. Is. 17:12–13; Jer. 6:23).

This understanding should be applied to other passages in Revelation as well. In this, we will see much more clearly how Revelation not only describes the end of the whole world, but also the judgment of Jerusalem in AD 70. For example, the judgment of the first trumpet in 8:7, can be understood as a judgment that specifically comes on Jerusalem once we see that "hail and fire . . . fell on the [*land*]."

10:4. The opening of the "little scroll" here in Revelation 10 has many similarities to the opening of the scroll of chapter 5.

—both are opened (cf. Chapters 6–8;10:2)
—both are held by Christ (5:7; 10:2)
—in both situations Christ is depicted as a lion (5:5; 10:3)

—both accounts involve a "strong / mighty angel"[29] who "cries out" (5:2, 10:1, 3)
—God is described as the one who "lives forever and ever" (4:9; 10:6)
—in both visions someone approaches a heavenly being and takes a book out of the being's hand (5:6–7; 10:10)
—both concern the destiny of "peoples, nations, tongues, and tribes / kings" (5:9; 10:11).[30]

In this we have another image of God's covenant promises being fulfilled.

The fact that John is to "seal up" the seven thunders instead of "write them down" possibly refers to the fact that John does not tell us everything he saw. For whatever reason (and scholars love to speculate), God did not want John to write some things down. We can't know, therefore, what exactly this referred to.

The Oath

Rev. 10:5–7. 5 And the angel whom I saw standing on sea and land lifted up his right hand to heaven 6 and swore by him who lives for ever and ever, who created heaven and what is in it, the earth and what is in it, and the sea and what is in it, that there should be no more delay, 7 but that in the days of the trumpet call to be sounded by the seventh angel, the mystery of God, as he announced to his servants the prophets, should be fulfilled.

10:5–7. The angel lifts his right hand and swears an "oath." By swearing an oath one establishes a covenant.[31] Scholars have, therefore, understood the prophecy of the "little scroll" in terms of a covenant background.

But what covenant is established? John explains that it is through this oath that "the mystery of God, as he announced to his servants the prophets, should be fulfilled." For Paul, "the mystery" describes the salvation of Israel with the Gentiles: "When you read this you can perceive my insight into the mystery of Christ . . . that is, how the Gentiles are fellow heirs, members of the same body, and partakers of the promise in Christ Jesus through the gospel" (Eph. 3:4, 6; cf. Rom. 11:25–26; Col. 1:27). The image of the angel standing on the "land" and the "sea" might serve as a confirmation of this interpretation.

John Eats the Scroll

> **Rev. 10:8–11.** 8 Then the voice which I had heard from heaven spoke to me again, saying, "Go, take the scroll which is open in the hand of the angel who is standing on the sea and on the land." 9 So I went to the angel and told him to give me the little scroll; and he said to me, "Take it and eat; it will be bitter to your stomach, but sweet as honey in your mouth." 10 And I took the little scroll from the hand of the angel and ate it; it was sweet as honey in my mouth, but when I had eaten it my stomach was made bitter. 11 And I was told, "You must again prophesy about many peoples and nations and tongues and kings."

10:8–11. John eats the scroll much like Ezekiel did (cf. Ezek. 3:1–3). Like the scroll that Ezekiel swallows, the scroll is sweet in John's mouth. That the scroll then becomes sour, may be an allusion to Ezekiel as well, since after eating the scroll Ezekiel is told to foretell the coming destruction of Jerusalem and goes out in "bitterness" (Ezek. 3:14). In the same way, John proceeds in the next chapter to announce the destruction of the city "where their Lord was crucified," i.e., Jerusalem.

Courting Disaster

Interpreters debate whether the temple in Revelation 11 is the earthly or the heavenly temple. In some ways, it would seem to be the earthly temple. For example, the outer court of this temple is given over to the Gentiles to destroy. If we were talking about a heavenly temple, this would be impossible. Likewise, it seems absurd to suggest that those worshipping God in heaven need protection.

At the same time, the measuring of the temple in Revelation 11 is clearly drawing on Ezekiel 40–48, which speaks of the measuring of God's restored eschatological temple. It would be strange for John to draw imagery from this eschatological temple in a way that describes the destruction of this temple. It appears, then, that John has *both* temples in mind, the earthly *and* the heavenly.

As we have seen, the Jews believed the worship of the earthly temple, in some way, was connected with the worship in heaven. In fact, the angels in Revelation perform rituals that the Levitical priests carried out in Jerusalem (see commentary on Rev. 8:1). Furthermore, as we have seen, the earthly temple was understood as a "copy" of that heavenly temple.

In a way, the Jerusalem temple was truly like an "outer court" of the heavenly temple. It was connected to the heavenly temple in as much as it was built as a copy of it. Yet, like those who stood in the outer court of the earthly temple, unable to enter into the main sanctuary, those who worshipped in the Jerusalem temple did not actually enter into the heavenly liturgy.

The meaning of this chapter, then, could be understood as follows. Since the saints now enter into the heavenly liturgy, the earthly temple, which is a kind of "outer court" of the heavenly temple, is no longer necessary. Gentiles, namely, the Romans, will destroy it.

Counting the Days

Rev. 11:1–2. 1 Then I was given a measuring rod like a staff, and I was told: "Rise and measure the temple of God and the altar and those who worship there, 2 but do not measure the court outside the temple; leave that out, for it is given over to the nations, and they will trample over the holy city for forty-two months.

11:1–2. "Forty-two months" is equivalent to three and a half years or 1,260 days. These numbers will appear over and over again in the following chapters. The image is taken from Daniel 7:25, where the fourth beast will persecute the righteous for "a time, two times, and half a time." Closely related to this is Daniel 12:7, which uses the same time frame.

In John's day, Daniel 12:7 was understood as a prophecy concerning the conquering and desecration of the temple by Antiochus

Epiphanes, who persecuted the Jews for three and a half years. John's use, then, of phrases, such as "three and a half years" (or "days"), "forty-two months," or "1,260 days," evoke the prior desecration by Antiochus. By prophesying about a coming forty-two months, John compares the coming destruction by the Romans to something the Jews had already experienced.

In fact, Jesus spoke of the actions of Antiochus in reference to the coming destruction in the year 70 (Mt. 24:15; Mk. 13:14). Some have noted that the Jewish war itself was said to last for three and a half years.[32] Revelation scholar David Chilton also noted that variants on the number forty-months appear repeatedly throughout the next few chapters:

A. 11:2—forty-two months
    B. 11:3—twelve hundred and sixty days
        C. 11:9—three and a half days
        C. 11:11—three and a half days
    B. 12:6—twelve hundred and sixty days
A. 13:5—forty-two months[33]

The visions in the following chapters, which use these numbers, serve as a warning of the coming judgment on the temple, in a manner similar to the predictions in the book of Daniel.

The Two Witnesses

Rev. 11:3–6. 3 And I will grant my two witnesses power to prophesy for one thousand two hundred and sixty days, clothed in sackcloth."

4 These are the two olive trees and the two lampstands which stand before the Lord of the earth. 5 And if any one would harm them, fire pours out from their mouth and consumes their foes; if any one would harm them, thus he is doomed to be killed. 6 They have power to shut the sky, that no rain may fall during the days of their prophesying, and they have power over the waters to turn them into blood, and to smite the earth with every plague, as often as they desire.

11:3–6. The two witnesses are likened to two "olive trees" and two "lamps." This is probably a reference to Zechariah 4. There, two olive trees continually provide oil for the lamps in the temple. The meaning of the passage is explained to Zechariah: the temple in Jerusalem will be built despite the resistance of those who oppose it because it has God's anointing (Zech. 4:1–6). These two witnesses, therefore, come to warn of the destruction of the earthly temple. Anyone who clings to it instead of following Christ, refuses to admit that the Spirit has left the earthly temple and anointed a better temple.[34] The image of the two witnesses who "stand before the Lord" is also taken from Zechariah (4:14).

The two witnesses are those who have power to "stop the rain," "turn water into blood," and bring forth "plagues." These images are associated with Moses and Elijah. Moses was able to turn water into blood through the plagues. Fire also came down and consumed Moses' and Elijah's enemies (Num. 16:35; 2 Kings 1:12).[35] Elijah was able to seal off the sky so no rain could fall (1 Kings 17:1).

Together, Moses and Elijah symbolize the two major parts of the Old Testament—the Law and the Prophets.[36] Interpreters of the New Testament recognize this, seeing the vision of Moses and Elijah at the Transfiguration of Jesus as symbolizing Jesus' fulfillment of the Old Testament (Mt. 17:3; Mk. 9:4; Lk. 9:30).[37] There is also some evidence that people in the first century expected a return of Moses and Elijah in the new age (cf. Deut. 18:15).[38] Indeed, the Gospels present John the Baptist as a new "Elijah" and Jesus as a new "Moses."[39]

These two witnesses continually bear witness against the city in Revelation. "Sackcloth" (v. 3) is worn in the Bible as a sign of repentance, especially in the face of coming judgment.[40] The image here, therefore, is that the Old Testament is now bearing witness against Israel. Moreover, Christians who preach the Gospel in Jerusalem are God's witnesses against the city.[41]

The Death of the Two Witnesses

Rev. 11:7–10. 7 And when they have finished their testimony, the beast that ascends from the bottomless pit will make war upon them and conquer them and kill them, 8 and their dead bodies will lie in the street of the great city which is allegorically called Sodom and Egypt, where their Lord was crucified. 9 For three days and a half men from the peoples and tribes and tongues and nations gaze at their dead bodies and refuse to let them be placed in a tomb, 10 and those who dwell on the earth will rejoice over them and make merry and exchange presents, because these two prophets had been a torment to those who dwell on the earth.

11:7–10. Here the two witnesses (in Greek, the two "martyrs") are killed, as were those under the altar (Rev. 6:9–11). The way the wicked citizens neglect to bury the bodies of the witnesses evokes Psalm 79. Psalm 79 also describes unburied bodies of the faithful killed in Jerusalem.[42] Those who fail to give the righteous proper burials deserve God's wrath. Jerusalem, therefore, is pictured as that city which killed the prophets, rejecting their message.[43] That the city is called "Sodom" may be an allusion to Isaiah 1, which addresses the rulers in Jerusalem as "you rulers of Sodom" (1:10).

The beast that kills them bears a strong resemblance to the fourth beast in Daniel 7. Like the beast of Daniel, this beast arises from the abyss (cf. Dan. 7:3) and makes war against the saints (cf. Dan. 7:21). As in Daniel, the saints will receive the kingdom once the beast is defeated.

Again, we see the number "three and a half," which itself is related to Daniel (7:25). That their bodies lie in the street for three and a half days seems to imply a further warning of coming destruction. In other words, their shed blood cries out for justice, just as the souls under the altar do in 6:11.

The "peoples, tribes and tongues," against whom John was told to prophesy in Revelation 10:11, rejoice at the death of these witnesses. The prophets were a thorn in their side, constantly reminding them of the coming consequences of their actions. One is reminded of Jeremiah, whom the people wanted to kill, saying:

"Let this man be put to death, for he is weakening the hands of the soldiers who are left in this city, and the hands of all the people by speaking such words to them. For this man is not seeking the welfare of this people, but their harm" (Jer. 38:4). The death of the witnesses, then, symbolizes the prophets who warned Israel to repent and were killed.

The Assumption of the Witnesses and the Great Earthquake

> **Rev. 11:11–14.** 11 But after the three and a half days a breath of life from God entered them, and they stood up on their feet, and great fear fell on those who saw them. 12 Then they heard a loud voice from heaven saying to them, "Come up hither!" And in the sight of their foes they went up to heaven in a cloud. 13 And at that hour there was a great earthquake, and a tenth of the city fell; seven thousand people were killed in the earthquake, and the rest were terrified and gave glory to the God of heaven.
>
> 14 The second woe has passed; behold, the third woe is soon to come.

11:11–12. Like Christ, who rose from the dead after three days, these witnesses are raised after "three and a half days." John's description of this seems to echo Ezekiel's vision of the dry bones that come to life (a symbol of the restoration of Israel). Ezekiel watches as the "breath" enters into the bodies of the dead and causes them to stand on their feet (Ezek. 37:1–10).

These two witnesses, then, are taken up into heaven. In fact, this being taken into heaven harkens back to Moses and Elijah. In fact, the Bible records Elijah's assumption into heaven and makes reference to an extra-biblical account of Moses' assumption. 2 Kings 2:11 records that a fiery chariot took Elijah up into heaven. The New Testament Book of Jude alludes to a Jewish tradition, which spoke of Moses' "assumption" into heaven (cf. Jude 9).[44]

The reference to "a tenth of the city" is similar to the other trumpet judgments, which only bring partial destruction. The "seven thousand" deaths may also be a symbolic number of "many" deaths. On the other hand, it may be understood in terms of the seven thousand righteous in Elijah's day (1 Kings 19:18). The righteous, therefore, like the two witnesses, are martyred in the city.[45]

Shaking Things Up

There is also an interesting parallel here with Matthew's account of the events that coincided with Jesus' death: "[A]nd the earth shook and the rocks were split; the tombs also were opened, and many bodies of the saints who had fallen asleep were raised, and coming out of the tombs after his resurrection they went into the holy city and appeared to many" (Mt. 27:52–53). Just as John records that "the rest were terrified and gave glory to God" at the sight of the resurrection of the witnesses, so too, the centurion, upon seeing these events, states, "Truly this was the Son of God" (Mt. 27:54).

Christ, the True Witness, was killed, rose from the dead, and ascended into heaven. By rejecting Him and delivering Him into the hands of Pontius Pilate, Jerusalem set itself up for judgment. All that now remains is the final woe.

The vision of the rising of the witnesses and their assumption into heaven also foreshadows the resurrection on the Last Day, when the wicked of the world will be judged and the saints taken into heaven. "At the end of time, the Kingdom of God will come in its fullness. After the universal judgment, the righteous will reign for ever with Christ, glorified in body and soul" (*Catechism*, no. 1042). The Eucharist is a foretaste of this, in as much as those on earth are mystically taken up into the heavenly liturgy.

The Seventh Trumpet: The Saints Praise God

Rev. 11:15–19. 15 Then the seventh angel blew his trumpet, and there were loud voices in heaven, saying, "The kingdom of the world has become the kingdom of our Lord and of his Christ, and he shall reign for ever and ever." 16 And the twenty-four elders who sit on their thrones before God fell on their faces and worshiped God, 17 saying, "We give thanks to thee, Lord God Almighty, who art and who wast, that thou hast taken thy great power and begun

> to reign. 18 The nations raged, but thy wrath came, and the time for the dead to be judged, for rewarding thy servants, the prophets and saints, and those who fear thy name, both small and great, and for destroying the destroyers of the earth." 19 Then God's temple in heaven was opened, and the ark of his covenant was seen within his temple; and there were flashes of lightning, voices, peals of thunder, an earthquake, and heavy hail.

11:15–19. The motif of the kingdom being given over to the saints after a time of persecution by a beast completes the picture of Daniel 7. It is also interesting that the saints take this opportunity to give "thanks" to God. "Thanks" in Greek is the word from which we get "Eucharist." Within the Eucharistic celebration, then, Christians enter the kingdom of God and peer into God's temple in heaven.

It is also noteworthy that, whereas the Lord was previously referred to as the one who "was and is and is to come," He is now simply called the one who "art and wast" (Rev. 11:17). In this, John indicates that He has "begun" to reign because His judgment is underway. This sequence reaches its climax in chapter 16, where the final judgment of the chalices brings the divine judgment to completion, so that God is simply the one "who art and wast" (Rev. 16:5).

Applying the Lessons of Revelation 8–11 Today

Revelation 8–11 describes the destruction of the earthly city, which causes God's temple in heaven to be opened. In other words, "Out with the old, in with the new." Yet, as glorious as the New Jerusalem is, some still cling to the earthly city and reject Christ's kingdom.

In this there is a lesson for all of us: you can't go to heaven without dying. This is true in the physical sense of death, but even more so in the sense of dying to oneself. We must constantly detach ourselves from worldliness and set our sights on heavenly realities. Thus, as great and glorious as earthly goods can be, they become evil when they stand in the way of our heavenly goal.

By keeping her "pilgrim" status in mind, the Church must always focus on her heavenly calling. Christians, therefore, must learn to prioritize their lives. A good job must be turned down if it endangers one's spiritual life. An old friendship must be scorned if it leads us away from the Lord. If even the holy city of Jerusalem can become an obstacle in God's plan—nothing on this planet is safe from being corruptible.

* * *

Multiple Choice

1. The half hour of silence refers to __________.
(a) the period before the anti-Christ
(b) the rite of the offering of incense in the temple
(c) the Old Testament
(d) Jesus' silent years before His ministry

2. The incense offered to God by the angel symbolizes the __________.
(a) prayers of the saints
(b) wrath of the Lamb
(c) smoke of the burning city
(d) victory over sin

3. The judgment of the seven trumpets recalls the destruction of __________.
(a) Jericho
(b) Tyre
(c) the Moabites
(d) Gomorrah

4. Wormwood was frequently used as a symbol of __________ in warnings to Israel in the Old Testament.
(a) peace

(b) mercy
(c) judgment
(d) mourning

5. The "land" is a symbol of __________.
(a) Israel
(b) the nations
(c) Galilee
(d) Rome

6. Both the persecution of the Jews under Antiochus and the Jewish war that led up to the destruction of Jerusalem lasted __________.
(a) one day
(b) one hour
(c) three and half years
(d) seven years

7. The two witnesses represent __________.
(a) the Law and the Prophets
(b) the northern and southern kingdoms
(c) Peter and John
(d) the Old and New Testaments

Answers) 1. b; 2. a; 3. a; 4. c; 5. a; 6. c; 7. a.

* * *

Discussion/Study Questions

1. How are the trumpet judgements reminiscent of the plagues of the Exodus? (See page 123)

____

____

____

____

2. Explain the image of the mountain being cast into the sea. (See page 125)

____

____

____

____

3. How are the images of three and a half years, forty-two months, and 1,260 days connected? To what do they refer? (See page 137–138)

____

____

____

____

4. What lesson does the destruction of the temple teach us? What can we learn from those who rejected Christ and clung to the temple? (See page 143)

____

____

____

____

THE ARCHETYPICAL WOMAN

The Woman Clothed with the Sun (Rev. 12:1–17)

Mistaken Identity?

Traditionally, Catholics have seen the woman in Revelation 12 as Mary. Of course, just as other passages in Revelation have multiple meanings, Catholics affirm that the woman doesn't *only* represent Mary.[1] As we shall see, the "woman" must also be understood as "Daughter Zion," depicted in Isaiah. What reasons are there for recognizing the woman as Mary at all? When one examines the way Revelation 11 leads into Revelation 12, the reasons for such an interpretation are clearly seen.

Indiana John

The ark of the covenant is the last thing John sees before the events of Revelation 12. The ark's importance can't be stressed enough. During the Exodus, God's presence appeared over the ark in the tabernacle, making it holy (Ex. 40:34–38). When the ark was captured by the Philistines, it was said, "The glory has departed from Israel, for the ark of God has been captured" (1 Sam. 4:22). The Philistines returned the ark, however, because they broke out in tumors after they took it (1 Sam. 5:6–12).

The ark was also holy because it contained (1) God's word, that is, the Ten Commandments, written on the stone tablets; (2) bread from heaven, that is, the manna; and (3) the staff of Aaron, the high priest. Nothing ritually unclean could touch the ark. When one man named Uzzah tried to catch the ark to prevent it from falling into the mud, he was killed on the spot for touching it (cf. 2 Sam. 6:6–7). Moreover, it was the "ark" that led Israel through the desert on their way to the Promised Land (cf. Num. 10:33–35).

When this ark was lost after the Babylonian invasion, it was nothing less than a national tragedy. People still speculate about its whereabouts today. Now John, looking into God's temple in the heavenly Jerusalem, sees that ark. But he just mentions it and moves on. This is surprising. You'd at least expect a little more about it, right? Yet John never mentions it again—or does he?

Lucan Parallel

In Luke 1, Catholics find two stories familiar to them from the Rosary—the Annunciation of the angel Gabriel to Mary and Mary's Visitation to her cousin Elizabeth. Both accounts evoke ark of the covenant imagery. In the Annunciation, Mary is told, "The Holy Spirit will come upon you, and the power of the Most High will overshadow you" (Lk. 1:35). The Greek word for "overshadow" is the same word used to describe God's presence "overshadowing" the ark in the tabernacle in the Old Testament (LXX, Ex. 40:34–38).

Mary is also compared to the ark in the story of the Visitation. Luke describes Mary's visit to Elizabeth in ways that echo the story of David's carrying the ark into Jerusalem:

Luke 1	**2 Samuel 6**
"Mary arose and went with haste into the hill country, to a city of Judah" (v. 39)	"And David arose and went with all the people who were with him from Baalejudah" (v. 2)
"[Elizabeth] exclaimed with a loud cry, 'Blessed are you among women'"(v. 42)	"[David] blessed the people in the name of the LORD" (v. 18)
"And why is this granted me, that the mother of my Lord should come to me?" (v. 43)	"[David] said, 'How can the ark of the LORD come to me?'" (v. 9)

"For behold . . . the babe in my womb leaped for joy" (v. 44)	"Michal . . . looked out the window and saw King David leaping and dancing before the LORD" (v. 16)
"And Mary remained with her about three months" (v. 56)	"And the ark of the LORD remained in the house of Obededom the Gittite three months" (v. 11)[2]

Mary, then, is the new ark, because she bears within herself Jesus, who is (1) God's Word in flesh, (2) the true Bread from heaven, and (3) the heavenly High Priest.[3]

The early Fathers also noticed the parallels between Mary and the ark. Saint Methodius writes:

> For if to the ark, which was the image and type of thy sanctity, such honour was paid of God that to no one but to the priestly order only was the access to it open, or ingress allowed to behold it . . . what sort of veneration is due to thee from us who are of creation the least, to thee who art indeed a queen; to thee, the living ark of God, the Lawgiver; to thee, the heaven that contains Him who can be contained of none? For since thou, O holy virgin, hast dawned as a bright day upon the world and hast brought forth the Sun of Righteousness, that hateful horror of darkness has been chased away.[4]

Similarly, Saint Ephraim referred to Mary in his hymns, comparing her to the ark.[5] Saint John Damascene also preached on Mary's role as the new ark, giving a spiritual interpretation to 2 Samuel as a foreshadowing of the Assumption.

Given the parallels of Mary and the ark, it should be no wonder that in Revelation 12, a vision concerning "a woman" who bears the Messiah follows a vision of the ark of God. And it shouldn't surprise us that John simply calls her "woman" and doesn't use the name "Mary." In the Fourth Gospel, John *never* mentions Mary's name, but usually refers to her as "woman" (Jn. 2:4; 19:6).

Saint John Damascene and other Fathers may have been right, then, in understanding this passage as confirmation of the doctrine of the Assumption. Damascene preached a homily on Revelation 12, in celebrating the Assumption, saying, "This day the Holy and Singular Virgin is presented in the sublime and heavenly Temple. . . . This day the sacred and living Ark of the Living God, who bore within her womb her own Creator, took up her rest within that Temple of the Lord that was not made with hands. . . . And David her forefather, and her father in God, dances with joy."[6] Thus, Damascene understood Revelation 12 to mean that, just as David brought the ark into Jerusalem, so too Christ brings the new ark, Mary, into the New Jerusalem of heaven. So after we read in chapter 11 about the two witnesses who are taken into heaven, we then read in chapter 12 of the "woman" in heaven. In effect, we read about three people who have been assumed into heaven—Moses, Elijah and Mary.

The Woman

> **Rev. 12:1–2.** And a great portent appeared in heaven, a woman clothed with the sun, with the moon under her feet, and on her head a crown of twelve stars; 2 she was with child and she cried out in her pangs of birth, in anguish for delivery.

12:1–2. The image of a "sign" [or "portent"] of a woman giving birth recalls Isaiah's famous prophecy, "Therefore the Lord himself will give you a sign. Behold, a young woman shall conceive and bear a son, and shall call his name Immanuel" (Is. 7:14).[7] This is not the only allusion to Isaiah found in Revelation 12.

Labor of Love

The image of a woman giving birth is reminiscent of the image that Isaiah used to describe the restoration of God's people. Isaiah depicted Israel, on the verge of restoration, as a woman in labor: "Like a woman with child, who writhes and cries out in her pangs when she is near her time" (Is. 26:17). At the end of his book, he again uses similar imagery: "Before she was in labor she gave birth; before her pain came upon her she was delivered of a son" (Is. 66:7).

Who, then, is this woman? Does John think of Isaiah's prophecy in reference to Daughter Zion or to Mary? The answer, in short, is both. John is alluding to both Mary and Daughter Zion because Mary personifies Isaiah's Daughter Zion.[8] Through Mary, the people of Israel give birth to the Messiah.[9]

Travail Mixed Allusions

In Isaiah, those who return from the exile in the New Exodus are described as sons of "Daughter Zion." Isaiah 66:8 reads, "For as soon as Zion was in labor she brought forth her sons." Here in chapter 12, John tells us that the "woman" is the mother of "those who keep the commandments of God and bear testimony to Jesus" (Rev. 12:17). Of course, the Church, as Mother of all Christians, is the fulfillment of Isaiah's Daughter Zion prophecies. Moreover, Isaiah's Daughter Zion prophecies are also fulfilled in Mary, who is the icon of the Church, mother of all believers.[10]

In his Gospel, John tells us how Jesus wanted all believers to recognize Mary as their mother. There, dying on the Cross, Jesus gives His mother to be the mother of the beloved disciple, who represents all Christians: "When Jesus saw His mother, and the disciple whom He loved standing near, he said to his mother, 'Woman, behold your son!' Then he said to the disciple, 'Behold, your mother!'" (Jn. 19:26–27). Mary, then, is the fulfillment of daughter Zion.

But what of the labor pains? In John 16, Jesus explains His Passion in terms of a woman in travail. "When a woman is in travail she has sorrow, because her hour has come; but when she is delivered of the child, she no longer remembers the anguish" (Jn. 16:21). The woman's travail, then, is a symbol for the Passion—the suffering through which the Redemption comes.[11]

Furthermore, not only did Isaiah prophesy that Daughter Zion would be the mother of those redeemed from the nations, he also mentions that God will marry her—and her sons! Daughter Zion is both virgin bride and fruitful mother: "For as a young man marries a virgin, so shall your sons marry you, and as the bridegroom rejoices over the bride, so shall your God rejoice over you" (Is. 62:5). This prophecy is fulfilled in Jesus, the God-Man, who becomes the new Adam, making Mary the new Eve. She is both virgin and mother.

Starting Over

In the Gospel of John, the first two chapters describe Jesus' mission in terms of a new creation, much like Isaiah describes the restoration of Israel (cf. Is. 66:22). There are many parallels between the opening of John's Gospel and the Book of Genesis:

—both start, "In the beginning"
—both speak of "life," "light," and "darkness"
—as Genesis describes God's Spirit moving over the waters, John describes the Spirit hovering over Jesus in the waters of the Jordan.[12]

And the parallels don't stop here. Just as Genesis describes a seven-day week of creation, John seems to do so as well. John begins by telling us about John the Baptist baptizing in the Jordan. He then introduces Jesus, telling how Jesus came toward John on "the next day" (Jn 1:28–34). After this, on "the next day," Andrew, Peter and another disciple, decide to follow Jesus (Jn. 1:35–42). And then, "on the next day," Phillip meets Jesus and follows after Him (Jn. 1:43–51).

Now, this may sound like a high school math problem, but how many days has John described here? Since John begins, "on the next day," a first day is implied—the day before the next one. The first time he says "the next day," he's speaking about the second day. Add to those two days the two more references to "the next day," and we see John has described four days. It is interesting, then, that John begins the following story, "On the third day . . ." (Jn. 2:1). The third day from the last day mentioned, the fourth day, equals the seventh day. John is describing the seven days that begin the new creation:

Day 1 John the Baptist baptizes in the wilderness;
Day 2 (*the next day*) (Jn. 1:28–34) Jesus meets John the Baptist and is called "Lamb of God;"
Day 3 (*the next day*) (Jn. 1:35–42) Andrew, Simon Peter and another disciple follow after Jesus;
Day 4 (*the next day*) (Jn. 1:43–51) Phillip and Nathaniel follow Jesus;
Day 7 (*on the third day*) (Jn. 2:1–11) Jesus and Mary at a wedding.

Did John really mean to tell us that this "third day" was also the "seventh day"? Consider the following evidence. Jesus works a miracle on this day, in which He transforms the water used for purification into wine. Numbers 19 gives us the directions for performing this rite of purification; a person must "cleanse himself with the water on the *third day* and on the *seventh day*" (Num. 19:12). When John begins the story with the "third day," he also alludes to this ritual prescription—showing its fulfillment by Jesus' miracle on the "third day," which was also the "seventh day."

A Biblical Type of Woman

Adam was created with the beasts on the sixth day of creation (Gen. 1:24–2:1). Eve was not created until later. When Adam fell into a deep sleep, she was formed from his side (Gen. 2:21). The ancient rabbis believed that this deep sleep indicated the passing of one night. They understood that it was on the seventh day that Adam awoke and found his bride, the woman, Eve. John 1–2 must be read in light of all this.

It is no coincidence, therefore, that we find a wedding on the seventh day of John's creation week. Interestingly, John never tells us the names of the couple married that day. Jesus and Mary are the only two persons named in the story. Surely, two people were married at Cana, but John uses the context to reveal Jesus and

Mary's role in the new creation. Jesus addresses His mother as "woman" (Jn. 2:4), reminiscent of Eve in the Genesis story. Jesus is even referred to as the "Bridegroom" in the next chapter (Jn. 3:29). John is showing us that Jesus is the New Adam and Mary is the New Eve.

Starting Over

This imagery is found not only in John. Saint Paul refers to Jesus as the New Adam (1 Cor. 15:45). Likewise, from the earliest times, Mary was understood as the New Eve. In the 2nd century AD, Saint Justin Martyr wrote, "For Eve, who was a virgin and undefiled, having conceived the word of the serpent, brought forth disobedience and death. But the Virgin Mary received faith and joy . . . wherefore also the Holy Thing begotten of her is the Son of God."[13] Likewise, Saint Jerome wrote, "[N]ow the chain of the curse is broken. Death came through Eve, but life has come through Mary."[14]

In Revelation 12, this New Eve imagery is continued. The mother of Jesus, Mary, is referred to again as "woman," calling to mind the Genesis narrative. There is even a reference to the devil as, "that ancient serpent" (12:9), which clearly shows us that John had the story of the fall in the back of his mind.

Isaiah had prophesied that Daughter Zion would marry her sons (Is. 62:5). Mary fulfills this prophecy in as much as she is both the Mother of Christ, the New Adam, and the New Eve—the icon of the Bride of Christ, the Church. In Revelation 12, all of these Old Testament types come together to form a beautiful mosaic—John's theological picture of Mary.

Here it is important to note that the description of the woman also seems to be based on the bride of the son of David, Solomon. Solomon writes of his beloved, "Who is this that looks forth like the dawn, fair as the moon, bright as the sun?" (Song 6:10). Here again we see how the woman of Revelation 12 is depicted as not only the mother of the Davidic king, but also the bride of the son of David.

Royal Pangs

Speaking of the Davidic kingdom, let us now turn our attention towards the woman's crown (Rev. 12:1). Like the twenty-four elders, the "woman" wears a crown, indicating that she, like them, has been faithful and received the "crown of life" (Rev. 2:10, cf. commentary on 20:4–6). Yet her crown is unique.

It might seem odd to non-Catholics that the Mother of the Messiah should receive such a prominent status as to even wear a special crown. But, in fact, there is precedent for recognizing a "Queen Mother." It goes back to the Old Testament tradition of the *gebirah*—the Great Lady.

Recall that the king of Israel was a son of David. But who was the queen? Immediately, you might think that it must have been the wife of the son of David. But that would have gotten complicated, since Solomon, a son of David, had many wives—700 of them (1 Kings 11:3)! Instead, the queen was always the mother of the king. And her role was very important. She symbolized the unity of the Davidic line. In fact, when the Chronicler mentions each new Davidic king, he almost always identifies the Queen Mother.[15]

The most striking account of the Davidic Queen Mother is the account of Bathsheba, wife of David and mother of Solomon. Solomon erected a throne for her at his right hand and even bowed down to her (1 Kings 2:19). Requests for the king were taken to the Queen Mother, who, interceding on behalf of the requisitioner, would speak to her son (cf. 1 Kings 2:13–35).

In Revelation 12:2, we see the birth of the Davidic King. Revelation's description of Him as the One who "is to rule all the nations with a rod of iron" (Rev. 12:5), is drawn from Psalm 2:9, a Psalm about the Davidic king. Over time, this Psalm was understood as a prophecy describing the Davidic-Messiah.[16] Given this Davidic background, we should not be surprised that the mother of the Davidic King is presented as a Queen, crowned with twelve stars. She is the Davidic Queen Mother, raised up by grace and glorified by her Son.

Of course, Mary is nothing without Jesus. But Jesus, like Solomon, knows how to keep the commandment: "Honor thy Father and Mother." In fact, how much more would the Son of God honor His Holy Mother! Moreover, if those in the Old Testament could take their requests before the King through Bathsheba, how much more can we take our prayers to the King of kings through Mary? If Mary would ask Jesus to help the bride and groom with their supply of wine at the wedding of Cana, how much more will she go to Him in the heavenly throne room with our heartfelt requests!

The Red Dragon

> **Rev. 12:3–4.** 3 And another portent appeared in heaven; behold, a great red dragon, with seven heads and ten horns, and seven diadems upon his heads. 4 His tail swept down a third of the stars of heaven, and cast them to the earth. And the dragon stood before the woman who was about to bear a child, that he might devour her child when she brought it forth;

12:3–4. The great red dragon is obviously the devil (Rev. 12:9). Once again, Isaiah seems to be in the background. After speaking of a woman "in travail" in chapter 27, Isaiah describes the defeat of the wicked in terms of crushing the Leviathan. Like Revelation 12, the Leviathan in Isaiah 27 is described as a "dragon" (Is. 27:1; Rev. 12:3) and a "serpent" (Is. 27:1; Rev. 12:9). Although Isaiah does not mention the number of his heads, the Leviathan was commonly known in the Bible and ancient literature as having multiple heads (cf. Ps. 74:14).[17]

As we have repeatedly seen in Revelation, stars are symbols of angels. The casting of the stars to earth, then, is a symbol for the fallen angels.[18] The seven diadems indicate that Satan is the chief fallen angel, since diadems were understood as crowns in antiquity.[19] Indeed, the image of political power is present in the dragon's ten horns, which is drawn from the fourth beast (the fourth kingdom) in Daniel's vision (Dan. 7:7).

Edom Up

However, the imagery may even penetrate deeper into the historical events of Christ's birth. If the male child born is Christ, and the woman is Mary, the red dragon may represent Herod. Since "Edom" actually means "red," the "red" dragon, may refer to the fact that Herod was an Edomite, (cf. Gen. 25:25, 30). The dragon, therefore, seeks to destroy the infant Christ as Herod did. Just as the Holy Family fled to Egypt, so the "woman" also takes flight into the wilderness (12:6, 14).[20]

Herod's kingship, then, is the antithesis, the very opposite, of Christ's. Herod gained his throne through murder, was not the rightful heir to the throne, and established an earthly temple. Christ is the rightful heir, as God's true Son and as the Son of David. His kingdom is not of this world, and His temple is in heaven. Herod represents everything that must be destroyed when the new creation is ushered in.

The Birth of the Male Child

> **Rev. 12:5–6.** 5 she brought forth a male child, one who is to rule all the nations with a rod of iron, but her child was caught up to God and to his throne, 6 and the woman fled into the wilderness, where she has a place prepared by God, in which to be nourished for one thousand two hundred and sixty days.

12:5–6. As stated above, the woman's flight into the wilderness recalls the escape of the Holy Family from Herod's murderous attempts to kill the infant Christ. Yet, it also recalls Israel, who fled into the desert to escape Pharaoh. In fact, Psalm 74:12–14 compares the defeat of Pharaoh at the parting of the Red Sea to the defeat of the Leviathan.

The two interpretations are not exclusive of each other, since the events in the life of Jesus are presented as the true fulfillment of Old Testament accounts. Thus, just as Jesus escaped Herod, Israel escaped Pharaoh.

The fact that Christ is depicted as "caught up to God," a reference to His Ascension, demonstrates that the visions in Revelation, although describing historical events, are not necessarily chronological. Likewise, the vision goes on to explain the fall of the angels (Rev. 12:7–8), which John already mentioned in 12:4. From all this we can see how John is inter-weaving several different themes and ideas, which tell us the spiritual meaning behind historical events—but not necessarily in their chronological order.

The Flight of the Woman into the Wilderness

Twelve hundred and sixty days brings us back to the "forty-two months" and "three and a half days" symbolism. No doubt the symbolism is meant to describe a time of tribulation, and probably more specifically, the chaos surrounding the events in the year 70 (see commentary on Rev. 11:1–2). Indeed, the Church fled into the wilderness and found refuge on Pella during the siege of Jerusalem. Mary's flight into Egypt, thus, symbolizes the escape of the early Christians during the year 70. In all of this, we see God's protection of His people, and not only in the year 70—here we have an image of His constant protection of the Church from the evil one.

The War of Heaven

Rev. 12:7–9. 7 Now war arose in heaven, Michael and his angels fighting against the dragon; and the dragon and his angels fought, 8 but they were defeated and there was no longer any place for them in heaven. 9 And the great dragon was thrown down, that ancient serpent, who is called the Devil and Satan, the deceiver of the whole world—he was thrown down to the earth, and his angels were thrown down with him.

12:7–9. Michael is the guardian of God's people (cf. Dan. 12:1). It is no surprise then that he appears here to foil the devil's attempt to make war on the woman (the Church) and Christ. The passage demonstrates that there is a spiritual battle waging behind the scenes of history.

The Fall before the Fall

Furthermore, the Fathers interpreted this passage in terms of the angelic fall at the dawn of creation. Irenaeus explained that the devil fell because he was "envious of man."[21] Indeed, the Book of Wisdom tells us that the devil tempted Adam and Eve out of envy (Wis. 2:24). It would seem then that the fall had something to do with the devil's disgust for God's love for man. Some of the Fathers speculated, therefore, that the devil refused to be a part of God's plan to make men share in the life of grace with the angels. Because of this he revolted.[22]

The fact that Revelation 12 closely associates the birth of Christ and the fall of the angels is also interesting. Upon seeing the close link between the angelic fall and the Incarnation the Fathers speculated that the angels fell because they rejected the notion of a God-Man, whom they would have to worship.[23]

The Accuser Is Cast Out

> **Rev. 12:10.** And I heard a loud voice in heaven, saying, "Now the salvation and the power and the kingdom of our God and the authority of his Christ have come, for the accuser of our brethren has been thrown down, who accuses them day and night before our God.

12:10. Once again, Christ's victory is associated with the ushering in of the "kingdom," evoking the fulfillment of the vision of the "son of man" in Daniel 7. As we have mentioned, there are close parallels between the dragon and the beasts of Daniel 7 (see commentary on Revelation 12:3–4). John sees the accuser thrown out—out of court, if you will—just as Daniel saw "the court" sitting in judgment of the beast (Dan. 7:26).

This is also the only place where the "brotherhood" of the saints is mentioned. The saints in heaven refer to the martyrs on earth (cf. Rev. 12:11) as their "brethren." That brotherhood is closely connected here to the establishment of the kingdom. This is because the restoration of the Davidic kingdom is the fulfillment of God's plan to bring all nations into His covenant family.[24]

This family, this kingdom made present on earth, is the Church—the Family of God. This kingdom is established in the work of Christ, through which Satan is defeated. The defeat of Satan occurs on multiple levels.

Exorcising Regularly

First, Satan is cast down at the beginning of time. This is evident from the fact that the fall of the angels is presented before Christ's birth in the image of a third of the stars falling from heaven. As we have seen, the Fathers also spoke of a primordial angelic fall.

Yet it is primarily through Christ's work on earth that Satan is "cast out." John sees here the spiritual war behind Christ's work. Thus when Christ speaks of His own death, He says, "[N]ow shall the ruler of this world be *cast out*" (Jn. 12:31).

It is also noteworthy that in the previous chapter, Revelation 11, the destruction of the temple is spoken of in terms of being "cast out" (11:2). Christ's victory over Satan and establishment of a New Covenant is manifested in the judgment on wicked Jerusalem. It further indicates that the Jewish leaders, who preferred the earthly temple to Christ, were truly acting in concert with Satan and were thus judged with him (cf. Jn. 8:44; Rev. 3:9).

The devil is here called the "accuser." This draws on a tradition in the Old Testament that understands Satan as a kind of "prosecutor" or legal "adversary" in the heavenly courtroom (Job. 1:6ff; Zech. 3:1ff.). Indeed, the word "satan" literally means "adversary" in Hebrew.[25] The "casting out" of Satan, then, symbolizes what God does with the "case" against the saints—He throws it out of court.

Those Who Conquered

> **Rev. 12:11.** And they have conquered him by the blood of the Lamb and by the word of their testimony, for they loved not their lives even unto death.

12:11. The saints have conquered through the offering of their own lives—"they loved not their lives unto death." They have learned to give God life-giving love—pouring themselves out to

God, holding nothing back—and, therefore, have defeated Satan, who seeks to make them like himself, selfish and proud. In so doing, these saints realize the calling Adam first received but failed to obey (see chapter 4, "Love of Your Life"). Whereas Adam failed as a priest-king, the saints learn to offer their own priestly sacrifice, themselves, obtaining the "crown of life" (Rev. 2:10).

In the Mass we are given the grace through the sacrament of the Eucharist to learn life-giving love, by offering ourselves up in union with Christ. Moreover, Pius XII explained how this self-offering is made by the faithful through their participation in the Eucharistic liturgy: "[T]he people unite their hearts in praise, impetration, expiation and thanksgiving with the prayers or intention of the priest, even of the High Priest Himself, so that in the one and same offering of the victim and according to a visible sacerdotal rite, they may be presented to God the Father."[26]

Likewise, just as the Church offers up the "Body of Christ" in the Eucharist, so too do the faithful receive Him in Holy Communion, which not only transforms the Church into Christ's Mystical Body, but also enables her to be offered as His Mystical Body. The Church, as we will see when we look at Revelation 19–22, is Christ's Body—not as a headless torso—but as His Bride (cf. Eph. 5:23–33). In the Eucharist, the Church enters into intimate communion of one flesh with her Bridegroom. Christ pours out His life in her and through her, so that just as He once offered Himself through His earthly body, so now He offers Himself through the Church. When the Church offers herself up in the liturgy, Christ is presenting Himself to the Father through her.

The Devil Is Cast Down to Earth

> **Rev. 12:12.** Rejoice then, O heaven and you that dwell therein! But woe to you, O earth and sea, for the devil has come down to you in great wrath, because he knows that his time is short!"

12:12. The "heavens"[27] rejoice because Satan has been defeated. Yet a woe comes upon the earth because Satan is now angry at being cast down and looks to take out his frustration on man. However, his time is "short." This can be understood two different ways.

In Short

The "short time" mentioned by John would be the time from Christ's Ascension to the destruction of Jerusalem. Like Israel, who wandered for forty years in the desert, a forty-year period extends from Christ's Resurrection to the destruction of the temple. Those in Jerusalem, therefore, must make a decision between "Egypt" and the "New Jerusalem."

In another sense, the passage refers to the casting down of Satan after Christ has defeated him.[28] The devil's time to tempt man will be cut short when the Son comes in glory and casts him into the lake of fire, for eternal punishment. Until then, the devil has a "short time" in which he roams the earth, trying to take as many people with him as possible.

One does not have to decide between the different possible meanings. Since creation, Israel, and the Church all come together in the figure of the "woman" whom the devil targets, the imagery gives us a kind of panoramic view of salvation history.

The Dragon Pursues the Woman

> **Rev. 12:13–14.** 13 And when the dragon saw that he had been thrown down to the earth, he pursued the woman who had borne the male child. 14 But the woman was given the two wings of the great eagle that she might fly from the serpent into the wilderness, to the place where she is to be nourished for a time, and times, and half a time.

12:13–14. The "woman," God's people symbolized in the person of Mary, flees into the wilderness for protection, recalling the Holy Family's flight into Egypt and Israel's Exodus. Both events mark the deliverance of God's people from an evil king (e.g., Herod and Pharaoh). One might also include the Church's flight to Pella in the year 70. In a certain sense, the Exodus is a template for all the various ways God brings deliverance. Indeed, the "wings of an eagle" is frequently used in the Old Testament to describe the Exodus (Ex. 19:4; Deut. 32:10–12). This became a symbol of God's protection of His people (e.g., Ps. 55:6–8; Is. 40:31).

The nourishment of God's people in the desert also evokes the imagery of God's people being fed on the "manna" (cf. Ex. 16:32; Deut. 8:16). Given the close connection in John's Gospel between the manna and the Eucharist (cf. Jn. 6:32–58), the image may also be understood as a picture of the Church fed by the Blessed Sacrament during her earthly pilgrimage. This is what the Catechism teaches when it speaks of the Eucharist, which "sustains our strength along the pilgrimage of this life, . . . and unites us even now to the Church in heaven." (*Catechism*, no. 1419).

Not Too Hard to Swallow

Rev. 12:15–17. 15 The serpent poured water like a river out of his mouth after the woman, to sweep her away with the flood. 16 But the earth came to the help of the woman, and the earth opened its mouth and swallowed the river, which the dragon had poured from his mouth. 17 Then the dragon was angry with the woman, and went off to make war on the rest of her offspring, on those who keep the commandments of God and bear testimony to Jesus. And he stood on the sand of the sea.

12:15–16. There are multiple places in the Old Testament, where the deliverance of God's people is described in terms of rescue from floodwaters. Undoubtedly this evokes the story of Noah's Ark, when God quite literally saved His people from the flood. Here, given the prominent use of Exodus imagery, two passages come to mind.

The first passage comes from the song that Moses sang when God delivered Israel through the Red Sea: "Thou didst stretch out thy right hand, the earth swallowed them" (Ex. 15:12). The second is drawn from Numbers 16. There, Korah and his sons rebel against Moses and seek to usurp him. God vindicates Moses, however, when the earth "swallows" them up, sending them down to Sheol. This parallels John's account in Revelation, since Sheol itself was believed to be the place of subterranean waters.[29]

In light of John's heavy dependence on Isaiah, we should also mention Isaiah 51, where God's promise of the New Exodus is backed up by a reminder of the first one. The account there of Israel's redemption bears striking similarities to the rescue of the "woman" in Revelation 12. "Was it not thou . . . that didst pierce the dragon? Was it not thou that didst dry up the sea, the waters of the great deep; that didst make the depths of the sea a way for the redeemed to pass over?" (Is. 51:9–10). Both Isaiah and Revelation speak of the defeat of the "dragon" and salvation from the "waters."

Our Mother

12:17. The "woman," who is the mother of "all those who keep the commandments of God and bear testimony to Jesus," is the Church and Mary, who is an icon of the Church. The reference here also evokes imagery of the "New Eve," who is also called "the mother of all the living." The Fathers, as mentioned before, understood this as referring to Mary (see chapter 10, commentary on Rev. 14:1-5).[30]

Applying the Lessons of Revelation 12 Today

First and foremost, we have seen how Mary is an icon of the Church. She is the "model" believer. When the angel comes to her, and she says, "*Fiat*," Mary gives herself completely to God in an act of self-giving love. She holds nothing back. Everything she is, from that moment on, is given to God. "Let it be done to me according to your will" (Lk. 1:38). If only we could learn to pray this.

Yet, so often, we hold things back from God. We even try to make deals with God, saying, "Okay, you can have this and that, but then there's this one thing—that's for me. I know I should give it to you too, but look, I've given you everything else." This won't fly because God demands *total* self-giving love. Everything we have and everything we are must be given over to Him. If there's something we are unwilling to give up, it might be because we love that thing more than God.

Mary doesn't celebrate her grace-filled status. She doesn't sit around in Nazareth, saying, "Well, now that I've given everything over to God and become the Queen Mother, I at least deserve to be waited on and treated like the Queen I am." No! Mary doesn't take a moment's time to congratulate herself. Instead, she takes off to serve her pregnant cousin, Elizabeth, even as she is pregnant herself.

So often we look for the things we "deserve." Commercials often remind us, "You deserve it. Treat yourself." But Mary reverses that logic. She shows us how to radiate the glory of the Trinity. It's not in being served or gawked at, but in serving others. The Visitation follows the Annunciation. Mary's example of life-giving love, therefore, shows us that the greatest glory is not in being served, but in serving others.

* * *

Multiple Choice

1. The image of the woman represents __________.
(a) Mary only
(b) Israel, the Church, and Mary
(c) the Church only
(d) Daughter Zion only

2. The last thing John sees before the woman is ___________.
(a) the garden of Eden
(b) the ark of the covenant
(c) two witnesses
(d) the red dragon

3. Saint John Damascene believed Revelation 12 depicted Mary being taken into heaven as David brought ___________.
(a) the ark into the temple

(b) the people into the Promised Land
(c) the menorah into the holy of holies
(d) the book of the Law to Zion

4. The labor pains of the woman symbolize __________.
(a) Mary's martyrdom
(b) the Passion of Christ
(c) the suffering Jerusalem in the year 70
(d) a difficult birth

5. As mother of the living, who defeats the serpent, the woman is a type of __________.
(a) Eve
(b) Rachel
(c) warrior
(d) Daughter Zion

6. The flight of the woman into the wilderness, who is given the wings of the eagle, recalls _________.
(a) the deliverance of Eve
(b) the Exodus
(c) the Queen Mother
(d) Jerusalem

Answers) 1. b; 2. b; 3. a; 4. b; 5. a; 6. b.

* * *

Discussion/Study Questions

1. What is the connection between the ark of the covenant and Mary? (See pages 148–149)

____

____

____

____

2. How is the "woman" a symbol of Mary? In what way is she presented here as the embodiment of Daughter Zion? As icon of the Church? (See pages 150–154)

____

____

____

____

3. How is Mary depicted as the Queen Mother? (See pages 155–156)

____

____

____

____

4. How is Mary an example to all believers? What can we learn from her? (See pages 164–165)

____

____

____

____

BEAUTY AND THE BEASTS

The Church and Her Enemies (Rev. 13:1–15:8)

Beasts of Burden

Even before we begin our analysis of the two beasts in Revelation 13, it is important to note the fundamental meaning of "beast." The "beast" is a symbol of sinful humanity. Adam was created on the sixth day with the "beasts" (Gen. 1:24–31). Yet God set up the seventh day as the goal towards which Adam was to strive. For six days he was to work and reign as king, having dominion over creation. The seventh day, however, represented his priestly calling, whereby he would enter into God's rest. By failing to choose God's ways, Adam remained in the sixth day. The sixth day is the day of the beast, and, as we shall see, the number of the beast. At the most basic level, "beast" symbolizes man's fallenness.[1]

Furthermore, as we have seen throughout the Book of Revelation, John's visions often contain multiple layers of meaning. The vision of the two beasts is no different. As we have already mentioned, the first beast, which is characterized by the number "666," is Rome, headed by Caesar Nero. However, this does not exhaust the meaning of "666."

Rome itself is a symbol of any nation throughout history that has turned its back on God. But before we can apply Revelation to our day, we must first grasp the original meaning it had for John's first-century audience. Only then can we see how it relates to us today.

The First Beast

Rev. 13:1–3. 1 And I saw a beast rising out of the sea, with ten horns and seven heads, with ten diadems upon its horns and a blasphemous name upon its heads. 2 And the beast that I saw was like a leopard, its feet were like a bear's, and its mouth was like a

> lion's mouth. And to it the dragon gave his power and his throne and great authority. 3 One of its heads seemed to have a mortal wound, but its mortal wound was healed, and the whole earth followed the beast with wonder.

13:1–2. The beast that comes out of the sea is very similar in appearance to the "dragon" of Revelation 12. Like the dragon, it has "seven heads and ten horns" (Rev. 12:3). However, the beast is not exactly like the dragon. This shows that the beast is an instrument of the devil—a kind of demonic agent.

The vision of the beast here is taken from Daniel 7, from which John has already drawn. The beasts seen by Daniel, like the beasts in this vision, come up "out of the sea" (see commentary on Rev. 1:12–13). The fact that the beast comes out of "the sea" implies its Gentile origin, since as we have seen; "the sea" is often a symbol for the nations (see commentary on 10:4).

The beast seen here is a combination of all the beasts seen by Daniel.

Daniel 7	**Revelation 13**
First Beast: "like a lion" (v. 4)	"a mouth like a lion" (v. 2)
Second Beast: "like a bear" (v. 5)	"its feet were like a bear's" (v. 2)
Third Beast: "like a leopard" (v. 6)	"like a leopard" (v. 2)
Fourth Beast: "it had ten horns (v. 7)	"with ten horns" (v. 1)

The beast John sees, then, is probably the fourth beast, which Daniel also describes as the climactic combination of all its predecessors.

The four beasts were a sign to Daniel of the four nations who would come to oppose Israel: Babylon, Medo-Persia, Greece, and Rome (see commentary on Rev. 1:12–13). This beast in Revelation, therefore, symbolizes Rome.

Yet, as we have said, this beast does not only symbolize Rome. The "horns" and the "heads" are symbols of political authority (cf. Dan. 7:24; Rev. 17:9). Thus, Rome becomes a symbol for any state that turns away from God and persecutes His people.

13:3. As mentioned before, the beast is Rome, and yet, there is fluidity in the image of the beast. In one sense, it identifies the Roman Empire in general, since its seven heads are described as its seven kings (Rev. 17:9). However, the beast is also identified by one of its heads in particular—one of the kings, who receives a mortal wound (cf. Rev. 13:3, 12).[2] So which of the Roman kings is signified?

Head Count

As we have shown in chapter 1, the king must be Nero. A number of reasons could be cited in support of interpreting Nero as the king. First, one of the few things scholars agree upon is that Revelation was written during a time of persecution. Most evidence indicates that it was written during Nero's persecution.[3] (See Chapter 1, "Seizure by Caesar," and following)

Secondly, Revelation 17:8 describes the seven heads in terms of seven kings: five who have fallen, one who is reigning, and a future seventh, whose reign will last "only a little while." The idea that Nero is the sixth king—"the one who is"—would have been nothing new to the historians in John's day. They began counting the Roman Emperors with Julius Caesar, making Nero the sixth king.[4] In fact, as John prophesied, Nero was succeeded by Galba, who did in fact reign "only a little while"—about six months.

The "number of the beast" also points to Nero, since "666" is the numeric value of "Nero Caesar" in Hebrew. John's frequent transliteration of Hebrew words, such as "Abaddon" (Rev. 9:11), "Amen" (Rev. 3:14), "Armageddon" (Rev. 16:16), and "Hallelujah"

(Rev. 19:1), demonstrate that the author of Revelation often "thinks" in Hebrew.[5] Moreover, evidence that the early Christians saw "666" as Nero Caesar, is found in the fact that other early manuscripts often changed the number to 616, which is the numerical value of the Nero's name in Hebrew according to its Latin spelling.[6]

The End of the Line

Moreover, the depiction of one of the beast's heads receiving a mortal wound, causing some to expect the downfall of the beast itself, is also reminiscent of Nero's death. Nero was in the dynastic line of Julius Caesar, as all the Roman Emperors had been. This unbroken line of succession was a symbol of the stability of the Empire.[7] However, the Julian line ended when Nero killed himself, running himself through with a sword.[8]

This threw the Empire into chaos and a state of civil wars.[9] Josephus omitted a detailed account of these events, explaining that they were already well-known to all.[10] The ancient writer Tacitus explained that this time "well nigh brought the commonwealth to an end."[11] Nonetheless, the Empire recovered with the rise of Vespasian, regained its stability, and continued its dominance of the ancient world.

This is very much like John's vision. One of the beast's heads—one of the kings—receives a mortal wound by a sword, just like Nero did (Rev. 13:14). Although all expect the beast to die, the beast recovers. Similarly, all expected the Roman Empire to fall with the death of Nero,[12] yet somehow the Empire (the beast) survived, which seemed miraculous.[13]

The Second Beast

> **Rev. 13:4.** Men worshiped the dragon, for he had given his authority to the beast, and they worshiped the beast, saying, "Who is like the beast, and who can fight against it?"

13:4. The reference to the worship of the beast is probably borrowed from Daniel 3. There the king of Babylon sets up an image of himself to be worshipped. Similarly, an image of this beast is set up to be adored (Rev. 13:14–15). Furthermore, the worship of the beast describes the widespread custom whereby Roman emperors were worshipped as gods. As we saw in Revelation 2–3, many temples were erected throughout Asia Minor for this express purpose.

Wanna Be-ast

The beast is a kind of demonic parody of the Lamb. This is seen in the many parallels of the Lamb and the beast.

—Like the Lamb, who receives authority from God (Rev. 5:7, 12), the first beast receives authority from the dragon (13:2).
—Just as the Lamb is the ruler over people from "every tribe and tongue and people and nation" (5:9), so too the beast rules over every "tribe and people, tongue and nation" (13:7).
—Just as the cherubim and twenty-four elders "worshipped" the Lamb (5:14), so too "men worshipped the beast" (13:4).
—As the Lamb appears as one who has been slain (5:6), the beast lives in spite of a "mortal wound" (13:3, 12, 14).
—Like those who belong to the Lamb, those who belong to the beast are marked with a sign on their foreheads (7:2; 13:16).[14]

Rome, therefore, embodies a world power, which sets itself up as an evil substitute for Christ. Its close association with the dragon, who is the devil, shows that Rome's dominion comes from Satan.

Yet the image is not simply limited to Rome. It reveals the true demonic nature of any world power that opposes God and His Church.[15] That Satan has power to give earthly political authority is clear from Satan's third attempt to tempt Christ: "Again, the devil took him to a very high mountain, and showed him all the kingdoms of the world and the glory of them; and he said to him, 'All these I will give you, if you will fall down and worship me.' Then Jesus said to him, 'Begone, Satan! for it is written, 'You shall worship the Lord your God and him only shall you serve.'" (Mt. 4:8–10). Notice that Jesus does not correct Satan, saying something like, "You don't have that kind of power!" The temptation is dangerous because Satan, the dragon, does in fact confer power on those who worship him.

The Beast Is Given Authority for Forty-Two Months

Rev. 13:5–10. 5 And the beast was given a mouth uttering haughty and blasphemous words, and it was allowed to exercise authority for forty-two months; 6 it opened its mouth to utter blasphemies against God, blaspheming his name and his dwelling, that is, those who dwell in heaven. 7 Also it was allowed to make war on the saints and to conquer them. And authority was given it over every tribe and people and tongue and nation, 8 and all who dwell on earth will worship it, every one whose name has not been written before the foundation of the world in the book of life of the Lamb that was slain. 9 If any one has an ear, let him hear: 10 If any one is to be taken captive, to captivity he goes; if any one slays with the sword, with the sword must he be slain. Here is a call for the endurance and faith of the saints.

13:5–10. Again, we see the symbolic number, "forty-two months," derived from Daniel's "a time, two times, and a half a time." As in Daniel, this image signifies a time of tribulation (Dan. 7:25; see commentary on Revelation 11:1–2). Here the number symbolizes a time wherein the beast (Rome) persecutes the Church. It appears that Nero's persecution of Christians in Rome actually lasted about forty-two months.[16]

A warning, however, is issued to the churches so that they will "endure": "If any one is to be taken captive, to captivity he goes; if any one slays with the sword, with the sword must he be slain." Scholars have recognized this as an allusion to Jeremiah 15:2 and 43:11. In both places God explains that He will use the king of Babylon to destroy Jerusalem. Here, then, the Roman emperor is like the king of Babylon, as he comes to destroy the Jerusalem temple. Since destruction is coming, the saints must not give up—they must endure their tribulation a little longer.

The Second Beast

Rev. 13:11–15. 11 Then I saw another beast which rose out of the earth; it had two horns like a lamb and it spoke like a dragon. 12 It exercises all the authority of the first beast in its presence, and makes the earth and its inhabitants worship the first beast, whose mortal wound was healed. 13 It works great signs, even making fire come down from heaven to earth in the sight of men; 14 and by the signs which it is allowed to work in the presence of the beast, it deceives those who dwell on earth, bidding them make an image for the beast which was wounded by the sword and yet lived; 15 and it was allowed to give breath to the image of the beast so that the image of the beast should even speak, and to cause those who would not worship the image of the beast to be slain.

13:11–15. Like the first beast, this second beast is a parody of the Lamb. Though it looks "like a Lamb," it's really another agent of Satan. Its two horns may be an allusion to the ram-beast seen in Daniel 8.

The Worst in the Land

As the first beast symbolized Gentile powers, arising out of the sea, the second beast, which comes from the "land," represents the corrupt religious leaders in Jerusalem. Furthermore, whereas the first beast represented a corrupt political government, the second beast represents false religious authority. In fact, this beast is also identified by John as the "false prophet" (Rev. 16:13; 19:20; 20:10).[17]

As the "false prophet," this beast sets himself up against God's prophets and therefore mimics the two witnesses of chapter 11. Like the witnesses, the beast demonstrates his power by special fire (11:5; 13:13). As the two witnesses stood "before the Lord" (11:4), the beast stands in the presence of the dragon (13:12). The false prophet "gives breath" to a statue of the beast, making it come to life (13:15), mirroring John's account of the "breath of God" reviving the dead bodies of the witnesses (11:11).

The second beast, as a false prophet and religious leader, causes the inhabitants of the earth to worship the first beast instead of God. This is much like the corrupt Jerusalem leaders who incited the people of the city to shout out the blasphemous words, "We have no king but Caesar" (Jn. 19:15). As Scott Hahn explains,

"[Caesar] wanted more than respect. He demanded sacrificial worship, which the chief priests gave him when they handed over the Lamb of God."[18] Therefore, instead of leading the people to recognize Christ as King, the high priest taught the people to pledge their allegiance to the Roman emperor.

The "false prophets" in league with the beast may reflect the situation of places like Smyrna, where anti-Christian Jews incited the persecution of Christians. The Book of Acts tells us how anti-Christian Jews often brought Christians to Roman authorities (cf. Acts 17:5–8; 14:5; 18:12–13). In this, "false religion" teams up with "corrupt political authority" in persecuting God's people.

"666"

> **Rev. 13:16–18.** 16 Also it causes all, both small and great, both rich and poor, both free and slave, to be marked on the right hand or the forehead, 17 so that no one can buy or sell unless he has the mark, that is, the name of the beast or the number of its name. 18 This calls for wisdom: let him who has understanding reckon the number of the beast, for it is a human number, its number is six hundred and sixty-six.

13:16–17. Like the sealing of the saints in Revelation 7, the sealing of those who worship the beast is an image of allegiance. In other words, those who are sealed by the mark of the beast are those who have given themselves to Satan. Here again we see how the devil mimics God's dealings with man.

A certain lesson, which is applicable to our day, might be learned from this. Many false religions and false moralities have been established, which on the surface have similarities with God's true Church and her teachings. Yet, they are only demonic parodies. In Jesus' words, they are "wolves in sheep's clothing" (cf. Mt. 7:15).

13:18. Much has already been said about the cryptic "666." However, in addition to Nero, there lies a deeper meaning we have not yet considered. Indeed, though "666" is the numeric value of Nero's name in Hebrew, there is a more subtle point here. John tells his readers that one needs "wisdom" to comprehend his point—a point drawn from a much overlooked Old Testament allusion that we shall now examine.

Prodigal Son of David

It is important to point out that "666," in addition to equaling "Nero," is also the numeric value of the word "beast" in Hebrew.[19] This brings us back to what we were saying at the beginning of the chapter. "Six" and "beast" both represent man's fallen state. Thus, "six" is often used in connection with evil men. Goliath stood *six* cubits and a span tall and used a spear that weighed *six hundred* shekels (1 Sam. 17:4, 7). The king of Babylon erected a statue that was *sixty* cubits high and *six* cubits wide (Dan. 3:1).

This brings us to the deepest meaning of "666." 1 Kings tells us that Solomon amassed "*six hundred and sixty six* talents of gold" in taxes (1 Kings 10:14). This is the only other place in the Bible where "666" occurs. Solomon, king of Israel, known for his great and holy wisdom, slowly slipped into sin and went from being a type of Christ to a symbol of the Antichrist. He, who was called to be a priest-king like Melchizedek, ultimately chose to be king instead of priest. The connection with Solomon is underscored by John's mention that "wisdom" is necessary to discern the beast's identity, something famously attributed to Solomon.

Solomon, then, like Adam, failed to fulfill his vocation by preferring earthly goods to heavenly ones. This translates into the perverted two beasts of Revelation—the corrupt state and the false prophet. All kingship must be ordered to God, or else it becomes tyrannical. All priesthood must be directed to the true King, or else it becomes false, serving only the interests of human rulers.

When John uses "666," he refers, at the most basic level, to fallen humanity. The number value of "beast," "666," echoes Adam's sin. Instead of realizing his calling to be God's son, Adam was relegated to be like the "beasts" he was made with on the sixth day. Solomon also falls, forsaking his call to be God's son (2 Sam. 7:14).

And yet there's more to this riddle. For in John's day, the notion of corrupt kingship would no doubt remind the people of another wicked king of Jerusalem: Herod. Herod was himself a counterfeit ruler. Indeed, Jerusalem was home not only to the corrupt religious leadership symbolized by the second beast, but also to an evil king symbolized by the first beast. Thus, the emperor of Rome, a corrupt ruler, will be used by God to bring judgment on this city characterized by such intense wickedness. This city, which has gone from holiness to wickedness, like Solomon, under the rule of evil kings like Herod, will now be judged.[20]

The 144,000 on Mount Zion

> **Rev. 14:1.** 1 Then I looked, and lo, on Mount Zion stood the Lamb, and with him a hundred and forty-four thousand who had his name and his Father's name written on their foreheads.

14:1. Isaiah and the prophets envisioned the restoration of Israel in Jerusalem, on Mount Zion. Yet, when John sees the righteous remnant that is saved, he beholds a restoration that is truly remarkable. The prophets were right. Jerusalem would be the focal point of the restoration. Little did Israel realize, however, that God was talking about bringing the redeemed into the true Mount Zion in heaven, of which the earthly Jerusalem was only a copy.

This vision reminds the reader that, though Jerusalem has become wicked, not all from Israel will be condemned. The reader is reminded that not all have bowed to the beast and received his image. Some are marked with the sign of the Lamb.

The vision of the 144,000 on Mount Zion shows that God has not failed Israel, even if they have failed him. In the final chapters of Revelation, the last curses of the Mosaic covenant come upon Israel—but not all of Israel. Earlier we looked at the 144,000 in terms of God's promise to restore the lost tribes. But some of these saints come from Judah (Jerusalem) as well. Though Jerusalem will be judged, God has spared a remnant.

The Song of the 144,000

> **Rev. 14:2–3.** And I heard a voice from heaven like the sound of many waters and like the sound of loud thunder; the voice I heard was like the sound of harpers playing on their harps, 3 and they sing a new song before the throne and before the four living creatures and before the elders. No one could learn that song except the hundred and forty-four thousand who had been redeemed from the earth.

14:2–3. As in chapters 4 and 15, the remnant of Israel here sings a "new song." Just as Moses led Israel in singing a song of praise to God after delivering them through the Red Sea, so now the saints sing a song of praise as they enter into the true Promised Land of heaven (see commentary on Rev. 5:7–13).[21]

The Virgins

> **Rev. 14:4.** It is these who have not defiled themselves with women, for they are chaste; it is these who follow the Lamb wherever he goes; these have been redeemed from mankind as first fruits for God and the Lamb,

14:4. In contrast to the earthly Jerusalem, later described as a harlot (see chapter 12, "The Whore-able City"), holding a cup of "abominations" and "the impurities of fornication" (Rev. 17:4), the saints in the heavenly Jerusalem are "chaste," and have not "defiled themselves with women"; in a word, they are "spotless" (Rev. 14:5). Those marked with the name of God on their foreheads, who "follow the Lamb wherever He goes," are the exact opposites of those who "follow the beast" (Rev. 13:3).

Kingdom of Priests

The image of the "virgins" on Mount Zion is first and foremost a symbol of the Church's purity. Since harlotry is associated with idolatry in John's Apocalypse, the image of the saints as "pure" may indicate their resistance to worshipping the beast. Moreover, priests of the Old Testament were required to abstain from sexual activity before entering into God's temple. Likewise, the virgins here are clearly masculine, since "they have not defiled themselves with women." This, therefore, depicts the Church as the "kingdom of priests" established by Christ. This image is further strengthened by the fact that they are given the role of the Levitical priests, who sang in the temple of God.

In fact, if the vision of the 144,000 in Revelation 14 seems familiar, it might be because the scene John describes is almost exactly like the one he recorded in chapter 5.

Rev. 14:1–5 "Then I looked, and lo, . . . stood the Lamb" (v. 1)	**Rev. 5:6–11** "I saw a Lamb standing" (v. 6)
"before the throne and before the four living creatures and before the elders" (v. 3)	"between the throne and the four living creatures and among the elders" (v. 6)
"the voice I heard was like the sound of harpers playing on their harps" (v. 2)	"and the twenty four elders . . . each having a harp" (v. 8)
"and they sing a new song" (v. 3)	"they sang a new song" (v. 9)
"these have been redeemed from mankind as first fruits for God and the Lamb" (v. 4)	"[For the Lamb] didst ransom men for God" (v. 9)[22]

The 144,000, therefore, are like the twenty-four priestly elders who offered their lives as a priestly sacrifice to God (see commentary on Rev. 4:4).

Further evidence for this interpretation may lie in the fact that the saints are called the "first fruits." In the Old Testament the first fruits were to be an offering to the Lord (cf. Ex. 34:26). These who "have been redeemed" have offered themselves to God as a sacrificial offering.

Finally, soldiers who were about to go into battle were also forbidden to engage in sexual relations (Lev. 15:16; Deut. 23:10; 1 Sam. 21:5; 2 Sam. 11:11). The saints in heaven therefore represent God's army, which fights against the enemy on earth through the celebration of the heavenly liturgy. The prayers of the saints effect the judgments from God that are then sent to destroy the enemy.

Celebrating Celibacy

Although this image is first and foremost a symbol of the Church as God's holy kingdom of priests, we cannot say that it is *only* a symbol. Christ Himself foretold of the ministry of celibate men in the Church saying, "there are some who have made themselves eunuchs for the sake of the kingdom" (Mt. 19:12). Eunuchs were usually entrusted with the wives of the king in the ancient world (cf. Esther 2:14). Following this tradition, Catholic priests remain celibate, as to them the Bride of Christ, the Church, is specially entrusted.[23]

Therefore, just as Mary is an icon of the Church as Virgin Bride and fruitful Mother, so too celibate priests and religious embody the Church's vocation as the chaste spouse of the Lamb. Indeed, consecrated virginity is an "eschatological sign," since there will be no marriage in eternity (Mk. 12:25; cf. *Catechism*, no. 1619). By offering up the goods of marriage, these holy men and women make an act of life-giving love. They are able to "follow the Lamb wherever he goes" (cf. *Catechism*, no. 1618).

Description of the Saints

Rev. 14:5. and in their mouth no lie was found, for they are spotless.

14:5. That "no lie has been found in their mouths" links these saints with the "faithful witnesses" of chapter 11. Isaiah similarly portrayed the suffering servant as one who had "no deceit in his mouth" (Is. 53:9). As is well known, the prophecy of the suffering servant is frequently applied to Christ in the New Testament (cf. Mt. 8:17; Lk. 22:37; Acts 8:32–33; 1 Pet. 2:22; 1 Pet. 2:24–25). Yet, through the Mystical Body of Christ, the Church, Jesus offers His life through the lives of the faithful (cf. Col. 1:24; Gal. 2:20; Rom. 8:17; 1 Pet. 2:4–5, 21; 4:13).[24]

Similarly, Psalm 110 envisions the people of God standing on the holy mountains where they "offer themselves freely" with the Davidic king, who is described as a priest like Melchizedek (Ps. 110:4). In this, Catholics hear echoes of the Eucharist, where Christ offers Himself as a sacrifice under the appearances of bread and wine, the sacrifice of Melchizedek. Furthermore, it is in the liturgy that the faithful unite their sufferings with Christ the King and "offer themselves freely" as they partake in the liturgy of the heavenly Jerusalem.[25]

The Proclamation of the Angel

> **Rev. 14:6–7.** 6 Then I saw another angel flying in midheaven, with an eternal gospel to proclaim to those who dwell on earth, to every nation and tribe and tongue and people; 7 and he said with a loud voice, "Fear God and give him glory, for the hour of his judgment has come; and worship him who made heaven and earth, the sea and the fountains of water."

14:6–7. At first glance it may seem that this angel is an angel of comfort, since he announces the "gospel," which means, "good news." In reality he brings judgment, since he announces a gospel that the people reject. This once again brings us back to the New Exodus proclaimed by Isaiah, since it was Isaiah who first coined the term "Gospel" ("good news"). "The Spirit of the Lord is upon me, because the Lord has anointed me, to bring good tidings ["gospel" in Greek] to the afflicted . . . to proclaim liberty to the captives . . . and the day of vengeance of our God" (Is. 61:1, 2). Isaiah explains that the "good news" is a two-edged sword, since to the righteous it speaks of deliverance, but to the wicked it is the announcement of condemnation.

It should be no surprise that this angel brings judgment. This angel is spoken of in the same terms used to describe the angel who announced the three woes in Revelation 8:13. Both speak in a loud voice (8:13; 14:7), fly in midheaven (8:13; 14:6), and direct their message to the unbelievers of the land (8:13, those who "sit on the land"). The term "the land" is always a description of the wicked in the Apocalypse (3:10; 6:10; 8:13; 11:10; 13:8, 12, 14; 17:2, 8).[26]

The Fall of Babylon Predicted

> **Rev. 14:8.** Another angel, a second, followed, saying, "Fallen, fallen is Babylon the great, she who made all nations drink the wine of her impure passion."

14:8. Jerusalem is given the title, "Babylon," the name of one of the most wicked cities in the Old Testament. More importantly, Babylon was the nation that destroyed the Jerusalem temple in 586 BC. Jerusalem is like Babylon because it destroyed the true Temple, Christ.

The words of the angel also recall Isaiah 21:9. There the prophet describes the fall of Babylon in terms of the destruction of its idols. In a certain sense, the temple itself has become an object of idolatry for those who choose it over Christ, the true Temple.

The angel says the city has "fallen," though John has not yet seen it destroyed. The angel is speaking like the prophets, announcing the coming judgment as though it had already happened. By doing this he indicates that devastation is inevitable.

If the city is Jerusalem, how is it that "all the nations" are said to drink from her cup of impure passion? It is because Jerusalem was to be the capital city of God's holy people, acting as God's light to the nations. In failing in their vocation, the inhabitants of Jerusalem scandalize the people of the world, giving them an example they shouldn't follow. As Jesus taught, "Whoever causes one of these little ones who believe in me to sin, it would be better for him to have a great millstone fastened round his neck and to be drowned in the depth of the sea" (Mt. 18:6).

The Fate of the Followers of the Beast

Rev. 14:9–13. 9 And another angel, a third, followed them, saying with a loud voice, "If any one worships the beast and its image, and receives a mark on his forehead or on his hand, 10 he also shall drink the wine of God's wrath, poured unmixed into the cup of his anger, and he shall be tormented with fire and sulphur in the presence of the holy angels and in the presence of the Lamb. 11 And the smoke of their torment goes up for ever and ever; and they have no rest, day or night, these worshippers of the beast and its image, and whoever receives the mark of its name."

12 Here is a call for the endurance of the saints, those who keep the commandments of God and the faith of Jesus.

13 And I heard a voice from heaven saying, "Write this: Blessed are the dead who die in the Lord henceforth." "Blessed indeed," says the Spirit, "that they may rest from their labors, for their deeds follow them!"

14:9–13. In chapter 13, the false prophet threatened that anyone refusing to worship the beast would be killed. Yet the angel shows that anyone who aligns himself with the beast will suffer a much worse fate: "[H]e shall be tormented with fire and sulphur . . . and the smoke of their torment goes up for ever and ever; and they have no rest, day or night." To drink from the cup of the beast's "impure passion" is also to drink from the cup of "wrath."

The saints who do not drink from this cup—even though they are persecuted—will finally receive true rest. The use of the term "rest" here underscores what we said above concerning the link between Adam's fall, the image of "666," and the "beast." The saints are those who will indeed enter into that seventh day rest. By offering their lives they have become priests and thereby realize their calling to be "life-giving" sons of God.[27]

Love Hurts

It is also noteworthy that death is absolutely required of the Christians. The ones who are blessed are those who "die." The martyrs don't have some masochistic desire to suffer, but rather, they have learned total self-offering. Christians are not required to pick up their belongings and move to lands where belief in Jesus is punishable by execution. Their calling may even be more difficult than martyrdom—they have to live every day, every moment of their lives, as an offering to the Lord. They must learn to die to their own selfish desires and be transformed according to the will of Christ.

This explains the holy logic of mortification. Mortification is the practice of making small sacrifices to God in an effort to, as Paul said, put to death the desires of the flesh (cf. Gal. 5:24). In the original context, Paul was telling Christians to abstain from grave sins of immorality. Yet, at a spiritual level, this points to Christ's calling to love Him more than oneself. This is expressed through small sacrifices.

Couples often make these kinds of small sacrifices out of love for each other. For example, a husband takes his wife to an Italian restaurant, though he dislikes it himself, because he knows she really enjoys the food. The wife joins her husband in watching a football game, though she doesn't understand anything other than the halftime show.

In the same way, Christians should learn to deny themselves small pleasures, as acts of love for God. Thus, one might give up watching his favorite television show for a month, or listening to the radio, or putting salt on his food, etc., as a sacrifice. As Saint Josemaría Escríva said, "Where there is no mortification, there is no virtue."[28]

The Harvest of the Son of Man

Rev. 14:14–16. 14 Then I looked, and lo, a white cloud, and
seated on the cloud one like a son of man, with a golden crown
on his head, and a sharp sickle in his hand. 15 And another angel
came out of the temple, calling with a loud voice to him who sat
upon the cloud, "Put in your sickle, and reap, for the hour to reap
has come, for the harvest of the earth is fully ripe." 16 So he who
sat upon the cloud swung his sickle on the earth, and the earth
was reaped.

14:14–16. In keeping with John's interpretation of Christ as the Son of Man from Daniel, the figure who "comes on a cloud" is Christ. His golden crown is a symbol of His kingship over the earth. Those who have followed the beast have, therefore, rejected the true King. They are ripe for judgment.

The "sickle" in Jesus' hand is a tool used for harvesting. Christ Himself described His Second Coming in "harvest" terminology in Matthew 13, where the righteous are separated from the wicked as wheat from weeds (Mt. 13:30). Jesus goes on to explain that the wicked (the weeds) shall be burned up. This picture resembles John's vision concerning the fate of Jerusalem, which is also "burned with fire" (Rev. 17:16; also cf. Rev. 8:8).

Judgment as a harvest also evokes Joel 3:13, where God judges the nations who threaten Jerusalem. Ironically, judgment is now coming upon that same earthly city once protected by God because it has begun persecuting those who belong to the New Jerusalem of heaven. This passage in Joel also resonates with John's vision, since it also portrays judgment as the Lord's treading on the wine presses (Joel 3:13; Rev. 14:20).[29]

The Wine Press Is Trampled

Rev. 14:17–20. 17 And another angel came out of the temple in heaven, and he too had a sharp sickle. 18 Then another angel came out from the altar, the angel who has power over fire, and he called with a loud voice to him who had the sharp sickle, "Put in your sickle, and gather the clusters of the vine of the earth, for its grapes are ripe." 19 So the angel swung his sickle on the earth and gathered the vintage of the earth, and threw it into the great wine press of the wrath of God; 20 and the wine press was trodden outside the city, and blood flowed from the wine press, as high as a horse's bridle, for one thousand six hundred stadia.

14:17–18. Christ's judgment—the casting of His sickle—is carried out by the angels who follow His actions. This is much like the angel at the beginning of chapter 10, who enacted what the Lamb did in chapter 5. Furthermore, the fact that this angel comes "with fire" and "from the altar" links this judgment with that brought by the angel of 8:5, who was also associated with the altar and who also set the earth on fire.

14:19–20. John describes the judgment of Jerusalem as the destruction of a wine press or vineyard, just as Isaiah 5 and Lamentations 1:15 do. The description of blood flowing as high as "a horse's bridle" paints a horrific picture of a massive slaughter. Once again, Josephus' account of the Jewish war has an amazing correspondence with John's prophecy, as he recounts the sheer carnage of the war, "[For] the ground did nowhere appear visible, for the dead bodies that lay on it; but the soldiers went over heaps of these bodies, as they ran upon such as fled from them."[30] Indeed, the measurement of the winepress as one thousand six hundred stadia corresponds to the dimensions of the land of Israel.[31]

Those beside the Sea of Glass

> **Rev. 15:1–4.** 1 Then I saw another portent in heaven, great and wonderful, seven angels with seven plagues, which are the last, for with them the wrath of God is ended.
>
> 2 And I saw what appeared to be a sea of glass mingled with fire, and those who had conquered the beast and its image and the number of its name, standing beside the sea of glass with harps of God in their hands. 3 And they sing the song of Moses, the servant of God, and the song of the Lamb, saying, "Great and wonderful are thy deeds, O Lord God the Almighty! Just and true are thy ways, O King of the ages! 4 Who shall not fear and glorify thy name, O Lord? For thou alone art holy. All nations shall come and worship thee, for thy judgments have been revealed."

15:1–4. Chapter 15 ushers in the sequence of the last seven plagues. In Revelation 14:2–3, we saw New Exodus imagery in the "new song" sung. Here that theme is picked up in greater detail. As in chapter 5, the saints sing a "new song" beside the "sea of glass" just as Moses sang a song with Israel on the other side of the Red Sea (Ex. 15).[32] Here the link is made more explicit, however, by the reference to the "song of Moses."

The words of the new song are even taken from Moses' song: "Who is like thee, O LORD, among the gods? Who is like thee, majestic in holiness, terrible in glorious deeds, doing wonders?" (Ex. 15:11). Moreover, the Old Testament compares the victory at the Red Sea to God's crushing the great sea monster (cf. Ps. 74:13–14). It is therefore appropriate for a new song of the sea to be sung in Revelation 15 once the dragon and the beast of the sea are defeated.[33]

Seven Angels with Seven Chalices

> Rev. 15:5–8. 5 After this I looked, and the temple of the tent of witness in heaven was opened, 6 and out of the temple came the seven angels with the seven plagues, robed in pure bright linen, and their breasts girded with golden girdles. 7 And one of the four living creatures gave the seven angels seven golden bowls full of the wrath of God who lives for ever and ever; 8 and the temple was filled with smoke from the glory of God and from his power, and no one could enter the temple until the seven plagues of the seven angels were ended.

15:5. In this verse, the New Exodus theme continues. The term "the tent of witness" evokes the tabernacle in which Israel worshipped during their wilderness journey. Likewise, the seven "plagues" evoke the plagues sent on Egypt in the Exodus.

15:6–8. The word for "bowls" here may also be translated "cups."[34] Furthermore, since the Greek word used here specifically describes a liturgical vessel, one may even translate the word "chalice."[35] This liturgical element is highlighted further once we read that the angels come out of the temple. It is also underscored in the way their white clothes and golden girdles mirror John's description of Christ as High Priest in Revelation 1.[36] Here, then, we once again see how the liturgy of heaven is what sets into motion the events on earth.

The "chalice" judgments may also be connected with the angel's announcement in 14:10: "[H]e also shall drink the wine of God's wrath, poured unmixed into the cup of his anger."[37] It may also be connected with the golden "bowl" or "chalice" of the saints' prayers in 8:3, which we understood in terms of the saints' petition for vengeance in 6:9–10. The chalice judgments, therefore, represent the answer to their prayers. Back in Revelation 6, they were told to "rest a little longer" until the "full number" of those to be slain had been realized. With that number, the 144,000, now completed and standing safely on Mount Zion, the final judgment comes.

The vision also carries themes from Isaiah 6. There Isaiah has a vision of the throne room of God wherein the angels come forth, as "smoke" fills the temple (Is. 6:1–5).[38] Upon witnessing this, Isaiah is commissioned to pronounce a coming judgment on the people of Jerusalem. John also stands in the throne room where he will see the chalices of wrath poured out on the once holy city. With these, the final destruction will come.

Applying the Lessons of Revelation 13–15 Today

It would be nice to read that any one who tries to persecute Christians will immediately be zapped by God. Indeed, many well-meaning believers think in these terms. They think that the wrong candidate won't be elected. The good one will necessarily win since he has God on his side. They think that a professional athlete who leads an immoral life will immediately suffer defeats and failure. In short, they think that good things will always happen to good people, and bad things will always happen to bad people. The Cross shatters this image.

In chapters 13–15, God allows Christians to be killed by the beast. They suffer and die with no recognizable deliverance. Does this mean that goodness has been defeated? No. It simply redefines victory.

Actual victory is found not in earthly vindication, but in entering into God's Triune life in heaven. By learning to offer their lives, the saints are truly victorious—perhaps not in the eyes of this passing world—and their victory is real and eternal. We must recognize that this world is not meant to be our home.

It is very tempting to evaluate our success by this world's standards. This is especially true when worldly goods are set up as counterfeits for heavenly ones. This is the strategy of the beasts. A politician, for example, may pass himself off as a real "reformer," one who apparently is in touch with the needs of his constituents. Indeed, he may do many good things for the community. Yet he may only be doing these good things to gain popular support for himself and divert attention away from his wicked agenda. He may give a lot of money to a school to appear caring for children, all the while aggressively supporting the murder of thousands of babies in abortion.

Indeed, Saint Paul warns us that Satan disguises himself as an "angel of light" (2 Cor. 11:14). Christians must always be on their guard. They must avert their vision from the deceptive beauty of the harlot and look down to see the beast she is riding on.

* * *

Multiple Choice

1. The beast comes from the "sea," symbolizing that it is __________ in origin.
(a) Gentile
(b) Jewish
(c) evil
(d) mysterious

2. The four beasts of Daniel 7 represented ____________.
(a) Babylon, Medo-Persia, Assyria, and Greece
(b) Babylon, Assyria, Greece, and Rome
(c) Babylon, Medo-Persia, Greece, and Rome
(d) Babylon, Assyria, Medo-Persia, and Rome

3. The seven kings represent the first seven _____________.
(a)Herodian kings

(b) Caesars
(c) governors of Judah
(d) nations

4. __________ is like Babylon, since it also will destroy Jerusalem and its temple
(a) Rome
(b) Persia
(c) Egypt
(d) Jericho

5. Another image for the two beasts in Revelation 13 is ___________.
(a) the beast and the false prophet
(b) the two witnesses
(c) the seven stars and the seven churches
(d) Wormwood and Screwtape

6. The prophets envisioned the New Exodus leading to __________.
(a) Mount Sinai
(b) Mount Zion
(c) Mount Megiddo
(d) Mount Carmel

7. The word "gospel" was first used by __________.
(a) Abraham
(b) the psalmist
(c) Isaiah
(d) Jesus

8. Jerusalem is like Babylon because it destroyed the ___________.
(a) true Temple, Christ
(b) Romans

(c) Upper Room
(d) hope

Answers) 1.a; 2.c; 3.b; 4.a; 5.a; 6.b; 7.c; 8.a.

* * *

Discussion/Study Questions

1. How does the beast symbolize the fallen state of man? (See page 177?)

2. How does the first beast mimic the Lamb? (See page 173)

3. What does the second beast symbolize? (See page 175)

4. What does "666" symbolize? How does it symbolize something more than Nero? (See page 177)

5. What do the virgins on Mount Zion symbolize? (See pages 179–180)

____

____

____

____

6. What does the wine press symbolize? (See pages 186–187)

____

____

____

____

WHEN HE REIGNS, HE POURS

The Chalice Judgments and the Fall of "Babylon"
(Rev. 16:1–16:21)

Chalice'n Up

The chalice judgments bring to completion the partial judgments of the seven trumpets. This can be seen in the way the two judgments parallel each other. Moreover, just as the seven trumpets evoked the imagery of the plagues of Egypt, so too, do the chalice judgments.

The 7 Chalices	The 7 Trumpets	Plagues of Egypt
1. On the land, becoming sores (16:2)	On the land; 1/3 of the earth, trees, grass burned (8:7)	Boils (sixth plague: Ex. 9:8–12)
2. On the sea, becoming blood (16:3)	On the sea; 1/3 sea becomes blood; 1/3 sea creatures die; 1/3 ships destroyed (8:9)	Waters become blood (first plague: Ex. 7:17–21)
3. On rivers and springs, becoming blood (16:4–7)	On the rivers and springs; 1/3 waters become wormwood (8:10–11)	Waters become blood (first plague: Ex. 7:17–21)
4. On the sun, causing it to scorch (16:8–9)	1/3 of the sun, moon and stars darkened (8:12)	Darkness (ninth plague: Ex. 10:21-23)
5. On the throne of the Beast, causing darkness (16:10–11)	Demonic locusts tormenting men (9:1–12)	Locusts (eighth plague: Ex. 10:4–20)

6. On the Euphrates, drying it up to make way for kings of the east; invasion of frog-demons; Armageddon (16:12–16)	Army from Euphrates River kills 1/3 of mankind (9:13–21)	Invasion of frogs from the Nile River (second plague: Ex. 8:2–4)
7. On the air, causing storm, earthquake, and hail (16:17–21)	Voices, storm, earthquake, and hail (11:15–19)	Hail (seventh plague: Ex. 9:18–36)[1]

The trumpets were only partial judgments. While the trumpets only brought judgments on a third of the land, the chalices bring about total devastation.

Furthermore, the chalices are not interrupted like the other judgments were. Between the fifth and sixth seals, John paused and narrated the vision of the 144,000 and the great multitude. Similarly, the vision of the mighty angel from heaven and the two witnesses separated the sixth and seventh trumpets. Here, however, the chalices are seen in rapid-fire succession with no analogous intermission.

The First Three Chalices Are Poured Out

Rev. 16:1–7. 1 Then I heard a loud voice from the temple telling the seven angels, "Go and pour out on the earth the seven bowls of the wrath of God."

2 So the first angel went and poured his bowl on the earth, and foul and evil sores came upon the men who bore the mark of the beast and worshiped its image.

3 The second angel poured his bowl into the sea, and it became like the blood of a dead man, and every living thing died that was in the sea.

4 The third angel poured his bowl into the rivers and the fountains of water, and they became blood. 5 And I heard the angel of water say, "Just art thou in these thy judgments, thou who art and wast, O Holy One. 6 For men have shed the blood of saints and prophets, and thou hast given them blood to drink.

It is their due!" 7 And I heard the altar cry, "Yea, Lord God the Almighty, true and just are thy judgments!"

16:1–7. Since these plagues, unlike the trumpets, bring full judgment, the saints change the words of their prayer. In previous chapters, the Lord was described as the One who "was, is and is to come" (1:4, 8; 4:8). Now, as in 11:17, He is simply called the One "who art and wast"—His coming is no longer anticipated. He has arrived.

Who exactly are the "men [who] have shed the blood of saints and prophets"? They can be no other than the inhabitants of Jerusalem, for it is there that prophets were killed. In the Gospel, Jesus explained that He must go to Jerusalem and be crucified there, "for it cannot be that a prophet should perish away from Jerusalem" (Lk. 13:33). Furthermore, Revelation 11:8 describes Jerusalem as the place "where their Lord was crucified."

Coming like a Plague

Just as old Egypt persecuted God's people and held them in slavery, so now Jerusalem, having turned on God's people, is described as the new Egypt (cf. Rev. 11:8). It is wholly appropriate, therefore, that the judgment upon this new Egypt is described in terms of the plagues that fell upon the old Egypt.[2]

The first plague has a slight ring of poetic justice. Those who once bore the mark of the beast now bear the marks of sores and boils. In this we see the true effect of the mark of the beast—it is disfiguring, a punishment that fits the crime.

As for the second and third chalices, we see how the water, a basic necessity for life, is slowly but surely taken away—first with the sea, then with the water remaining in the rivers and fountains. As in the Exodus the water turns to blood. Blood is all that is left to drink, recalling Isaiah's prophecy concerning Israel's enemies: "[T]hey shall be drunk with their own blood as with wine" (Is. 49:26).

The Fourth and Fifth Chalices Are Poured Out

Rev. 16:8–11. 8 The fourth angel poured his bowl on the sun, and it was allowed to scorch men with fire; 9 men were scorched by the fierce heat, and they cursed the name of God who had power over these plagues, and they did not repent and give him glory.

10 The fifth angel poured his bowl on the throne of the beast, and its kingdom was in darkness; men gnawed their tongues in anguish 11 and cursed the God of heaven for their pain and sores, and did not repent of their deeds.

16:8–11. The fifth chalice brings intense heat, which is all the more unbearable due to the fact that all the water has turned to blood. With no fresh water, the people have no way to refresh themselves. The fate of the wicked is the exact opposite of that of the saints, of whom it is said: "[T]he sun shall not strike at them, nor any scorching heat" (Rev. 7:16).

As the chalice is poured out on the throne of the beast, darkness comes upon the beast's empire. Darkness was the ninth plague that fell upon Egypt. It was the last plague before the final judgment—the death of the firstborns. Similarly, darkness appears here as one of the last chalice judgments before the final destruction of the city.

History Lessons

Some have seen the plague of darkness as reflecting the historical situation of Rome. When Nero died, there was utter confusion and chaos in the Roman Empire. There judgment came upon the "throne of the beast," casting the "kingdom" into a state of "darkness."[3]

There is reason, however, to see this as a description of Jerusalem before the destruction of the temple. The recurring image of the wicked refusing to repent, even in the face of calamities and plagues, paints a picture of Jerusalem as the "New Egypt." Even though God sent plague after plague on Egypt, and despite Moses' pleading, Pharaoh remained obstinate in his hard heart. Likewise, the wicked of the "New Egypt" refuse to acknowledge the Lord.

This theme of obstinacy also dominates Josephus's description of the destruction of the temple. Josephus explains that, when it was clear that Jerusalem would be destroyed, the Romans continually urged the people to surrender and repent of their rebelliousness. He records how Titus tortured the leaders of the rebel movement in full view of the city so "that they would now at length leave off [their madness], and not force him to destroy the city, whereby they would have those advantages of repentance, even in their utmost distress, that they would preserve their own lives, and so fine a city of their own, and that temple which was their peculiar."[4] Josephus himself even pleaded with them to repent and surrender.[5] Just as John speaks of the people of the "New Babylon" cursing God, Josephus writes, "[T]hey seem to me to have cast a reproach upon God himself, as if he were too slow in punishing them."[6]

The Sixth Chalice Is Poured Out

> **Rev. 16:12.** The sixth angel poured his bowl on the great river Euphrates, and its water was dried up, to prepare the way for the kings from the east.

16:12. The marching army, which comes from the "east," draws on the imagery from the prophets Isaiah and Daniel, both of whom referred to judgment as coming from this direction (Is. 46:11; Dan. 11:44). And this is what happened in AD 70. The Romans crossed over the Euphrates on their way to demolish Jerusalem, coming from the east.[7]

Another Old Testament allusion may be found in John's description of the water drying up. The Old Testament prophets frequently linked judgment with such an occurrence.[8] Here in Revelation, the water is dried up so that a path can be made for the coming armies. This recalls the parting of the Red Sea, which God worked on Israel's behalf. Now, however, God has turned His power against the wicked in Israel.

The Evil Frogs

Rev. 16:13–14. 13 And I saw, issuing from the mouth of the dragon and from the mouth of the beast and from the mouth of the false prophet, three foul spirits like frogs; 14 for they are demonic spirits, performing signs, who go abroad to the kings of the whole world, to assemble them for battle on the great day of God the Almighty.

16:13–14. According to the Levitical code of law, frogs are "unclean," and thus an appropriate symbol for demons (Lev. 11:9–12, 41–47). The three unclean spirits proceed from the three primary figures: the dragon, the beast, and the false prophet. With this plague of demonic frogs, demonic activity reaches its climax, and wickedness envelops the land.

These spiritual realities were the impetus behind the indescribable madness and ruthlessness that seized both the Jews and the Roman soldiers in AD 70. Josephus explains how soldiers acted without orders—and even against them—taking their hatred out on the Jews with savage results: "Then did Caesar, both by calling to the soldiers that were fighting . . . and by giving a loud signal to them with his right hand, order them to quench the fire [that began to burn down the temple], but they did not hear what he said . . . neither any persuasions nor any threatenings could restrain their violence, but each one's own passion was his commander at this time. And as they were crowding into the temple together, many of them were trampled by one another, while a great number fell among the ruins. . . . Now, round about the altar lay dead bodies heaped one upon another; as at the steps going up to it ran a great quantity of their blood."[9]

Yet the wickedness of the Romans pales in comparison to what Josephus says about his own people. Josephus explains how a certain group of Roman soldiers followed the smell of food in the city into one woman's house. Upon entering her house, they were horrified to discover a mother who had taken her own infant son, nursed him, and cooked his flesh to eat. Chillingly, she reassured the soldiers "that she had saved a very fine portion of it for them."[10] In this, we recall Isaiah's prophecy, "I will make your oppressors eat their own flesh" (Is. 49:26).

False prophets frequently rise up to proclaim deliverance in time of divine judgment. Pharaoh consulted his "magicians," who worked signs similar to Moses' (Ex. 8:7, 18; 9:11). Similarly, before the Babylonians came to destroy Jerusalem, false prophets reassured the people, saying, "Peace, peace" (Jer. 6:14).

Not surprisingly, then, false prophets arose in Jerusalem in AD 70, foretelling victory over the Romans. Even as the city was burning down, the people were urged to persist in suicidal attempts to recover the city. Josephus records: "Now, there were a great number of false prophets suborned by the tyrants to impose upon the people . . . that they should wait for deliverance from God; and this was in order to keep them from deserting."[11]

The Call to Not Be Caught Exposed

Rev. 16:15. ("Lo, I am coming like a thief! Blessed is he who is awake, keeping his garments that he may not go naked and be seen exposed!")

16:15. The warning to not be caught exposed recalls Jesus' warning to the Laodiceans in chapter 3. There Jesus says, "Therefore I counsel you to buy from me . . . white garments to clothe you and to keep the shame of your nakedness from being seen" (Rev. 3:18). The imagery of nakedness calls to mind the sin of Adam and Eve and the fallen state that resulted from it.[12]

The Battle of Armageddon

Rev. 16:16. And they assembled them at the place which is called in Hebrew Armageddon.

16:16. Much has been made of the Battle of Armageddon. Some of the wildest apocalyptic theories have centered on this battle. I have vivid memories of people, in 1991, predicting that the Gulf War was leading up to this event. They were wrong, but what is John *really* talking about?

Dreadin' Armageddon

"Armageddon" comes from the Hebrew words, *Har-Magedon*, which mean, "Mount of Megiddo."[13] Yet, the city of Megiddo was not built on a mountain, but a plain. Interpreters therefore recognize that John is combining different images.

First, Megiddo is mentioned because it was the site of one of Israel's most famous tragic battles. The beloved King Josiah, having disobeyed God, went out to fight with the king of Egypt and was killed on the battlefield (2 Chron. 35:20–25). This war and the shocking death of Josiah made such a lasting impression on Israel that its people were still mourning the event centuries later (2 Chron. 35:25). This battle had become the symbol of a war in which Israel would suffer terrible defeat.

Secondly, Zechariah links Megiddo with an apocalyptic battle in which the enemies of Jerusalem will be destroyed (Zech. 12:9–11).[14] It is clear that John is thinking of this passage, since Revelation 16 has many parallels with the final prophecies in Zechariah:

—Both speak of the nations being gathered for battle against the city of Jerusalem (Zech. 12:3; 14:2; Rev. 16:14)
—Both speak of an earthquake and the splitting of the city (Zech. 14:4–5; Rev. 16:18–19)
—Both speak of false prophets and evil spirits (Zech. 13:2; Rev. 16:13)
—Both describe the Lord sending "plagues" (Zech. 14:12; cf. parallels of Rev. 16:1–21 and the plagues of Egypt)

Some have speculated that the "Mountain" of Megiddo is Mount Carmel, which is near the city. John's imagery, however, is probably the result of a combination of several Old Testament passages, something we have seen John do frequently throughout the Apocalypse.

By alluding to Megiddo, John recalls a war in which the people of Jerusalem were defeated. By adding the image of a battle on a mountain, he evokes passages from the prophets, which spoke of final devastation. Isaiah prophesied that Babylon's destruction would occur on "the mount of assembly" (Is. 14:13). Ezekiel predicted the apocalyptic battle would occur on the "mountains of Israel," where God's enemies would be crushed once and for all (Ezek. 39:4). The term "Armageddon" thus symbolizes that Jerusalem is the New Babylon, receiving its final catastrophic judgment. Here the enemies of God's people will be defeated.

Babylon Is Split

> **Rev. 16:17–19.** 17 The seventh angel poured his bowl into the air, and a loud voice came out of the temple, from the throne, saying, "It is done!" 18 And there were flashes of lightning, loud noises, peals of thunder, and a great earthquake such as had never been since men were on the earth, so great was that earthquake. 19 The great city was split into three parts, and the cities of the nations fell, and God remembered great Babylon, to make her drain the cup of the fury of his wrath.

16:17–19. As mentioned above, Zechariah also predicted an earthquake, which would split the city of Jerusalem apart (Zech. 14:4–5). Ezekiel also was told to prophesy that Jerusalem would be divided into thirds for its unfaithfulness:

> Therefore thus says the Lord GOD: Because you are more turbulent than the nations that are round about you, and have not walked in my statutes or kept my ordinances, but have acted according to the ordinances of the nations that are round about you; therefore thus says the Lord GOD: Behold, I, even I, am against you; and I will execute judgments in the midst of you in the sight of the nations. And because of all your abominations I will do with you what I have never yet done, and the like of which I will never do again. Therefore fathers shall eat their sons in the midst of you, and sons shall eat their fathers. . . . A third part of you shall die of pestilence and be consumed with famine in the midst of you; a third part shall fall by the sword round about you; and a third part I will scatter to all the winds and will unsheathe the sword after them (Ezek. 5:7–10, 12).

This long citation aptly describes all that we have seen so far concerning Jerusalem's judgment.

The reference to fathers eating their sons, as we have seen, accurately describes the horrors of AD 70. Even the three categories of judgments mentioned by Ezekiel—those killed by famine and pestilence, those killed by the sword, and those scattered—also resonate with Josephus's account. Once the soldiers broke through the wall and came in to destroy those left in the city, Josephus describes what happened: "[T]he Romans slew some of them, some they carried captives. . . . There were also found slain there above two thousand persons, partly by their own hands, partly by one another, but chiefly destroyed by the famine."[15] Indeed, Jerusalem was defeated in part because the people of the city themselves were divided among three warring factions.[16]

The Islands Flee—The Great Hailstones

> **Rev. 16:20–21.** 20 And every island fled away, and no mountains were to be found; 21 and great hailstones, heavy as a hundred-weight, dropped on men from heaven, till men cursed God for the plague of the hail, so fearful was that plague.

16:20–21. The portrayal of islands vanishing and mountains disappearing may call to mind passages in the Old Testament that speak of the coming of the Lord (Ps. 97:5; Is. 40:5; 42:15; 45:2; 54:10; Ezek. 38:20). It may also be a way of saying, "There's nowhere to run," since the mountains are described as hiding places in time of God's judgment (Gen. 19:30; Mt. 24:16; Mk. 13:14; Lk. 21:21; Lk. 23:30; Rev. 6:15).[17] The fiery hail that falls down to destroy the city reminds us not only of the plagues of Egypt, but also of Sodom, which was destroyed by fire from heaven (Gen. 19:24). Thus, just as Jerusalem's wickedness is described as resembling Sodom and Egypt, so too, it receives a similar judgment in the plagues and the fire from heaven. With the hail, God's judgment is completed. The final judgment of burning hailstones is described as the most "fearful" of all the plagues since it brings about the worst devastation.[18]

The Son Cometh

Josephus describes the Romans catapulting burning stones into the city. These stones weighed a "talent," which is the same weight as the hail that falls on the city in John's vision (a "hundredweight" can also be translated "talent").[19] Even more striking are the words uttered by the people upon seeing the fiery-stones: "The Son cometh."[20]

Applying the Lessons of Revelation 16 Today

Revelation 16 describes God's final seven-fold judgment. Notice that, prior to this final judgment, God has already sent judgments through the seals and the trumpets. By sending judgment in stages, God gives us ample opportunity to repent.

This can be applied to our own lives. God does not delight in judging His people. He is not an angry, vengeful God, simply waiting for us to cross the line so that He can zap us. God loves us. His judgments are meant to bring us to our knees in penance. In this, God's judgment is revealed as mercy. The Book of Hebrews explains, "For the Lord disciplines him whom he loves, and chastises every son whom he receives" (Heb. 12:6). Judgment comes, then, to get us to repent. The psalmist states, "It is good for me that I was afflicted that I might learn thy statutes" (Ps. 119:71).

God's punishment is often simply letting us have what we want. If a man refuses to admit that he has a drinking problem, God may allow him to lose all he has worked for and hit rock bottom. Only by hitting the bottom does he then look up and see the need to change. By suffering the consequences of his actions, a person learns why God condemns sin.

At times God's punishment comes as shock—invasion, war, suffering. Some people might suppose these kinds of trials indicate that God has abandoned His people. In fact, God draws close to them by shaking them up and bringing them to repentance. In all of this, God is love. His wrath is simply an expression of His mercy.[21]

* * *

Multiple Choice

1. Armageddon comes from the Hebrew words for ____________.

(a) Mountain of the Battle
(b) Mountain of Jerusalem
(c) Megiddo's plains
(d) Mountain of Megiddo

2. Megiddo was the place where the righteous king Josiah ____________.

(a) defeated Gog
(b) was killed
(c) made a covenant with God
(d) was anointed

3. Megiddo reminded Israel of ____________.

(a) a great victory
(b) a tragic defeat
(c) an old promise
(d) their vocation to be a first-born son to the nations

4. The removal of mountains and the vanishing of islands symbolizes the absence of ____________.

(a) hiding places
(b) God
(c) angelic protection
(d) hope

Answers) 1. d; 2. b; 3. b; 4. a.

* * *

Discussion/Study Questions

1. In what ways are the judgments of the seven chalices like the seven trumpets and the plagues of Egypt? (See pages 195–196)

2. In sending plagues upon Jerusalem similar to those He sent on Egypt, what does God teach us about the judgment of Jerusalem? How are the two places similar? (See page 197)

3. What is the meaning of the Battle of Armageddon? (See pages 202–203)

4. How did Josephus describe the spiritual state of the people of Jerusalem? (See pages 200–201)

5. How is divine wrath really an expression of God's love? (See page 205)

THE WHORE-ABLE CITY

(Rev. 17:1–19:21)

Out with the Old, In with the New

In Revelation 17, the wicked city is described as a harlot. This is not a new city or a different city than the ones judged throughout Revelation. This is the same "great city" where the Lord was crucified (cf. 11:8; 16:19; 17:18).

Throughout this commentary, I have shown that the wicked city destined for destruction is Jerusalem. One of the most compelling indications of this is the way in which John shows how the wicked city, symbolically called "Babylon," is replaced by a "new" Jerusalem. The emphasis on a "new" Jerusalem indicates that the "old" one has been replaced.[1]

Through subtle clues, we can see how John connects the two cities. The wicked city is the photographic negative of the New Jerusalem. This can be seen in the numerous ways John describes the similarity of the two cities:

"Babylon" (= Old Jerusalem) Seventh chalice: destruction of Babylon (16:17–21)	**The New Jerusalem** Final Seventh Vision:[2] descent of the New Jerusalem (21:1–8)
"Then one of the seven angels who had the seven bowls came and said to me . . ." (17:1)	"Then came one of the seven angels who had the seven bowls full of the seven plagues, and spoke to me . . ." (21:9)
"Come, I will show you" (17:1)	"Come, I will show you" (21:9)
"the great harlot" (Rev. 17:1)	"the Bride, the wife of the Lamb" (21:9)

"And he carried me away in the Spirit" (17:3)	"And in the Spirit he carried me away" (21:10)
"I saw a . . . woman arrayed in purple and scarlet, bedecked with gold and jewels and pearls" (17:4)	"having the glory of God, its radiance like a most rare jewel, like jasper, clear as crystal" (21:11)
"on her forehead was written a name of mystery: 'Babylon the great, mother of harlots'" (17:5)	"on the gates the names of the twelve tribes of the sons of Israel were inscribed" (21:12)
"It has become a dwelling place of demons" (18:2)	"Behold, the dwelling of God is with men" (21:3)
"mother of harlots and of earth's abominations" (17:5) or "falsehood" (21:27)	"nothing unclean shall enter it, not anyone who practices abomination" (21:27)
"[those] whose names are not written in the book of life from the foundation of the world, will marvel to behold the beast" (17:8)	"only those who are written in the Lamb's book of life [shall enter]" (21:27)[3]

It is, then, John's intention to describe the *new* Jerusalem as the antithesis of the old one.[4]

Sitting Pretty Dangerously

If the city is Jerusalem, though, what are we to make of John's vision of the city "sitting upon the seven hills" (Rev. 17:9)? Rome, of course, is famously built on seven hills. Because of this, many are convinced that the wicked city is Rome rather than Jerusalem. However, it is important to situate this vision within the larger symbolic framework of the chapter and the book itself.

First of all, it is clear that the harlot in chapter 17 is an image of the "city" (17:18). Secondly, the harlot is not the beast, but symbolizes something separate from it. This is clear from the fact that the "beast" devours the "harlot" (17:16). Furthermore, the harlot "sits" upon the beast (17:3).

Now we can consider the "seven hills" (17:9). John tells us that the seven hills are the seven heads of the beast (17:8). Thus, the harlot-city sits on the seven hills, just as the woman sits upon the beast with seven heads. As mentioned above, Rome was the city of seven hills. In Revelation 17, we have an image of Jerusalem (= the harlot) "propped" up on Roman authority (= the beast with seven heads). In other words, Jerusalem had become an instrument, a puppet, controlled by the beast. This is also evident in the words of the chief priests at Christ's trial: "We have no king but Caesar" (Jn. 19:15).

Furthermore, this interpretation reflects the true historical situation of the Herodian dynasty. Herod, as we have said, was not the rightful king—he wasn't even a Jew! He and his sons were appointed by the Roman emperor.[5] Therefore, Jerusalem is the city that "sits" upon Rome.

The Harlot

> **Rev. 17:1–2.** 1 Then one of the seven angels who had the seven bowls came and said to me, "Come, I will show you the judgment of the great harlot who is seated upon many waters, 2 with whom the kings of the earth have committed fornication, and with the wine of whose fornication the dwellers on earth have become drunk."

17:1–2. In looking at John's image of the city "seated upon many waters," many scholars rightly point to Jeremiah 51:13, which says that Babylon sits by "many waters."[6] By borrowing this imagery, John is describing Jerusalem, the New Babylon, in terms identical to the old. Yet John may also have a subtler point.

As we have already mentioned, the symbols of "sea" and "waters" represent Gentile nations. The "many waters" that the woman sits on is yet another way of showing how Jerusalem has set itself up on Gentile authority (cf. 17:15). It is another way of presenting the same message conveyed in the portrayal of the "harlot riding the beast" and the "city sitting on seven hills" (17:3, 8).

Trouble with the Mrs.

Because Israel was supposed to be in a covenant relationship with God, its unfaithfulness was often painted in terms of an adulterous wife. In the first chapter of Isaiah, we read concerning Jerusalem, "How the faithful city has become a harlot, she that was full of justice! Righteousness lodged in her, but now murderers" (Is. 1:21). Her participation in the idolatrous ways of the nations was also understood in terms of harlotry. Ezekiel explains that, when the city engaged in the idolatrous practices of the pagans, she was "playing the harlot" (Ezek. 16:15ff). This is also a major theme of Hosea's message (cf. Hos. 1:2; 4:16–19; 5:3–5; 6:10).

The image of Jerusalem being "drunk" evokes Isaiah's prophecy: "Stupefy yourselves and be in a stupor . . . Be drunk but not with drink!" (Is. 29:9). There is a lesson to be learned in this.

As Saint Thomas Aquinas taught, sin darkens the intellect and impedes understanding. This is because the more one sins, the more that person has to justify his sin in his mind, rationalizing the guilt away. Hosea likewise explains; "Wine and new wine take away the understanding. My people inquire of a thing of wood, and their staff gives them oracles. For a spirit of harlotry has led them astray, and they have left their God to play the harlot" (Hos. 4:11–12). Sin, then, is a slippery slope. In the end, the sinner has convinced himself so thoroughly that he is doing no wrong, that he no longer can discern true good from evil.

The Harlot Riding the Beast

Rev. 17:3. And he carried me away in the Spirit into a wilderness, and I saw a woman sitting on a scarlet beast which was full of blasphemous names, and it had seven heads and ten horns.

17:3. John, much like Isaiah, is carried out into the wilderness to see the fall of the harlot. Isaiah also had a vision of God's coming judgment, which was also associated with the desert (cf. Is. 21:1). John again borrows from this chapter of Isaiah when he states: "Fallen, fallen is Babylon" (Is. 21:9; Rev. 18:2).

This beast is the first beast that arises out of the sea in Revelation 13, which we saw was Rome.[7] As in Revelation 13, this beast has seven heads and ten horns (Rev. 13:1; 17:3) and has "blasphemous names" (Rev. 13:1; 17:3). Its scarlet color stands in stark contrast to the "white robed" saints.

The Apparel of the Harlot

Rev. 17:4–5. 4 The woman was arrayed in purple and scarlet, and bedecked with gold and jewels and pearls, holding in her hand a golden cup full of abominations and the impurities of her fornication; 5 and on her forehead was written a name of mystery: "Babylon the great, mother of harlots and of earth's abominations."

17:4–5. The jewels that the woman wears (17:14) are a subtle contrast to the splendor of the Bride of the Lamb (cf. 17:4, 21:11). Likewise, these jewels are mentioned in chapter 18 as the goods the harlot city traded as part of her prosperous economy (18:12). The harlot, then, is literally "wrapped up" in her own wealth. Jeremiah uses similar imagery to describe Jerusalem dolling herself up to seduce the nations (cf. Jer. 4:30). John's description mirrors Jeremiah's words: "Babylon was a golden cup in the LORD's hand, making all the earth drunken; the nations drank of her wine, therefore the nations went mad" (Jer. 51:7).

Furthermore, precious jewels and gold were also used as part of the temple services in Jerusalem. The high priest wore "gold," "scarlet," and "precious stones" (Ex. 28:5, 15–23).[8] These items were part of the temple's furnishings (cf. Ex. 25:3–7; 26:1; 26:31, 36; 27:16). Some scholars have seen temple imagery in the "golden cup" and have connected the inscription on the harlot's forehead to the high priest, whose miter also had words written across the forehead (Ex. 28:36–37).[9] Cups, in fact, were used in the temple for sacrifice. However, the blood poured out in the harlot's cup is not from animals, but the martyrs. In a sense, then, Jerusalem has "sacrificed" the saints.[10]

When John speaks of the "mystery" of the words written on the harlot's forehead, he alludes to Daniel's visions. There "mystery" is associated with the destruction of the wicked kingdom. It is also connected with the establishment of God's kingdom by the Son of man. Here, therefore, the "mystery" is applied to the destruction of the wicked city—Jerusalem. Once this earthly city has been destroyed, God's true bride, the New Jerusalem, will come down from heaven (21:11). As Jerusalem is judged, God begins to reign (cf. Rev. 11:15–17).[11] Similarly, God's temple in heaven is opened once the earthly city is judged (cf. Rev. 11:19).

John Marvels

Rev. 17:6. And I saw the woman, drunk with the blood of the saints and the blood of the martyrs of Jesus. When I saw her I marveled greatly.

17:6. The Greek word here, *martys*, is translated as "witness" everywhere else in John's vision. In this, we can better see the link between those who are killed by the harlot here in Revelation 17 and the two "witnesses" who lie dead in the streets of the wicked city of Revelation 11. The wicked city's responsibility for the deaths of these saints is also mentioned in Revelation 18: "And in her was found the blood of prophets and of saints" (18:24). Clearly, this describes the prophets and saints killed in Jerusalem.

The Seven Mountains and the Seven Kings

Rev. 17:7–11. 7 But the angel said to me, "Why marvel? I will tell you the mystery of the woman, and of the beast with seven heads and ten horns that carries her. 8 The beast that you saw was, and is not, and is to ascend from the bottomless pit and go to perdition; and the dwellers on earth whose names have not been written in the book of life from the foundation of the world, will marvel to behold the beast, because it was and is not and is to come. 9 This calls for a mind with wisdom: the seven heads are seven hills on which the woman is seated; 10 they are also seven kings, five of whom have fallen, one is, the other has not yet come, and when he comes he must remain only a little while. 11 As for the beast that was and is not, it is an eighth but it belongs to the seven, and it goes to perdition.

17:7–11. John's wonder at the beast reminds the reader of those in Revelation 13 who "follow the beast with wonder" (Rev. 13:3). John is similarly captivated by the woman, albeit only temporarily. Her beautiful appearance, which shares so much in common with the Bride of the Lamb, is truly compelling (cf. Rev. 21:10–23). The harlot is very seductive. Yet the angel rebukes John for admiring her skin-deep beauty. The angel turns John's focus to the beast that carries her.

The beast parodies the Lord, who is called the One who "was and is and is to come" (Rev. 1:8; 4:8), by being called the One who "was, and is not, and is to ascend from the bottomless pit." Furthermore, the prediction of the beast who will die ("is not") and then be revived from the pit refers to the re-emergence of the Empire after the chaos that followed the death of Nero (see commentary on 13:3). At that time, those who thought Rome would fall will "wonder" in amazement at its resurgence.

"Eight Is Enough"

Here John tells us wisdom is needed to discern the meaning of the seven heads. This is reminiscent of the beast in 13:18, where wisdom is required to know the meaning of "666." The seven hills represent the first seven emperors of the Roman Empire. When we begin counting with Julius, as the historians of John's day did, we learn that Nero is the sixth king, the one who is reigning at the time John writes Revelation; this is who John is referring to by the phrase, "the one who is." The Caesar who reigned after Nero, Galba, only reigned six months, fulfilling what John said, "[W]hen he comes he must remain only a little while."

But who is the "eighth"? At the outset, it is noteworthy that John does not call him "*the* eighth," but simply, "*an* eighth." This is because he only saw *seven* heads and *seven* hills. The "eighth," therefore, is not to be understood in the same way that the other seven are. He is not necessarily the successor of the seventh king. At the same time, he does "belong to the seven."

In connection with this, it is important to realize that, though John has foretold the collapse and resurgence of the Empire, his list of seven kings stops short of the reign of Vespasian, the tenth Caesar, who brought about its revitalization. John is using the number "eight," then, symbolically. "Eight" was a symbol of resurrection and new beginnings in first century Judaism and Christianity.[12] The Christians especially understood this in reference to Christ, who was raised from the dead on the "eighth" day. In fact, if one calculated the numeric value of Jesus' name, one would find that it equals "888."[13] The "eighth" king, therefore, is likely a reference to the reestablishment of the Empire—its "resurrection"—under Vespasian.[14]

The Ten Horns of the Beast

Rev. 17:12–14. 12 And the ten horns that you saw are ten kings who have not yet received royal power, but they are to receive authority as kings for one hour, together with the beast. 13 These are of one mind and give over their power and authority to the beast; 14 they will make war on the Lamb, and the Lamb will conquer them, for he is Lord of lords and King of kings, and those with him are called and chosen and faithful."

17:12–14. Drawing on Daniel 7:4–7, John uses the imagery of ten horns to signify ten kings. These ten horns derive their authority from the beast. Some have seen these ten kings as representing ten rulers appointed by Caesar. The Herodian dynasty would be included with these "client-kings."[15]

What is harder to explain is what John means when he says that they have not yet received "royal" power. I have found no interpretation that satisfactorily explains this. Regardless, the "ten horns" represent the sum total of those who receive their power from the Roman Emperor and rule under him.

The Beast Devours the Harlot

Rev. 17:15–18. 15 And he said to me, "The waters that you saw, where the harlot is seated, are peoples and multitudes and

> nations and tongues. 16 And the ten horns that you saw, they and the beast will hate the harlot; they will make her desolate and naked, and devour her flesh and burn her up with fire, 17 for God has put it into their hearts to carry out his purpose by being of one mind and giving over their royal power to the beast, until the words of God shall be fulfilled. 18 And the woman that you saw is the great city which has dominion over the kings of the earth."

17:15–18. John's description of the waters as the peoples and nations confirms our interpretation above that the meaning of the harlot sitting on the waters is Jerusalem, sitting atop and supported by Gentile authority. The image of the beast turning on the harlot and burning her down is a graphic description of the destruction of Jerusalem—for in the year 70, Rome truly did burn down the city.

But how did Jerusalem have dominion over the kings of the earth? On the surface it seems that Rome would fit this description much better than Jerusalem! Yet John is speaking of "spiritual" dominion. As God's holy city, Jerusalem had preeminence among the nations. Indeed, in the glory days of Solomon, the nations came to recognize this, coming to Jerusalem to learn the ways of God (cf. 1 Kings 10:24). The Old Testament contains numerous examples of pagan kings coming to understand the spiritual headship of Jerusalem (cf. 1 Kings 3:1; 10:2; 2 Chron. 6:6; 9:1; Is. 2:1–3; Jer. 3:17; Sir. 24:11).

Since she was called to lead the nations back to God as the Lord's light to them, she was given a sacred authority over them. Yet the "great city" turned sinful itself. Jerusalem became a hypocrite and a bastion of wickedness. She, to whom the other nations were to turn for guidance, led them astray. She is responsible for getting the other nations "drunk" with immorality (17:2). By forsaking her God, she has not only condemned herself to judgment but has also led the Gentiles into blindness. Jerusalem is the "false prophet."[16]

The Fall of Babylon

Rev. 18:1–5. 1 After this I saw another angel coming down from heaven, having great authority; and the earth was made bright with his splendor. 2 And he called out with a mighty voice, "Fallen, fallen is Babylon the great! It has become a dwelling place of demons, a haunt of every foul spirit, a haunt of every foul and hateful bird; 3 for all nations have drunk the wine of her impure passion, and the kings of the earth have committed fornication with her, and the merchants of the earth have grown rich with the wealth of her wantonness." 4 Then I heard another voice from heaven saying, "Come out of her, my people, lest you take part in her sins, lest you share in her plagues; 5 for her sins are heaped high as heaven, and God has remembered her iniquities.

Chapter 18 contains numerous parallels to Jeremiah's prophecy concerning the fall of Babylon:

Babylon's Fall in Revelation 18	**Babylon's Fall in Jeremiah 50–51**
"It has become a haunt of every foul spirit, a haunt of every foul and hateful bird" (18:2)	"And Babylon shall become a heap of ruins, the haunt of jackals." (Jer. 51:37)
"for all the nations have drunk the wine of her impure passion, and the kings of the earth have committed fornication with her" (18:3)	"Babylon was a golden cup in the LORD's hand, making all the earth drunken; the nations drank of her wine, therefore the nations went mad" (Jer. 51:7)
"Come out of her, my people, lest you take part in her sins, lest you share in her plagues" (18:4)	"Flee from the midst of Babylon, let every man save his life! Be not cut off in her punishment" (Jer. 51:6)
"For her sins are heaped high as heaven" (18:5)	"for her judgment has reached up to heaven, and has been lifted up even to the skies" (Jer. 51:9)

"Render to her as she herself has rendered" (18:6)	"Requite her according to her deeds, do to her according to all that she has done" (Jer. 50:29; cf. 51:6)
"she shall be burned with fire" (18:8)	"her dwellings are on fire" (Jer. 51:30)
"Rejoice over her, O heaven, O saints and apostles and prophets, for God has given judgment for you against her" (18:20)	"Then the heavens and the earth and all that is within them, shall sing for joy over Babylon; for the destroyers shall come against them out of the north" (Jer. 51:48)
"And in her was found the blood of prophets and of saints, and of all who have been slain on earth" (18:24)	"Babylon must fall for the slain of Israel, as for Babylon have fallen the slain of the earth" (51:49)

Babylon destroyed the earthly temple; Jerusalem destroyed the true Temple—Christ (cf. Jn. 2). Jerusalem will now fall as Babylon did.

18:1–3. Though the angel uses the past tense (Babylon has fallen) this should be understood as a prophetic announcement of a future event. This is clear from the warning to the saints to leave the city in the next verse, as well as the future orientation of the rest of the angel's words (e.g., 18:8: "so shall her plagues come in a single day"). In addition, the link between "harlotry" and trade is made in Isaiah's prophecy concerning the destruction of Tyre (Is. 23:17). It is appropriate that John draws on imagery from the destruction of Tyre, since it was Hiram from Tyre who originally helped Solomon build the temple (1 Kings 7:13–14).

18:4–5. John draws his imagery not only from Jeremiah, but also from the Exodus. The saints are to "come out of" this new Babylon, also called the new Egypt (Rev. 11:8), so that they do not share in its "plagues." Just as the Passover lamb delivered the

Israelites, the saints here are saved by the true Lamb of God. The Exodus is one example of God leading His people out of a city on the brink of judgment. Another example is God's deliverance of Lot's family from Sodom.

The Judgment of the Harlot

> **Rev. 18:6–8.** 6 Render to her as she herself has rendered, and repay her double for her deeds; mix a double draught for her in the cup she mixed. 7 As she glorified herself and played the wanton, so give her a like measure of torment and mourning. Since in her heart she says, 'A queen I sit, I am no widow, mourning I shall never see,' 8 so shall her plagues come in a single day, pestilence and mourning and famine, and she shall be burned with fire; for mighty is the Lord God who judges her."

18:6–8. The message God sends in judging Babylon is, as the well-known saying goes, "a punishment that fits the crime." Just as the harlot-city sought to kill the saints, now she herself will be destroyed. Just as Babylon prided herself as unbreakable, so she will be broken. And just as she indulged herself in illicit pleasures, she will now face painful judgment.

Moreover, the angel's message has an interesting parallel to Psalm 137, which is a prayer for judgment on Babylon. The psalmist prays: "Happy shall he be who requites you with what you have done to us!" (137:8). Yet at the time Psalm 137 was placed in the Psalter, the Babylonian exile had long been over. The return from "Babylon," then, was a symbol for the hope of God's restoration of Israel in the New Exodus. This is what John now describes.

Jerusalem became proud expecting to be the center for that glorious gathering of God's people. After all, hadn't the prophets said that it would take place in Jerusalem? In judgment, however, they had come to realize that the earthly city was only penultimate. It was only a scale model of something greater, something heavenly. Because they became attached to the earthly, they missed the heavenly—a lesson taught over and over, from Adam, to Solomon, to Jerusalem.

The Kings Mourn over the Harlot City

Rev. 18:9–10. 9 And the kings of the earth, who committed fornication and were wanton with her, will weep and wail over her when they see the smoke of her burning; 10 they will stand far off, in fear of her torment, and say, "Alas! alas! thou great city, thou mighty city, Babylon! In one hour has thy judgment come."

18:9–10. Three groups mourn the destruction of the city: the kings (18:9), the merchants (18:11), and the sailors (18:17). The description of the three groups parallel each other:

—They each "mourn" over the fall of the city (18:9, 15, 19).
—Each group "stands far off" as they watch (18:10, 15, 17).
—All three begin their lament, saying "Alas, alas" (18:10, 16, 19).
—The three groups also mention that the city is destroyed in "one hour" (18:10, 17, 19).

Although each group mourns at the sight of the harlot's judgment, they cry, not necessarily because of the city, but because of the negative effects its destruction has on them. They cry for themselves.[17]

This is manifest in the lament of the kings of the earth, who weep because they have now lost the one with whom they "committed fornication." They now must go and search for another who will indulge their perverted appetites. They don't pity her and try to help her. Rather, they stand far off, for fear that they will be judged as well, and watch as she burns.

The Merchants Mourn over the Harlot City

Rev. 18:11–17a. 11 And the merchants of the earth weep and mourn for her, since no one buys their cargo any more, 12 cargo of gold, silver, jewels and pearls, fine linen, purple, silk and scarlet, all kinds of scented wood, all articles of ivory, all articles of costly wood, bronze, iron and marble, 13 cinnamon, spice, incense, myrrh, frankincense, wine, oil, fine flour and wheat, cattle and sheep, horses and chariots, and slaves, that is, human souls. 14 "The fruit for which thy soul longed has gone from thee, and all thy dainties and thy splendor are lost to thee, never to be found again!" 15 The merchants of these wares, who gained wealth from her, will stand far off, in fear of her torment, weeping and mourning aloud, 16 "Alas, alas, for the great city that was clothed in fine linen, in purple and scarlet, bedecked with gold, with jewels, and with pearls! 17 In one hour all this wealth has been laid waste."

18:11–17a. As the lament of the kings was motivated by selfishness, so too are the cries of the merchants. They mourn because there is no one left to buy their goods. The destruction of the city hits these merchants hard financially, since they lose their best customer. They cry because they lose money.

The list of the goods that were sold is partly based on those included in Ezekiel's condemnation of Tyre (cf. Ezek. 27:12ff.).[18] In fact, Josephus explains that these were the very same items the Romans carried out of the temple: "The treasurer of the temple . . . shewed Titus the coats and girdles of the priests, with great quantities of purple and scarlet . . . as also a great deal of cinnamon and cassia, with a large quantity of other sweet spices."[19]

The list climaxes with the trading of "human souls," indicating Jerusalem's involvement in spiritual slavery. One is reminded of Paul's words, "Now Hagar is Mount Sinai in Arabia; she corresponds to the present Jerusalem, for she is in slavery with her children. But the Jerusalem above is free, and she is our mother" (Gal. 4:25–26). Now those earthly things, for which Jerusalem traded its soul, will be taken away from her.

The Sailors Mourn over the Harlot City

Rev. 18:17b–19. 17 And all shipmasters and seafaring men, sailors and all whose trade is on the sea, stood far off 18 and cried out as they saw the smoke of her burning, "What city was like the great city?" 19 And they threw dust on their heads, as they wept and mourned, crying out, "Alas, alas, for the great city where all who had ships at sea grew rich by her wealth! In one hour she has been laid waste.

18:17b–19. Finally, the last group, the sailors, mourns at the fall of Babylon because "all who had ships at sea grew rich by her." They put ashes on their heads, not because of true repentance, but out of self-pity. Like the merchants, they cry because they lose money. Again, John seems to draw from Ezekiel's imagery. Ezekiel speaks of sailors placing ashes on their heads at the fall of Tyre (cf. Ezek. 27:28–33).

Heaven Rejoices over the Judgment of Babylon

Rev. 18:20–24. 20 Rejoice over her, O heaven, O saints and apostles and prophets, for God has given judgment for you against her!" 21 Then a mighty angel took up a stone like a great millstone and threw it into the sea, saying, "So shall Babylon the great city be thrown down with violence, and shall be found no more; 22 and the sound of harpers and minstrels, of flute players and trumpeters, shall be heard in thee no more; and a craftsman of any craft shall be found in thee no more; and the sound of the millstone shall be heard in thee no more; 23 and the light of a lamp shall shine in thee no more; and the voice of bridegroom and bride shall be heard in thee no more; for thy merchants were the great men of the earth, and all nations were deceived by thy sorcery. 24 And in her was found the blood of prophets and of saints, and of all who have been slain on earth."

18:20–24. The prophets and saints rejoice at the destruction of the city that killed them. God has avenged their blood, as He promised in Revelation 6 (see commentary on 6:9–11). Jesus' promise that Jerusalem would finally be held accountable for the blood of all the prophets killed there is finally fulfilled (Lk. 11:50).

The image of the city being cast like a millstone into the sea, recalls John's description of a mountain cast into the sea in Revelation 8:8. However, it also vividly depicts Christ's warning: "Temptations to sin are sure to come; but woe to him by whom they come! It would be better for him if a millstone were hung round his neck and he were cast into the sea, than that he should cause one of these little ones to sin" (Lk. 17:1–2). John takes this imagery from Jesus Himself and applies it to Jerusalem.[20] So then, because the city seduced the nations as a harlot and led them into sin by its scandalous conduct, it is cast into the sea like a "millstone."

Mission Accomplished

There are many connections here between Revelation 4–5, the end of Revelation 11 and the vision presented here in chapter 19.

Chapters 4–5 "Then I looked, and I heard around the throne and the living creatures and the elders the voice of many angels, numbering myriads of myriads and thousands of thousands, saying with a loud voice, . . ." (5:11–12)	**Chapter 11** "There were loud voices in heaven." (11:15)	**Chapter 19** "I heard what seemed to be the mighty voice of a great multitude." (19:1)
"the twenty-four elders fall down before him who is seated on the throne . . . they cast their crowns before the throne" (4:10)	"And the twenty-four elders who sit on their thrones before God fell on their faces and worshipped God" (11:16)	"And the twenty-four elders . . . fell down and worshipped God who is seated on the throne" (19:4)
"Holy, holy, holy, is the Lord God Almighty" (4:8)	"We give thanks to thee, Lord God Almighty . . . thou hast begun to reign" (11:17)	"For the Lord our God, the Almighty reigns" (19:6)
"From the throne issue flashes of lightning, and voices and peals of thunder" (4:5)	"and there were flashes of lightning" (11:19)	"Like the sound of mighty thunder peals" (19:6)

Thus, three contexts are linked together:

1. the Lamb's opening of the scroll, symbolizing the fulfillment of God's covenant plan with the saints in heaven;
2. the seventh trumpet at the end of Revelation 11, which introduced the woman of chapter 12—who is Mary, the icon of the Church seen in heaven;
3. the vision of the Church, the Bride of Christ, coming down from heaven.

In all of this, then, John shows how Christ fulfills God's Old Testament promises through the Church. In the Church, the spotless Bride, God's plan from the dawn of time is accomplished and Christ's victory is realized. His victory over the devil is finally complete. And all of this converges in the event called the marriage supper of the Lamb.

Hallelujah!

Rev. 19:1–5. 1 After this I heard what seemed to be the mighty voice of a great multitude in heaven, crying, "Hallelujah! Salvation and glory and power belong to our God, 2 for his judgments are true and just; he has judged the great harlot who corrupted the earth with her fornication, and he has avenged on her the blood of his servants." 3 Once more they cried, "Hallelujah! The smoke from her goes up for ever and ever." 4 And the twenty-four elders and the four living creatures fell down and worshiped God who is seated on the throne, saying, "Amen. Hallelujah!" 5 And from the throne came a voice crying, "Praise our God, all you his servants, you who fear him, small and great."

19:1–5. In response to the fall of Babylon, the saints in heaven rejoice. The close resemblance between John's words here ("He has judged the great harlot . . . and he has avenged on her the blood of his servants") to the prayers of the souls under the altar in 6:10 ("how long before thou wilt judge and avenge our blood?") reveals that God has heard their prayer. With this all the saints and angels erupt in praise.

Psalm-Kind of Prayer

Revelation 19 is the only place in the New Testament where the word "Hallelujah" (or "Alleluia") occurs. The word comes from "praise the LORD" in Hebrew; *hallel*, meaning "to praise," and *jah*, short for "Yahweh" (the "j" functions as a "y"). The word is well-known to Catholics, who regularly use it at Mass. Yet few realize the deep significance of the word.

The word was used to refer to Psalms 111–118, which are called the "Hallel Psalms."[21] These psalms function as praise for the coming and triumph of the messiah, which is depicted in Psalms 108–110. To best see this, a little background is necessary.

The Book of Psalms is carefully arranged. The psalms move from songs of lament, which make up the majority of the first half of the book, to psalms of praise, a theme that abounds in the second half.[22] In fact, the Psalter (the Book of Psalms) is arranged into five books.

Book 1:	Psalms 1–41
Book 2:	Psalms 42–72
Book 3:	Psalms 73–89
Book 4:	Psalms 90–106
Book 5:	Psalms 107–150.

There is a traceable movement in these psalms as well.

Book 1 is primarily made up of psalms about David and seems to end with a prayer the king sang as he lay on his deathbed.[23] Book 2 ends with Psalm 72, a song about Solomon, the successor of David, at the height of his reign. Going on, Psalm 89, which ends Book 3, recounts the defeat of the Davidic king and Israel's exile.

With Israel in exile, Moses enters the scene in Book 4. Psalm 90 is, in fact, a "Prayer of Moses." Throughout this book, Israel's wilderness experience is recalled, forming the basis for the hope of the New Exodus. Book 5 subsequently pictures the restoration of Israel. After the first psalm of Book 5, Psalm 107, which celebrates the deliverance of Israel, the Davidic king, the messiah, returns to sing Psalms 108–110. After appearing in 108, he suffers in 109, only to be glorified in 110. Indeed, the New Testament points to Psalms 109 and 110 as prophecies concerning Christ's death, Resurrection, and Ascension.[24]

Shedding Some Paschal Light on the Subject

With the messiah's victory, Israel explodes into the praise of the "Hallel" psalms (111–118). These psalms function as a response to the triumph of the messiah in Psalm 110. They represent a kind of climax, toward which the entire Book of Psalms has been moving.[25]

Because these psalms celebrate the return of Israel in the New Exodus, it should be no surprise that they were used during the Passover Meal, which celebrated the first Exodus. The "Hallel" psalms were divided up into two parts, one sung before and one after the meal.[26] In fact, it was believed that the messiah would come to restore the kingdom on the Feast of Passover. In this, the first Exodus was linked to the new one.[27]

The Book of Revelation manifests these hopes. After the plagues, which bring about the destruction of the city called the new Egypt, God's saints in heaven rejoice. They sing to God the "new song" sung by Moses, at the edge of the sea (Rev. 15:2–3). They burst into celebration, singing "Hallelujah." Furthermore, all this is done in the context of a "supper." This has led some scholars to see the Passover liturgy, which later became the Eucharistic celebration, as the background for John's vision in Revelation 19.[28]

The Marriage Supper of the Lamb

Rev. 19:6–9. 6 Then I heard what seemed to be the voice of a great multitude, like the sound of many waters and like the sound of mighty thunder peals, crying, "Hallelujah! For the Lord our God the Almighty reigns. 7 Let us rejoice and exult and give him the glory, for the marriage of the Lamb has come, and his Bride has made herself ready; 8 it was granted her to be clothed with fine linen, bright and pure"—for the fine linen is the righteous deeds of the saints.

9 And the angel said to me, "Write this: Blessed are those who are invited to the marriage supper of the Lamb." And he said to me, "These are true words of God."

19:6–9. There is a profound contrast between the "spotless" Bride, who wears her "righteous deeds" as garments, and the harlot who was the "mother . . . of the earth's abominations" (17:5). And yet the harlot inadvertently plays an important role. For God used her persecution of the saints as a means to "prepare" His Bride. Truly, then, the Bride has cooperated with God's grace, so that she is not simply prepared by God, but, we are told, "has made herself ready."

Furthermore, the garments in which she is clothed are reminiscent of the garments of the high priest, who also wears linen garments as a sign of holiness (cf. Zech. 3:5–6; Ex. 27:2–5).[29] Isaiah similarly combines the image of a bridegroom wearing priestly garments and a bride bedecked with jewelry to describe restored Israel: "I will greatly rejoice in the LORD, my soul shall exult in my God; for he has clothed me with the garments of salvation, he has covered me with the robe of righteousness, as a bridegroom decks himself with a garland, and as a bride adorns herself with her jewels" (Is. 61:10). The righteous deeds of the saints, therefore, are understood in terms of a priestly offering, which, in turn, makes the Church ready for her wedding to the Lamb.[30]

"We Can Work It Out"

In this passage of Revelation, we see part of the Scriptural basis for the Catholic understanding of salvation. Contrary to Luther, Scripture teaches us that we are not saved by faith alone. The Church's glory is revealed when she is clothed with her "righteous deeds" (19:8).

But doesn't this downplay Christ's work? How is one to understand Paul's statement, "[B]y grace you have been saved through faith; and this is not your own doing, it is the gift of God—not because of works lest any man should boast" (Eph. 2:8–9)?

At the outset, it must be said that the Catholic Church teaches that grace is not earned. The *Catechism of the Catholic Church* explains, "Grace is *favor*, the *free and undeserved help* that God gives us to respond to his call to become children of God, adoptive sons." (*Catechism*, no. 1996, emphasis in original). No one earns the gift of salvation—no one can merit heaven.

At the same time, though, Christ's work is so effective it merits our ability to merit. Jesus allows us to participate in His work of redemption. He turns our worthless deeds into saving acts by uniting them to His works. So Paul says, "Work out your salvation in fear and trembling; for God is at work in you" (Phil. 2:12–13).

This does not mean that Catholics have a lower view of Christ's work. Not at all! Far from diminishing Christ's role, Catholics have a much greater appreciation for the power of His love. When Christ crowns our good deeds and makes them meritorious, His work is not lessened but glorified, since our works are only possible because of His. In reality, then, when Christ crowns our work, He is simply glorifying His own work!

Then Comes Marriage

This brings us to the image of the Church as the Bride of Christ. Christ truly reproduces His life in the Church, so that the Church is the Mystical Body of Christ. Yet the Church is not simply His Body, forming some kind of torso connected to Him as Head. Though a surface reading of some of Paul's letters may lead to that conclusion, a deeper look reveals a much more profound mystery.

In Ephesians 5, the Apostle Paul gives us his most profound thoughts on the Church. He writes, "Even so husbands should love their wives as their own bodies. He who loves his wife loves himself. For no man ever hates his own flesh, but nourishes and cherishes it, as Christ does the church, because we are members of his body. 'For this reason a man shall leave his father and mother and be joined to his wife, and the two shall become one.' This is a great mystery, and I mean in reference to Christ and his church"

(Eph. 5:28–33). Paul cites Genesis 2:24, "and they shall become one flesh" and applies it to Christ and the church. Therefore, when Paul speaks of the Church being Christ's Body, he speaks in marital terminology.

The intimate communion in marriage, which occurs when the two become "one flesh," is a picture of Christ and the Church. Christ unites Himself to the Church so that His life is reproduced in her. The Church, therefore, becomes "Mother Church." Furthermore, just as husband and wife are united in an intimate communion of one flesh, so too the Church is wedded to Christ at the marriage supper of the Lamb, which is the Eucharist, where she enters into Holy Communion with the Flesh of our Lord.[31]

An Offering Fit for a King

The image in chapter 19 of a supper celebrated after a time of persecution also recalls the *todah* (meaning "thank") offering. This offering was comprised of three parts. It begins in a life-threatening situation. The afflicted would beseech God with a prayer for deliverance, attaching an oath by which he swore that he would offer God a sacrifice once he was saved.

Once the time of tribulation passed, the person who was saved would go to the temple and offer a sacrifice to God. Along with the animal to be slaughtered, bread would be brought to the temple, which was consecrated when the animal was killed. Finally, the person would gather his family and friends for a banquet, and over a cup of wine, he would recount how the Lord had rescued him from death. During the meal, the bread would be eaten. This is especially noteworthy, since the *todah* was the only time consecrated bread could be eaten by the Israelite people.

Although the Book of Leviticus makes provisions for the "thank offering," it became a prominent part of Israelite spirituality with the rise of David. The Book of Psalms contains numerous examples of *todah* offerings made by the great king. In fact, in the Psalms, the *todah* offering even seems to displace the sin offering as the superior sacrifice: "I will magnify [the Lord] with thanksgiving [*todah*]. This will please the Lord more than an ox or a bull with horns and hoofs" (Ps. 69:30–31).

Furthermore, the Psalms often depict "thanksgiving" as offered *before* deliverance has occurred (cf. Ps. 9:1–6). In this we see that the essence of the *todah* is not found simply in the sacrifice of the animal, but also in the sacrifice of praise made by the righteous who endure suffering. The *todah*, therefore, is an offering of self in sacrificial love to God.[32] Psalm 141 therefore says, "Let my prayer be counted as incense before thee, and the lifting up of my hands as an evening sacrifice" (Ps. 141:2).[33]

Mountaintop Experience

In the Book of Psalms, David acts as an example for Israel. As he offered up his sufferings and tribulations through sacrifice so too must Israel. In fact, a kind of "corporate" *todah* may be found in the Passover, where bread and wine are offered, as God's people recount His great deliverance.[34]

It's no surprise then that Isaiah envisions a messianic banquet on Mount Zion once the New Exodus is accomplished. "On this mountain the LORD of hosts will make for all peoples a feast of fat things, a feast of wine on the lees, of fat things full of marrow of wine on the lees well refined. . . . He will swallow up death for ever, and the Lord GOD will wipe away tears from all faces" (Is. 25:6, 8). The banquet of the restored kingdom is entirely appropriate. A new Passover meal should accompany the New Exodus.

In all of this we have a picture of what we find in Revelation. The saints celebrate the coming kingdom of God and their deliverance from the persecution of the harlot-city through a kind of corporate *todah*, the New Exodus' Passover meal. This messianic banquet is celebrated at every Mass.

It is important to note that the Greek word for *todah* is *eucharistia*, where we get the term "Eucharist." In the celebration of the Lord's supper, the Son of David offers His own *todah*, in which He offers Himself as a sacrificial offering and proclaims His deliverance from death. The Church, the restored kingdom of

Israel, participates by offering herself through her own sufferings and afflictions, as she wanders in this earthly pilgrimage, while also celebrating her redemption in the New Passover. In this she makes and fulfills her "oath"—in Latin, "sacrament"—to thank God in the banquet in the heavenly Mount Zion.

Worship God

> **Rev. 19:10.** Then I fell down at his feet to worship him, but he said to me, "You must not do that! I am a fellow servant with you and your brethren who hold the testimony of Jesus. Worship God." For the testimony of Jesus is the spirit of prophecy.

19:10. In Revelation 1:17, John fell down at Jesus' feet. Likewise, John falls down at the feet of the angel here in Revelation 19:10. However, the angel rebukes John for falling at his feet, saying, "Worship God!" Implied in all of this is the belief that Jesus truly is God. You can't worship an angel—he is not God. But you can worship Jesus—He is.

The angel's definition of the "testimony of Jesus" being "the spirit of prophecy" reveals that all the Old Testament prophets, whether they knew it or not, were ultimately speaking of Jesus. In this, the marriage supper of the Lamb in Revelation 19 accomplishes all that God promised He would do. And yet, while the angel's words explain the true mission of the prophets, they also bespeak a much more profound truth, for they also reveal the true identity of the Spirit.

Can I Get a Witness?

The angel's explanation has strong echoes of John's Gospel, where Jesus explains: "But when the Counselor comes, whom I shall send you from the Father, even the Spirit of truth, who proceeds from the Father, he will bear witness to me; and you also are witnesses, because you have been with me from the beginning" (Jn. 15:26–27). Similarly, in one of his letters, John writes: "And the Spirit is the witness, because the Spirit is the truth. There are three witnesses, the Spirit, the water, and the blood; and these three agree" (1 Jn. 5:7–8).

In all of this, we see that any testimony to Jesus comes through the Spirit. On one level, this teaches us that all prophecy comes through the Holy Spirit. However, on a deeper level it signifies the close association of the Spirit with the martyrs. "Martyr" in Greek means "witness," and the saints offer their lives as a "testimony" to Christ.

Earlier, in looking at the Trinity, we saw that the Holy Spirit is the Life-giving Love that unites the Father and the Son; indeed, He is the very Life They share. Because of this, when grace is given to believers, offering man a share in the life of God, it is done in the Spirit. In addition, when the saints offer their lives to God in self-donation, this too is done "in" and "through" that same Spirit, who is Life-giving Love itself.

In other words, since the Spirit is "Life-giving Love," He enables the saints to offer their lives in love, once He dwells within them. Paul explains: "It is the Spirit himself bearing witness with our spirit that we are children of God, and if children, then heirs, heirs of God and fellow heirs with Christ, provided we suffer with him in order that we may also be glorified with him" (Rom. 8:16-17). It is the Spirit, therefore, who reproduces Christ's life-giving love in the Church, making her alive, and enabling her to enter into God's inner life.

The Coming of Jesus on a White Horse

Rev. 19:11–16. 11 Then I saw heaven opened, and behold, a
white horse! He who sat upon it is called Faithful and True, and
in righteousness he judges and makes war. 12 His eyes are like a
flame of fire, and on his head are many diadems; and he has a
name inscribed which no one knows but himself. 13 He is clad
in a robe dipped in blood, and the name by which he is called is
The Word of God. 14 And the armies of heaven, arrayed in fine
linen, white and pure, followed him on white horses. 15 From
his mouth issues a sharp sword with which to smite the nations,

> and he will rule them with a rod of iron; he will tread the wine press of the fury of the wrath of God the Almighty. 16 On his robe and on his thigh he has a name inscribed, King of kings and Lord of lords.

19:11–16. The phrase, "Then I saw heaven opened," functions as an introduction to a new section. John now turns to see the final effects of the judgment on the harlot-city. Jesus' coming on a "white" horse should probably be understood in connection with the white robes given to those whom God avenged (cf. Rev. 6:11). Jesus is coming, therefore, as one who brings vindication.[35]

John now sees Jesus riding in as the triumphant King. This imagery of the Davidic King approaching His Bride is also found in Psalm 45, which was interpreted by ancient Jews as speaking about the coming of the messiah to the restored Jerusalem. Because of this, Psalm 45 may serve as the background for John's description.[36]

John's vision of Christ also draws heavily from Isaiah 62–63, which describe the restoration of Israel in terms of a marriage (Is. 62), when the Lord comes to crush her enemies (Is. 63). These parallels include:

—a "new name" (Is. 62:2; Rev. 19:12)
—a "crown" and "diadem" (Is. 62:3; Rev. 19:12)
—garments stained with blood (Is. 63:3; Rev. 19:13)
—the treading of the wine presses (Is. 63:2–3; Rev. 19:15)

Christ's judgment of the harlot city and His marriage to the Bride are, therefore, also spoken of in terms of God's promises to restore Israel when the messiah comes.

In fact, the description of Christ also serves as a reverse image of the harlot's wickedness. While Christ rides triumphantly on a white horse (19:11), she rides a scarlet beast that destroys her (17:3, 16). As the harlot had "a name of mystery" on her forehead, Jesus has a "new name" inscribed, apparently on the diadems on his head (19:12).[37]

Jesus' appearance here also echoes the description of Him in Revelation 1–3:

Revelation 1–3 "The faithful and true witness" (3:14)	**Revelation 19** "Faithful and True" (19:11)
"His eyes were like a flame of fire" (1:14)	"His eyes are like a flame of fire" (19:12)
"a new name written on the stone which no one knows except him who receives it" (2:17)	"He has a name inscribed which no one knows but Himself" (19:12)
"From His mouth issued a sharp two-edged sword" (1:16; cf. 2:12)	"From His mouth issues a sharp sword" (19:15)
"He shall rule the nations with a rod of iron" (2:27)	"to smite the nations, and He will rule them with a rod of iron" (19:15)

In chapters 1–3, Christ promises that He will surely bring condemnation unless the faithful of the seven churches repent of their deeds. Here John shows that Jesus did not issue an idle threat. He will be true to His words. Just like Jerusalem, each of the seven churches will receive judgment unless they reform their lives.

The Supper of God

Rev. 19:17–21. 17 Then I saw an angel standing in the sun, and
with a loud voice he called to all the birds that fly in midheaven,
"Come, gather for the great supper of God, 18 to eat the flesh of
kings, the flesh of captains, the flesh of mighty men, the flesh of
horses and their riders, and the flesh of all men, both free and
slave, both small and great." 19 And I saw the beast and the kings
of the earth with their armies gathered to make war against him
who sits upon the horse and against his army. 20 And the beast

> was captured, and with it the false prophet who in its presence had worked the signs by which he deceived those who had received the mark of the beast and those who worshiped its image. These two were thrown alive into the lake of fire that burns with brimstone. 21 And the rest were slain by the sword of him who sits upon the horse, the sword that issues from his mouth; and all the birds were gorged with their flesh.

19:17–18. The invitation to the birds to come to the supper of God, in which the wicked will be devoured, is a parody of the invitation to the marriage supper of the Lamb. In fact, several sacramental parodies may be found in John's account. As the New Jerusalem is connected with the "river of the water of life" (22:1), a baptismal image, so too the harlot-city sits upon "many waters" (17:1). The harlot is "drunk with the blood of the saints and the blood of martyrs" (17:6), and her "flesh" is later eaten by her foes, parodying the Eucharist (17:16; 18:3). Likewise, the followers of the beast are sealed, just as Christians are sealed with a mark in Baptism (Rev. 7:1–4; 13:16).[38]

The wicked are divided into seven categories, recalling the seven-fold judgments of God throughout the book. This passage also mirrors Ezekiel's vision of a similar feast, wherein the wicked shall be devoured: "Speak to the birds of every sort and to all beasts of the field, 'Assemble and come, gather from all sides to the sacrificial feast which I am preparing for you, a great sacrificial feast upon the mountains of Israel, and you shall eat flesh and drink blood'" (Ezek. 39:17). In this, the beast and the kings united with him will receive judgment.

Moreover, the general contexts of Ezekiel and Revelation are similar. In Ezekiel, the feast is called for the sake of God's holy "name," so that the nations will know "that I am the Lord" (Ezek. 39:7). This is paralleled here as the great supper of God is proceeded by the coming of Christ, who comes with a "new name," which is, "King of kings and Lord of lords" (Rev. 19:16).

19:19–21. While 17:16 envisions the beast turning against the harlot and devouring her, an image of Rome destroying Jerusalem, the idea here is that it is Christ who ultimately defeats them both. The alliance that was formed to kill Jesus—Pilate (the Roman governor) and the rulers of the Jews—is now judged. This is the same battle mentioned in 16:14, 19:19, and 20:8, as is apparent from the fact that all three contexts speak of the kings of the earth gathered for war.[39] All those who are associated with the beast therefore receive the judgment of God.

The description of God's condemnation here in Revelation 19 is different from that in chapters 17–18. There the battle is fought between earthly powers, resulting in earthly consequences: the harlot-city is burned with fire (17:16; 18:9, 18); the city becomes a haunt for animals (18:2); her wealth is obliterated (18:16–17), etc. With the exception of the birds who fly in mid-heaven eating the flesh of the kings, the judgment here is depicted in much more spiritual terms: the battle is fought by God's armies from heaven (19:14, 19); the beast and false prophet are thrown into the lake of fire (19:20); the wicked are slain by the sword that comes out of Christ's mouth (19:21).

Applying the Lessons of Revelation 17–19 Today

In Revelation 17–19 we read about an evil city that is destroyed for its wickedness. As we saw, "Babylon" was literally wrapped up with her own wealth. The harlot arrayed herself with the items that she traded. She was seductive—even, for a moment, to John! But then he saw the beast she was riding on. Her wealth and her sinfulness went hand in hand.

Nations cannot trust in their own wealth and strength. Countries can easily become wanton in their wealth as the wicked city in Revelation. The story is played out over and over again throughout history—Greece, Rome, etc. No nation, no kingdom, no country can last forever. Downfall is usually the result of arrogance and wantonness. Like a fatted calf, wealthy nations engorge themselves only to be destroyed.

Yet, there always remains the chance to repent. Think of Nineveh and how it repented when Jonah brought a warning of

God's impending judgment. In fact, the threat of destruction is actually part of God's mercy in that it can prompt us to repentance.

The terrorist actions in New York, the Pentagon, and Pennsylvania on September 11, 2001 marked the saddest day in American history. In May 2004, a similar attack shocked Spain. Thousands of good men and women lost their lives. Some even gave their lives heroically rescuing others. Indeed, America and Spain witnessed horrific evil—yet they also witnessed amazing, pious virtue.

In the aftermath of these events, both America and Spain turned out for public prayer vigils. Churches became jam-packed. Watching all of this, the image of an ancient city came to mind—Ninevah. Those terrible events taught us a valuable lesson. We are not immune from devastation. However, out of the ashes God can raise us up, if we will ask Him and be faithful.

Furthermore, Scripture gives us a model for how to offer up suffering in repentance—the *todah.* When we find ourselves in a situation that is dreadful, we can carry our crosses like Christ if we turn our affliction into a sacrificial offering. This is done through our *todah*, the "thanksgiving" feast of the New Covenant—the Eucharist. Active participation at Mass, then, is not primarily expressed through external enthusiastic responses or singing, but rather, by placing ourselves spiritually on the altar with Christ.[40] Our external responses simply express this offering.

* * *

Multiple Choice

1. The image of the beast devouring the harlot is a symbol of __________.

(a) the wickedness of Rome
(b) Rome destroying Jerusalem
(c) Jerusalem destroying Christ
(d) militant Islamic forces invading Europe

2. The image of the city sitting on seven hills is a symbol of __________.

(a) Jerusalem built on seven hills
(b) Rome built on seven hills
(c) Jerusalem propped up on Roman authority
(d) Jerusalem's seven-year war with the Romans

3. The image of the harlot was frequently applied to __________ in the Old Testament.

(a) Gentile nations
(b) David's enemies
(c) Jerusalem
(d) Egypt

4. The number "eight" was used to symbolize __________.

(a) holiness
(b) infinity
(c) resurrection
(d) ascension

5. The "Hallel" psalms were sung to celebrate the __________.

(a) restoration of the kingdom
(b) the defeat of Babylon in Jeremiah's day
(c) the crossing of the Red Sea
(d) the dedication of the temple

6. King David made the ______________ a prominent part of Israel's cultic life

(a) *todah*
(b) feast of Chanukah
(c) sin offering
(d) dance

Answers) 1. b; 2. b; 3. c; 4. c; 5. a; 6. a.

* * *

Discussion/Study Questions

1. How does John describe "Babylon" and the "New Jerusalem" in similar terms? Why does he do this? (See pages 209–210)

____

____

____

____

2. How does the destruction of Babylon in Revelation 18 recall Jeremiah 50–51? Why does John describe the destruction of Jerusalem in terms of the fall of "Babylon"? (See pages 218–219)

____

____

____

____

3. Explain the image of the Church as Bride of Christ. What connection does this have to the teaching that the Church is the Mystical Body of Christ? (See pages 229–230)

____

____

____

____

4. What is the connection between the *todah* and the Eucharist? How was the Passover a *todah*? How is the Mass the New Passover of the New Exodus? (See pages 230–232)

____

____

____

____

5. How is the supper of God a parody of the marriage supper of the Lamb? What other sacramental parodies are there in connection with the harlot? (See page 236)

____

____

____

____

6. What lesson can the Church in America learn from the destruction of the harlot city? (See pages 237–238)

____

____

____

____

Chapter Thirteen

THE PERENNIAL MILLENNIAL QUESTION

The Thousand-Year Reign (Rev. 20:1–15)

Why Too K O'd on Millennialism?

Revelation 20's description of the "thousand year reign" has traditionally been one of the most difficult parts of the Apocalypse to understand. Many people in the early Church even believed that this cryptic teaching was too strange for the Bible and concluded, therefore, that the Book of Revelation should be left out of the New Testament! Of course, the Church recognized it as a legitimately inspired book and placed it in the canon. Nonetheless, it is still a challenge to explain Revelation 20.

A common interpretation among Protestants today is that Christ will return and set up some kind of earthly reign.[1] Yet Christ explains, "My kingship is not of this world" (Jn. 18:36).

Because of this, it seems unlikely that John meant to say that Christ would set up an earthly kingdom. Instead, we will see how John's use of symbols and covenant terminology envision something much more than just a future reality. Revelation 20 gives us a kind of panoramic view of salvation history. In short, Revelation 20 is the summary of the story of Jerusalem, established by David, who began to reign in c. 1000 BC.[2]

Before we go on, let me add a brief note. Traditionally, Catholics have understood the "1,000 year reign" as referring to the age of the Church. In this interpretation, the "thousand" years are understood symbolically. The thousand years stand for the time Christ would reign through the Church—from the time of His first coming to the time of His Second Coming. Satan is restrained—the power of the sacraments administered by the Church hold him at bay. The first resurrection—the one prior to the final resurrection at the end of time— refers to the saints being taken up to God. At the end of time there will be a final confrontation between the Lord and the devil, wherein God will crush Satan once and for all. This view is well attested to in the Fathers of the Church.[3]

I whole-heartedly affirm this view. Nevertheless, I think we can also add to this view. As stated, the interpretation laid out here understands the Millennium in terms of the Davidic Covenant. Since the Davidic covenant is the Old Testament blueprint for the New Covenant, the Davidic kingdom foreshadows "the age of the Church." For example, in Solomon's concern to include all nations we have a foreshadowing of the way the devil will be bound and chained through the ministry of the Church. Likewise, just as the devil was loosed to wreak havoc in the last days the Old Testament world, which climaxed in the destruction of the temple, so too will he be loosed at the end of time. The "Davidic" interpretation laid out here, therefore, does not exclude the traditional explanation—it compliments it.

Satan Is Bound for a Thousand Years

Rev. 20:1–3. 1 Then I saw an angel coming down from heaven, holding in his hand the key of the bottomless pit and a great chain. 2 And he seized the dragon, that ancient serpent, who is the Devil and Satan, and bound him for a thousand years, 3 and threw him into the pit, and shut it and sealed it over him, that he should deceive the nations no more, till the thousand years were ended. After that he must be loosed for a little while.

20:1–3. The devil is locked in the "pit" by an angel, who uses the "key" to imprison him. These two images were loaded with meaning to Jewish readers. Understanding these two terms will be key (pardon the pun) to unlocking the meaning of this passage.

An "Abyssmal" Interpretation

Earlier we saw that the "key" is drawn from Isaiah 22, where it represents the authority of the Davidic kingdom (see commentary on 3:17–22). Indeed, John specifically identifies it as "the key of David" (Rev. 3:7). It is also referred to as the key of "Death and Hades" (Rev. 1:18).

The "key" is linked with the "pit." This "pit" (also called the "bottomless pit" in Rev. 9:1) is a word used in the Old Testament and Jewish tradition for the watery place of the dead, that is, the underworld, or "Sheol." Jonah speaks of how he was saved from it: "I called to the LORD, out of my distress, and he answered me; out of the belly of Sheol I cried, and thou didst hear my voice. For thou didst cast me into the deep, into the heart of the seas, and the flood was round about me; all thy waves and thy billows passed over me. . . . The waters closed in over me, the deep was round about me; weeds were wrapped about my head at the roots of the mountains. I went down to the land whose bars closed upon me for ever; yet thou didst bring up my life from the Pit, O LORD my God" (Jon. 2:2–3, 5–6)."[4]

This "pit," or "abyss," was also connected with the temple in Jewish literature. Although it is not recorded in Scripture, the temple, according to Jewish tradition, was built by David's son Solomon on top of a special rock, called the "foundation stone." This stone was said to be the "plug" to the netherworld.[5] Anyone who has ever seen a picture of Jerusalem can hardly miss the famous Muslim mosque called the Dome of the Rock, in which this famous "stone" or "rock" is located.[6]

In keeping with this, Rabbinic tradition passed on the story of how David almost inadvertently unleashed the waters of Sheol when he came to lay the foundation for the temple, which his son later built:

> When King David came to dig the foundations for the Temple around the Foundation Stone, he dug to a depth of fifteen hundred cubits. At length he found a projecting stone which he wished to remove. But the stone said to him: "This thou canst not do."
>
> David asked: "Why not?" and it answered: "I cover the mouth of the abyss!"

> . . . But David would not hearken and wished to remove the stone; and as he tried, the waters of the abyss rose in great torrents which appeared to be about to flood the world. Then David began to sing the Song of Degrees [Ps. 120–134] from the Book of Psalms, and the waters of the abyss returned to their place.[7]

The blood of the sacrifices was said to run down the shafts under the altar onto the foundation stone below, so that the blood would "cover" those in Sheol.

Ben Meyer, a famous scholar, showed how this tradition formed the background for Jesus' words in Matthew 16. There, Jesus builds His Church on Peter, the Rock, as Solomon built the temple on the foundation stone (Mt. 16:18).[8] Moreover, He gives Peter the "keys to the kingdom," which gives him power over the "gates of Hades," and in so doing, grants him the power to "free" souls from the power of the devil (Mt. 16:18–19).

Rock On

Whether or not David actually built the temple on a foundation stone that plugged up some watery pit, is not important. What is important is the truth this symbolism conveys. When God swore to David His covenant oath, establishing his kingdom, God brought to a partial fulfillment all the promises of the Old Testament. Through David's son, the effects of original sin would begin to be reversed. Jerusalem would become the center from which God's law would be taken to the nations. As the Lord promised, all nations would be blessed through Abraham's descendants.

When David understood this, he exclaimed, "[God] hast shown me a law for mankind" (2 Sam. 7:19).[9] Following in his father's footsteps, Solomon began to teach the Gentiles, who came from all over to hear his great wisdom. Because of God's oath, Satan was "bound" to deceive the nations no more.

Going In-Chain

This brings us to the angel's "chain." Just as the "key" was symbolic of the Davidic kingdom, so also a "chain" was associated with Solomon's courtroom. Right near the "Dome of the Rock" in Jerusalem, there is a smaller shrine called the "Dome of the Chain." This building commemorates an ancient legend, which says that a "chain" was used by the king in determining the truth of a witness' testimony. The person under oath would hold on to the chain and give his sworn statement. If he were not telling the truth, a link would fall so that all would know the lie he had told.[10]

The image of the devil being "bound" for "a thousand years," therefore, is a depiction of the incredible power of God's oath to establish the Davidic kingdom, through which the nations would be taught and the devil's deceptions unmasked. Indeed, the Davidic kingdom stood for one thousand years from David to Christ, since it was established in about 1000 BC.

Furthermore, it is interesting that the devil is "bound," a term often connected with exorcism. This is important because Solomon was well-known in Jewish tradition as the greatest exorcist who ever lived.[11] The Greek word for exorcism, *ex horkia*, literally means, "to oath out." Thus, because of God's sworn oath to David, the devil was exorcised—"bound"—so that he could no longer deceive the nations.

The Millennium, therefore, does not bespeak a future age of an earthly kingdom, but rather, summarizes God's work in salvation history. This is hinted at from the very beginning, since it is an angel who binds the devil. Angels were those through whom the Old Covenant economy was administered. This is why the author of Hebrews explains that the New Covenant is superior to the Old. The New is mediated by Christ, whereas in times past it was mediated by angels (cf. Heb. 2:2–5).[12]

Jail Break

So far we have seen that the one thousand year reign relates God's use of the Davidic kingdom and the king's own city,

Jerusalem, in His plan to save the nations. The image of the devil being "loosed" for a short time at the end of the thousand years, therefore, must be understood in connection with this. In fact, as we have seen, Jerusalem became increasingly evil in the first century. Its wickedness reached its peak at the time of its destruction in the year 70.

Jesus Himself testifies against the wickedness of His own generation, comparing it to the final state of wickedness: "When the unclean spirit has gone out of a man, he passes through waterless places seeking rest, but he finds none. Then he says, 'I will return to my house from which I came.' And when he comes he finds it empty, swept, and put in order. Then he goes and brings with him seven other spirits more evil than himself, and they enter and dwell there; and the last state of that man becomes worse than the first. So shall it be also with this evil generation" (Mt. 12:43–45).

Likewise, Josephus writes of his own people: "[N]or did any other age ever breed a generation more fruitful in wickedness than this was, from the beginning of the world."[13] Therefore, at the end of the thousand years, Satan was let loose to wreak his worst damage.

The First Resurrection

Rev. 20:4–6. 4 Then I saw thrones, and seated on them were those to whom judgment was committed. Also I saw the souls of those who had been beheaded for their testimony to Jesus and for the word of God, and who had not worshiped the beast or its image and had not received its mark on their foreheads or their hands. They came to life, and reigned with Christ a thousand years. 5 The rest of the dead did not come to life until the thousand years were ended. This is the first resurrection. 6 Blessed and holy is he who shares in the first resurrection! Over such the second death has no power, but they shall be priests of God and of Christ, and they shall reign with him a thousand years.

20:4–6. Just as the twenty-four elders sat on thrones, the saints sit on thrones here. But who are they? In keeping with our prior analysis that the thousand years represents the time from David to Christ, these are the prophets and Old Testament martyrs.

"Those who are beheaded" refers to John the Baptist, the final and greatest prophet, of whom Jesus said, "Truly, I say to you, among those born of women there has risen no one greater than John the Baptist" (Mt. 11:11). The Baptizer therefore embodies all the prophets who were killed for their witness to God. Likewise, those who did not "worship the beast or his image" refers to those Jews who refused to bow to the orders of pagan rulers to worship idols, such as those in Daniel 3.

All of these receive the "first resurrection." This resurrection is penultimate and awaits a "second resurrection" at the end of time. The first resurrection is not, therefore, the bodily resurrection of the saints at the end of time. The first resurrection is the ascent of the righteous souls to God at death. This is clear from the fact that the "first resurrection" is linked with the "first death" – physical death (cf. Rev. 2:10-11).[14]

These Old Testament martyrs have learned "life-giving" love in the fullest sense. They are made holy in their priestly self-offering and, in a special way, made ready for heaven. We too are called to prepare ourselves in this life for heaven by giving our lives to God—whether that means through martyrdom or through daily self-sacrifice.

Satan Is Loosed: The Battle of Gog and Magog

Rev. 20:7–8. 7 And when the thousand years are ended, Satan will be loosed from his prison 8 and will come out to deceive the nations which are at the four corners of the earth, that is, Gog and Magog, to gather them for battle; their number is like the sand of the sea.

20:7–8. At the end of the thousand years, Satan is loosed to "deceive" the nations. Thus, as Christ comes to replace the earthly Davidic kingdom and capital city (Jerusalem), with their heavenly realities, wickedness descends on the earthly city. Satan's "unbounded" work of deception seems to be evident in Jesus' condemnation of Jerusalem in His day (cf. Lk. 11:29–32, 49–51). Jesus says His generation is in the worst state of demonic possession: "When the unclean spirit has gone out of a man, he passes through waterless places seeking rest, but he finds none. Then he says, 'I will return to my house from which I came.' . . . Then he goes and brings with him seven other spirits more evil than himself, and they enter and dwell there; and the last state of that man becomes worse than the first. So shall it be also with this evil generation" (Mt. 12:43–45). As we have seen, Josephus also testifies to this intense wickedness.

Jerusalem was supposed to be a beacon of righteousness for the nations. When it becomes evil, the nations are set for shipwreck, as the devil is set free to deceive them as well. Because of this, Satan is able to deceive the nations, who are called Gog and Magog, and to bring them to fight against God's people.

"Gog" and "Magog" were originally spoken of by Ezekiel. In Ezekiel, "Gog" and "Magog" symbolize those who fight against the Davidic messiah and destroy Jerusalem. Gog and Magog later became symbols in the Jewish tradition for the enemies of the messiah.[15] These two symbols, then, represent those who persecute Jesus and God's people. They set out to destroy both Christ and the restored Israel (the Church), just as Gog and Magog did.

The Lake of Fire

Rev. 20:9–10. 9 And they marched up over the broad earth and surrounded the camp of the saints and the beloved city; but fire came down from heaven and consumed them, 10 and the devil who had deceived them was thrown into the lake of fire and brimstone where the beast and the false prophet were, and they will be tormented day and night for ever and ever.

20:9–10. The Church is here described as the "camp of the saints," recalling the "encampments" of Israel in the wilderness on their journey to the Promised Land. This image underlines the Church's pilgrim identity. Her dwelling on earth is only temporary—an "encampment" on the way to the true Promised Land.

The other term used to describe the saints, "the beloved city," anticipates the vision of chapter 21, where the Church is described as the New Jerusalem.

Those who oppose God's people face God's wrath and are consumed by fire. This is an apt depiction of the actual burning of Jerusalem. As the earthly enemies are defeated, so too is Satan, who is thrown into the lake of fire with the beast and the false prophet. Furthermore, hell's torment is graphically depicted as a place of never-ending suffering, lasting "day and night . . . forever!"

The One on the Great White Throne

> **Rev. 20:11.** Then I saw a great white throne and him who sat upon it; from his presence earth and sky fled away, and no place was found for them.

20:11. John now goes on to describe the "second resurrection" and the "second death." At first glance, it might seem strange that John moves from narrating the events of AD 70 to speaking about the final judgment. However, as we have seen, the destruction of Jerusalem points forward to that event. Because of this, John moves subtly between the two events.

The picture of Christ on the throne may evoke Daniel, where God is enthroned as the "Ancient of Days" (Dan. 7:9). Christ's kingship is also described in terms reminiscent of Solomon, who also sat enthroned on a white-ivory throne (cf. 1 Kings 10:18). Jesus, therefore, rules as the true Son of David, bringing to fulfillment God's plan for the Davidic covenant.

The flight of the earth and the sky evokes Old Testament descriptions of the Lord's coming (cf. Judg. 5:3–6; Ps. 18:6–16; Ps. 68:6–9; Amos 1:1–3; Mic. 1:2–5; Hab. 3:3–16). It also bears similarities with Isaiah's prophecy of God's deliverance of His people in the New Exodus. Isaiah states, "Lift up your eyes to the heavens, and look at the earth beneath, for the heavens will vanish like smoke, the earth will wear out like a garment" (Is. 51:6).

The Last Judgment

Rev. 20:12–15. 12 And I saw the dead, great and small, standing before the throne, and books were opened. Also another book was opened, which is the book of life. And the dead were judged by what was written in the books, by what they had done. 13 And the sea gave up the dead in it, Death and Hades gave up the dead in them, and all were judged by what they had done. 14 Then Death and Hades were thrown into the lake of fire. This is the second death, the lake of fire; 15 and if any one's name was not found written in the book of life, he was thrown into the lake of fire.

20:12–15. John sees the dead standing before the Lamb to be judged. Note that there is no distinction between the righteous and the wicked at this point. Both will, in some way, be resurrected on the last day (cf. *Catechism*, no. 998). Therefore, just as the righteous will somehow experience the joys of heaven in their bodies, the torment of hell is felt in both soul and body.

The opening of the books is taken from Daniel 7:10 and 12:1–2. In Daniel 7, the books are opened with the coming of the Son of man. Later, in Daniel 12:1–2, God promises to deliver all those whose names are "found written in the book." John thus foresees the Second Coming as the time when God's people will receive their eternal reward. Of course, those who are not written in the Book of Life will be cast with Satan and his minions into the fiery lake of hell.

What the Millennium Means For Us

Even though Y2K has now passed us by, there are still those who want to say that the new millennium signals an imminent return of Christ. There was even a television series (mercifully canceled), called "Millennium," in which strange events signaled the coming of the end of the world. So what does the "New Millennium" mean for us?

Though it doesn't tell us when Christ will come back, the calendar is important nonetheless. Our modern calendar began in the fifth century when a monk known as Dionysius, or simply

"Denis," did his best to determine the year Christ was born and started dating the years accordingly. He was a little off, but that's inconsequential. The symbolism was what mattered. But what was that symbolism?

It goes back to the Emperor Diocletian, who insisted that he was god. This Caesar decided to fully emphasize his all importance by introducing a new dating system, which started from the year he began to reign. He was saying, in effect, "History didn't matter until I became Emperor. Date everything starting from me. I am the new dawn." You might say he had a big ego.

By beginning his calendar with Christ's birthday, Denis made a bold and daring statement: Jesus is King—Caesar isn't. What Denis did was nothing less than to launch a revolution, which has lasted into our day. Whenever we celebrate the "new year," and especially a "millennium," we make a bold affirmation that the world recognizes Jesus as King above all others.

This gives us an incredible opportunity to share and celebrate our faith. New Year's parties are not anti-Christian (unless they are celebrated in a sinful way). Rather, they are a celebration of Jesus and a chance to evangelize. The calendar proclaims: Jesus is Lord![16]

* * *

Multiple Choice

1. The Davidic kingdom was established in about __________.
(a) 1000 BC
(b) 777 BC
(c) 2000 BC
(d) 586 BC

2. The key held by the angel is drawn from Isaiah 22, which speaks of the key of the kingdom of ___________.
(a) Babylon
(b) Greece

(c) David
(d) Samson

3. According to an ancient tradition, Solomon, the son of David built _________ over the bottomless pit, plugged up by a foundation stone.
(a) a shrine
(b) the palace
(c) the Upper Room
(d) the temple

4. According to an ancient tradition a great "chain" hung in the court of _____________,
(a) Solomon
(b) Pharaoh
(c) Caesar
(d) Nebuchadnezzar

5. The first resurrection refers to the ascent of the ________ of the martyrs in the Old Testament to God.
(a) bodies
(b) souls
(c) body and souls
(d) families

6. Gog and Magog were symbols in Jewish tradition of the enemies of the __________.
(a) Messiah
(b) Anti-Christ
(c) city of the beast
(d) great angel, Michael

Answers) 1. a; 2. c; 3. d; 4. a; 5. b; 6. a.

* * *

Discussion/Study Questions

1. How is the Davidic kingdom symbolized by the thousand years? How is the loosing of Satan at the end of that period to be understood? (See pages 247–248)

2. What are the first and second resurrections? (See page 249)

3. What are Gog and Magog? How do they symbolize the earthly Jerusalem? (See page 250)

4. What is the significance of Christ sitting on the white throne? (See page 251)

5. Why does John move so easily between descriptions of the end of the world and AD 70? (See page 251)

CITY OF ANGELS

The New Jerusalem (Rev. 21:1–22:21)

The Bride of the Lamb

Rev. 21:1–2. 1 Then I saw a new heaven and a new earth; for the first heaven and the first earth had passed away, and the sea was no more. 2 And I saw the holy city, new Jerusalem, coming down out of heaven from God, prepared as a bride adorned for her husband;

21:1–2. With the passing away of the old Jerusalem, the entire Old Economy—the temple, the Levitical priesthood, etc.—is replaced. A "new creation" is inaugurated with the vision of the "New Jerusalem." In one sense, this explains the spiritual significance of Christ's fulfilling all things in Himself and His Church, making the earthly Jerusalem obsolete. At the same time, it looks forward to the Last Day, in which the earth itself will pass away and the Church will receive her final heavenly glory.

Much of the imagery is taken from Isaiah's vision of the great restoration, which will occur under the messiah. We have already seen how the prophet envisioned the latter day deliverance of Israel in terms of a marriage (cf. Is. 62–63; see commentary on 19:11–16). In addition, Isaiah described God's salvation in the latter days as a "new creation:" "For behold, I create new heavens and a new earth; and the former things shall not be remembered or come into mind" (Is. 65:17).

Also, since we have seen that the "sea" was a symbol for evil, its passing away describes God's final victory over Satan. The image also recalls "new creation" terminology. The first creation arose out of the waters of chaos (cf. Gen. 1:1–2). It also evokes Noah's covenant with God, in which Noah is made to be a new Adam. In this, the "new creation" coincides with the subsiding of the waters of the "sea."

God Dwells with His People

Rev. 21:3. and I heard a loud voice from the throne saying, "Behold, the dwelling of God is with men. He will dwell with them, and they shall be his people, and God himself will be with them;

21:3. The New Jerusalem, as we have seen, describes both heaven and Christ's Bride, the Church. The New Jerusalem *comes down from heaven* to be with the saints on earth. The image here is this: through the Church, the people of God already share in the heavenly realities. This is especially true, of course, in the Eucharistic banquet, where our heavenly High Priest is present under signs and symbols. His dwelling *is* with men, as John says.

Furthermore, the word for the Lord's "dwelling" is the same word used for the "tabernacle" constructed by Moses in the wilderness. Leviticus 26:11–12 and Ezekiel 37:26–28 both anticipate the day when God will place His sanctuary in the midst of His people. In that day, God promises that the righteous "shall be his people," as John sees here.

Ezekiel depicted God's meeting with His people in the wilderness in terms of marital embrace (cf. Ezek. 16:8–10).[1] John, therefore, combines the marriage imagery with "tent" imagery to convey God's intimate union with the Church. God is not just close to us on earth—He communes with us.

John also borrows from Jeremiah's prophecy of the New Covenant when he says, "they shall be his people" (cf. Jer. 31:33). In so doing, he shows that Jeremiah's words are fulfilled as the Old Covenant has passed away with the establishment of the New City: "Behold, the days are coming, says the LORD, when I will make a new covenant with the house of Israel and the house of Judah, not like the covenant which I made with their fathers when I took them by the hand to bring them out of the land of Egypt, my covenant which they broke, though I was their husband, says the LORD. But this is the covenant which I will make with the house of Israel after those days, says the LORD: I will put my law within them, and I will write it upon their hearts; and I will be their God, and *they shall be my people*" (Jer. 31:31–33).

The only time Jesus referred to this "new covenant" was when He instituted the Eucharist. It is there that God's covenant union with His people is finally consummated. There the heavenly Jerusalem descends in our churches.

Death and Mourning Pass Away

Rev. 21:4–5. 4 he will wipe away every tear from their eyes, and death shall be no more, neither shall there be mourning nor crying nor pain any more, for the former things have passed away."
5 And he who sat upon the throne said, "Behold, I make all things new." Also he said, "Write this, for these words are trustworthy and true."

21:4–5. The source for much of the language in verse 4 is Isaiah's vision of the great messianic banquet. Isaiah 25:8 reads, "He will swallow up death for ever, and the Lord GOD will wipe away tears from all faces, and the reproach of his people he will take away from all the earth; for the LORD has spoken." Once again, a Catholic may read this passage in connection with the Eucharist, Christ's great banquet, through which death is defeated and truly "swallowed" up.

Verse 5, not surprisingly, continues with a reference to Isaiah, "Behold I am making a new thing" (Is. 43:19).[2] In the Greek, the word is present tense and may be translated "I am *making*," not simply, "I make." This is not, therefore, simply a vision of the Last Day, but God's work to remake the world through the Church on earth, which is happening now.

The Fountain of the Water of Life

Rev. 21:6. And he said to me, "It is done! I am the Alpha and the Omega, the beginning and the end. To the thirsty I will give water without price from the fountain of the water of life.

21:6. The words Jesus utters, "It is done," call to mind His words from the Cross, "It is finished" (Jn. 19:30). His name as

"Alpha and Omega," the first and last letters of the Greek alphabet, is another way of alluding to Isaiah's description of the Lord as "the first and the last" (cf. Is. 41:4; 44:6; 48:12). It also fittingly describes Him here, at the consummation of all things, as the Lord of history. The One through whom "all things were made" (Jn. 1:3) also brings them to fulfillment.

Holy Water

Jesus' promise that the righteous shall drink from "the fountain of water" evokes Jesus' words in John's Gospel: "If any one thirsts, let him come to me and drink. He who believes in me, as the scripture has said, 'Out of his heart shall flow rivers of living water'" (Jn. 7:37–38). Jesus says, in effect, that those who are thirsty will come to Him, and then living waters will flow not only from Himself, but also from them. In Revelation 22, this river is an image of the Holy Spirit (see commentary 22:1ff).

Those who drink, then, from the fountain of life are those who have received the Holy Spirit and enter into communion with the Triune God. As Jesus explains, "[W]e will come to him and make our home with him" (Jn. 14:23). Though the water is a symbol for God's presence, it is nonetheless an efficacious sign—a symbol that accomplishes what it represents. The water of Baptism isn't merely a symbol of rebirth—it is through water (and the word) that our rebirth in Christ is accomplished (cf. *Catechism*, no.1213). So Christ says, "Truly, truly, I say to you, unless one is born of water and the Spirit, he cannot enter the kingdom of God" (Jn. 3:5).[3]

The Inheritance of the Saints

Rev. 21:7. He who conquers shall have this heritage, and I will be his God and he shall be my son.

21:7. Salvation isn't just a legal transaction where God, the judge, says, "Not guilty!" Salvation is more than a legal declaration—it's entrance into the family. This is seen here as God says, "I will be his God and he shall be my son." Sonship is also implied in the promise of a "heritage," since "inheritance" is given, not to strangers, but to one's children. In fact, John may be borrowing from Psalm 2, where God promises His "son" an "inheritance" (Ps. 2:7–8).

The language, "I will be his God and he shall be my son," is closely related to the phrase, "I shall be their God and they shall be my people (Jer. 31:33)." Both are representative of covenant language. As we have seen, covenants involve the forging of family bonds. Covenants make families.

God's Covenant Kingdom

So how does one get into a covenant? By swearing an oath. In Latin, the word for oath is "sacramentum." This explains why one who wishes to enter into the New Covenant receives a sacrament, Baptism—it's the oath of initiation.

The Church isn't just the restored kingdom; it's God's covenant people. Covenants make families. So the Church, the restored Kingdom, is God's Family. Baptism doesn't simply grant "legal justification," but familial status. Through it, we are God's sons and daughters.

Therefore, our salvation cannot be understood simply in terms of "me and Jesus," but in the larger context of a family—His other sons and daughters, our brothers and sisters in Christ. Saint Paul therefore calls the Church not only the "pillar and bulwark of truth," but God's "household" (1 Tim. 3:15). This is the true meaning of the phrase "no salvation outside of the Church." This teaching does not mean that salvation is impossible for non-Catholics, but, rather, that all those who are saved are united in Christ's Mystical Body—whether they know it or not.

Taking the Easy Way

Rev. 21:8. But as for the cowardly, the faithless, the polluted, as for murderers, fornicators, sorcerers, idolaters, and all liars, their lot shall be in the lake that burns with fire and brimstone, which is the second death."

21:8. To be a sinner is to be a coward. Christians need strength and fortitude to profess their faith since the world is against them. In contrast, sin is easy. One simply goes along with one's own passions and desires to get immediate—though fleeting—pleasure. Sinners simply go with the flow, floating along. There is no effort in that. G. K. Chesterton once pointed out that a dead dog can do that! "A dead thing can go with the stream, but only a living thing can go against it. A dead dog can be lifted on the leaping water with all the swiftness of a leaping hound; but only a live dog can swim backwards."[4]

The Vision of the New Jerusalem

Rev. 21:9–11. 9 Then came one of the seven angels who had the seven bowls full of the seven last plagues, and spoke to me, saying, "Come, I will show you the Bride, the wife of the Lamb." 10 And in the Spirit he carried me away to a great, high mountain, and showed me the holy city Jerusalem coming down out of heaven from God, 11 having the glory of God, its radiance like a most rare jewel, like a jasper, clear as crystal.

21:9–11. As mentioned earlier, the introduction of the New Jerusalem parallels the vision of the harlot city, the old Jerusalem (see introduction to chapter 11, "The Whore-able City"). The vision of the New Jerusalem in Revelation 21 closely follows Ezekiel's vision of the temple in the latter days. Here, like Ezekiel, John is transported to a mountain from which he will receive his vision (cf. Ezek. 40:1–2).

The New Jerusalem has "the glory of God," the fiery cloud of the Spirit's presence, called the *Shekinah*, which once dwelled in the temple. Ezekiel saw its departure from the earthly temple before its destruction by the Babylonians (cf. Ezek. 10:4). Later, Ezekiel saw the Lord's glory return and dwell in the latter day temple (cf. Ezek. 43:4–5). Now John sees that same glory-presence dwelling in the New Jerusalem.

The Description of the Holy City

Rev. 21:12–14. 12 It had a great, high wall, with twelve gates, and at the gates twelve angels, and on the gates the names of the twelve tribes of the sons of Israel were inscribed; 13 on the east three gates, on the north three gates, on the south three gates, and on the west three gates. 14 And the wall of the city had twelve foundations, and on them the twelve names of the twelve apostles of the Lamb.

21:12–14. The city is perfectly symmetrical with three gates on each of its four sides. This is much like Ezekiel's vision of the restored city, which has three gates on each of its four sides. Obviously, the total number of gates, twelve, is symbolically significant. As in Ezekiel's vision, each of the twelve tribes' names is written on these gates (Ezek. 48:31–34; Rev. 21:12). Indeed, Israel may be described as a gate, since through God's promises to them, the whole world enters into His covenant family.

The foundations for the walls of the city have the names of the twelve apostles on them, signifying that the Church is built on them. This of course is an image borrowed from Jesus Himself, who made Peter the foundation rock upon which the Church is built (cf. Mt. 16:18). Likewise, Paul explains that the Church is "built upon the foundation of the apostles and prophets" (Eph. 2:20).

The close connection between the twelve apostles and the twelve tribes underscores the continuity of God's plan. The Church does not replace Israel. Rather, she is the fulfillment of God's Old Testament promises to the chosen people. In fact, Jesus picked "twelve" apostles, painting His mission with the colors of Old Testament hopes.

This is especially clear from Jesus' promise that the apostles would "sit on twelve thrones, judging the twelve tribes of Israel" (Mt. 19:28). Paula Fredricksen, a Jewish scholar at Yale, observes: "[I]f Jesus indeed taught that ultimately these twelve would judge the twelve tribes, then he was thinking eschatologically. To assemble the twelve tribes so many centuries after the Assyrian conquest would take a miracle. But that, I think, is what

Jesus was expecting."[5] In other words, since ten-twelfths of Israel were still in exile, the twelve in and of themselves represented the hope for the restoration of Israel.

The Holy City Is Measured

Rev. 21:15–16. 15 And he who talked to me had a measuring rod of gold to measure the city and its gates and walls. 16 The city lies foursquare, its length the same as its breadth; and he measured the city with his rod, twelve thousand stadia; its length and breadth and height are equal.

21:15–16. Once again, the image of measuring is drawn from Ezekiel's vision (cf. 40:3–5).[6] As in the verses above, the number twelve figures prominently, as all the measurements are multiples of twelve. However, the most profound truth of all is found in John's description of the city itself.

John learns once the measuring is complete that the city is built as a perfect cube. In this, the city is like the holy of holies, the sacred inner room of the temple, which was also a perfect cube (cf. 1 Kings 6:20).[7] The New Jerusalem, therefore, is one giant temple. And, not only is it a temple, but all who dwell within it live in the most sacred presence of God. John sees no court divisions, as in the earthly temple, which segregated the Gentiles from Israel, the men from the women, and the priests from the rest of the men. In heaven, all are given equal access to the holy presence of God.

The Walls and Gates of the City

Rev. 21: 17–21. 17 He also measured its wall, a hundred and forty-four cubits by a man's measure, that is, an angel's. 18 The wall was built of jasper, while the city was pure gold, clear as glass. 19 The foundations of the wall of the city were adorned with every jewel; the first was jasper, the second sapphire, the third agate, the fourth emerald, 20 the fifth onyx, the sixth carnelian, the seventh chrysolite, the eighth beryl, the ninth topaz, the tenth chrysoprase, the eleventh jacinth, the twelfth amethyst. 21 And the twelve gates were twelve pearls, each of the gates made of a single pearl, and the street of the city was pure gold, transparent as glass.

21:17–21. John's language here is confusing. What does it mean that the measurement is that of "a man, that is, an angel's"? The phrase probably refers to the fact that though the temple is spiritual, the description of its length is given according to human standards so that the reader will understand.[8]

Stone Hinge

The precious stones that decorate the city are drawn from the account of the construction of the tabernacle in Exodus (cf. Ex. 28:17–20; 39:10–13). It is also overlaid in gold as the temple was. In this, the heavenly city's identity as a temple is made clear.

In addition, many of these stones were also associated with the Garden of Eden, the first sanctuary, where Adam was called to be priest-king (Ezek. 28:13). The heavenly Jerusalem, therefore, is the place where God's people realize the calling of Adam, dwelling as a kingdom of priests in His presence (cf. Rev. 1:5–6). The connection between the heavenly city and the garden may also be seen in the fact that both the Garden and the heavenly city are guarded by angels (Gen. 3:24; Rev. 21:12).

Not surprisingly, there are twelve stones, in keeping with the number of the apostles and the tribes. In the Old Testament the high priest was to wear a breastplate that contained twelve precious stones when he went into the holy of holies (cf. Ex. 28:29). This was to symbolize Israel's entrance into God's presence.[9] In the New Jerusalem the Church truly does enter (and permanently resides) in that presence.[10]

The Temple in Heaven

Rev. 21:22. And I saw no temple in the city, for its temple is the Lord God the Almighty and the Lamb.

21:22. As we have seen, the heavenly Jerusalem is described as one giant holy of holies. Now we realize why all in the heavenly city dwell in the presence of the Lord—He *is* the Temple. The righteous dwell within the Lord God and the Lamb. In other words, they are taken into the inner life of God; they live in the Trinity.

The promise that the saints would dwell *within* the Lord Himself was also proclaimed by the prophets. Isaiah predicted, "[H]e will become a sanctuary" (Is. 8:14). Similarly, the Psalmist frequently refers to the Lord as a "refuge" (Ps. 2:12; 5:11; 7:1; 11:1; 14:6, etc.) Psalm 90:1 says that the Lord is a "dwelling place." The New Jerusalem represents the fulfillment of God's promise that the righteous would abide *in* Him.

How do they get there? How is one made worthy to enter into the self-giving life of the Blessed Trinity? By pouring out one's own life in life-giving love.

The Glory of God in the City

Rev. 21:23–27. 23 And the city has no need of sun or moon to shine upon it, for the glory of God is its light, and its lamp is the Lamb. 24 By its light shall the nations walk; and the kings of the earth shall bring their glory into it, 25 and its gates shall never be shut by day—and there shall be no night there; 26 they shall bring into it the glory and the honor of the nations. 27 But nothing unclean shall enter it, nor any one who practices abomination or falsehood, but only those who are written in the Lamb's book of life.

Isaiah 60	**Revelation 21**
"The sun shall be no more your light by day, nor for brightness shall the moon give light to you by night; but the Lord will be your everlasting light, and your God will be your glory" (v. 19).	"And the city has no need of sun or moon to shine upon it, for the glory of God is its light, and its lamp is the Lamb" (v. 23).
"And nations shall come to your light, and kings to the brightness of your rising . . . the wealth of the nations shall come to you" (vv. 3, 5).	"By its light shall the nations walk; and the kings of the earth shall bring their glory into it" (v. 24).

"Your gates shall be open continually; day and night they shall not be shut; that men may bring to you the wealth of the nations, with their kings led in procession" (v. 11).	"[A]nd its gates shall never be shut by day—and there shall be no night there; they shall bring into it the glory and the honor of the nations" (v. 25–26).

21:23–27. John's imagery is drawn from Isaiah's description of the restoration of Israel in the latter days. In both cases, God's universal salvation, real catholicity, is extended. All nations shall come to this New Jerusalem and offer all they have to the Lord. Here is yet another metaphor for the total life-giving love of the saints and for the "Catholic" Church.

The River of Life

Rev. 22:1–2. 1 Then he showed me the river of the water of life,
bright as crystal, flowing from the throne of God and of the
Lamb 2 through the middle of the street of the city; also, on
either side of the river, the tree of life with its twelve kinds of
fruit, yielding its fruit each month; and the leaves of the tree were
for the healing of the nations.

22:1–2. The image of water flowing out from the Lord God and the Lamb, who are the Temple, is taken from Ezekiel, who sees a similar vision. The prophet writes, "Then he brought me back to the temple and behold, water was issuing from below the threshold of the temple toward the east (for the temple faced east)" (Ezek. 47:1). Likewise, the prophet Zechariah saw water flowing out from the restored Jerusalem (Zech. 14:8–9, 16).

Next to the river is the tree of life. This mirrors Ezekiel's vision, in which trees are seen next to the river, whose leaves are also "for healing" (Ezek. 47:12). The image also recalls the first psalm, where the righteous man is described as a tree that bears fruit. "He is like a tree planted by streams of water, that yields its fruit in its season, and its leaf does not wither" (Ps. 1:3). The tree here has twelve kinds of fruit, indicating that it is a sign of God's people, the Church of the twelve apostles, the restored Israel.

River Giver

In the discussion above, we connected this river to Jesus' words in John 7:37–38, "If any one thirst, let him come to me and drink. He who believes in me, as the scripture has said, 'Out of his heart shall flow rivers of living water.'" Scholars are oftentimes perplexed over Jesus' assertion that He is quoting Scripture, since no Old Testament passage says, "Out of his heart shall flow rivers of living water."[11] So where is Jesus taking this from?

Although John may have Numbers 20:10–13 (cf. 1 Cor. 10:4) and Zechariah 14:8–9, 16 in the back of his mind, many think John is primarily drawing from Ezekiel's vision of the water flowing from the temple. Jesus' words in the Gospel of John are spoken in the context of the Feast of Booths, which celebrated the temple's dedication.[12] Jesus, whose body is the true Temple (Jn. 2:19–22), is therefore speaking of the water that will flow out of Him into believers. Through Him, the Holy Spirit will be given.

And yet Jesus insists that the waters will flow, not only from Him, but out of the heart of the believer as well. This is because the Church *is* His Body, and thus is also a temple. If Jesus' body is the temple, out of which living waters flow, the same is true of the Mystical Body. Christ does in us what He once did in His earthly body.

Here, then, we have something similar to Revelation 22, where the river flows from the Lord God and the Lamb, through the Church (through the city's street and the Tree of Life), to the nations. The fruit of the Tree of Life may be understood as the Eucharist, which fruitful Mother Church ministers to the nations. Likewise, the river of water is not simply the Holy Spirit, but Baptism, through which He is received.

The City's Everlasting Glory

Rev. 22:3–5. 3 There shall no more be anything accursed, but the throne of God and of the Lamb shall be in it, and his servants shall worship him; 4 they shall see his face, and his name shall be on their foreheads. 5 And night shall be no more; they need no light of lamp or sun, for the Lord God will be their light, and they shall reign forever and ever.

22:3–5. John's mention that there is no longer any "curse" is taken from Zechariah's vision of the restored Jerusalem, "And it shall be inhabited, for there shall be no more curse; Jerusalem shall dwell in security" (Zech. 14:11). The reason there is nothing unclean in the city is that the New Jerusalem represents the Church sharing in God's own glory. In fact, there is no need for any sun or moon—His glory burns bright enough to give light to the whole city.

Furthermore, the saints are said to "reign" there just as the twenty-four elders sat on thrones. Moreover, these saints are priests, bearing God's name on their foreheads as the high priest once did (cf. Ex. 39:30). Thus, by their self-offering, they fulfill mankind's original calling to a royal priesthood. They therefore enter fully into communion with God, as they "see his face," a hope expressed by the righteous of the Old Testament (Ps. 11:4–7; 27:4; Ps. 42:2). They bear their worthiness by the mark on their foreheads, which is the seal of their baptism (see commentary on 7:2–3).

What Must Soon Take Place

Rev. 22:6–7. 6 And he said to me, "These words are trustworthy and true. And the Lord, the God of the spirits of the prophets, has sent his angel to show his servants what must soon take place.
7 And behold, I am coming soon." Blessed is he who keeps the words of the prophecy of this book.

22:6–7. Verses 6–21 serve as the concluding message not only to the vision of chapters 21–22, but also to the book as a whole. The words here closely mirror the introduction of Revelation.

Revelation 1:1–3 "The revelation of Jesus Christ, which God gave him to show to his servants what must soon take place" (1:1).	**Revelation 22:6–10, 18** "the Lord the God of the spirits of the prophets, has sent his angel to show his servants what must soon take place" (22:6).
"Blessed is he who reads aloud the words of the prophecy… and who keep what is written therein" (1:3).	"Blessed is he who keeps the words of the prophecy of this book." (22:7).
"for the time is near" (1:3).	"for the time is near" (22:10).

In this, the beginning and end of the book are neatly tied together.

The reader is assured that the contents of the Apocalypse are "trustworthy and true," since it comes from the God of "the spirits of the prophets." On one hand, we could say that this refers to the "prophetic spirits" of the prophets (cf. 1 Cor. 14:32). However, the "spirit of the prophets" is also the Holy Spirit, the seven-fold Spirit, who inspired the prophets (cf. 1:4, 4:5, and commentary on 19:10).

The words here also echo the prophet Daniel.

Daniel 2:45 "A great God has made known to the king what shall be hereafter. The dream is certain and its interpretation sure."	**Revelation 22:6** "These words are trustworthy and true. And the Lord . . . has sent his angel to show . . . what must soon take place."

The overall context of Daniel 2 is itself similar to Revelation 22, since both describe the ultimate triumph of God's kingdom.

The "trustworthiness" of John's prophecy is bound up with the warning that Christ is coming "soon." This cannot simply be the end of time. It is imminent. He is just around the corner. His coming is as near to the Church as the next Eucharistic celebration. Furthermore, for John's audience of the late 60s, He is coming soon in the judgment of AD 70.

"Your Brethren the Prophets"

Rev. 22:8–9. 8 I John am he who heard and saw these things. And when I heard and saw them, I fell down to worship at the feet of the angel who showed them to me; 9 but he said to me, "You must not do that! I am a fellow servant with you and your brethren the prophets, and with those who keep the words of this book. Worship God."

22:8–9. John establishes himself as a "witness," one who has "seen" and "heard" the visions presented (cf. 1 Jn. 1:1–2). In so doing, John is saying, "These visions are true. Trust me, I've seen them, and I'm not lying." By making such testimony, John is putting himself under an oath, guaranteeing its truth.

As in Revelation 19:10, John is rebuked for falling down in worship at the feet of an angel. Only God is worthy of adoration. This reminds John that he is simply a "fellow servant." In this phrase we see how God raises up those who follow Him to the level of the angels, so that they worship and serve Him alongside of the angelic host.

Do Not Seal Up the Prophecy

Rev. 22:10–13. 10 And he said to me, "Do not seal up the words of the prophecy of this book, for the time is near. 11 Let the evildoer still do evil, and the filthy still be filthy, and the righteous still do right, and the holy still be holy."

12 "Behold, I am coming soon, bringing my recompense, to repay every one for what he has done. 13 I am the Alpha and the Omega, the first and the last, the beginning and the end."

22:10–13. The command not to "seal up the words . . . of this book" implies that its prophecies are soon to be fulfilled. Daniel was told just the opposite, "But you Daniel, shut up the words, and seal the book, until the time of the end" (Dan. 12:4). John, therefore, is told that the end is about to come.

Hang On

Because of the imminent coming of Jesus, John is told to let the wicked continue in their ways—their time is short. The righteous should continue to endure, because they don't have much longer to wait until God's judgment comes. In other words, "Just hang on a little longer!" At the same time, they should not fret about the wicked actions of God's enemies since Jesus, the Lord, will soon deal with them.

Indeed, the Old Testament makes it clear that God's judgment of the wicked is inevitable. Ecclesiastes states, "For God will bring every deed into judgment, with every secret thing, whether good or evil" (Eccl. 12:14). Furthermore, Jesus makes it clear that He Himself is the all-powerful God who will sit in judgment of them, identifying Himself as the "Alpha and Omega." This was the same title of "the Lord God" in Revelation 1:8.[13]

Those Who Wash Their Robes—Those Left Outside the City

Rev. 22:14–15. 14 Blessed are those who wash their robes, that they may have the right to the tree of life and that they may enter the city by the gates. 15 Outside are the dogs and sorcerers and fornicators and murderers and idolaters, and every one who loves and practices falsehood.

22:14–15. The description of the righteous as those who "*wash* their robes" and *eat* from "the tree of life," evokes the sacraments of Baptism and Holy Eucharist. It is through these two sacraments that believers come to enter into the Holy City, the Church. The Fathers understood these same sacraments in the symbolism of John 19, where "blood" and "water" flow from Christ's side (Jn. 19:34). The Fathers also saw this as an image of the Church, the New Eve, being formed from Christ's side in the sacraments of Baptism and Eucharist.

The Root of David and Morning Star

Rev. 22:16. "I Jesus have sent my angel to you with this testimony for the churches. I am the root and the offspring of David, the bright morning star."

22:16. Jesus has sent His angel to bear His testimony, much like the Old Testament depicts Yahweh sending His angel to bring His message (see Mal. 3:1, and commentary on Rev. 1:1 and 10:1). The testimony is specifically for "the churches," presumably the seven churches mentioned in Revelation 1–3. In other words, the Book of Revelation's prophecy concerning the destruction of Jerusalem is a warning for the seven churches: just as Jerusalem is judged for its unfaithfulness, so too will the Christian churches in Asia Minor be judged unless they repent.

Jesus' title, "the root and offspring of David," recalls Isaiah's prophecy, "There shall come forth a shoot from the stump of Jesse, and a branch shall grow out of roots" (Is. 11:1). Isaiah foresaw a time when the Davidic kingdom would be crushed. This happened in 586 BC. when the Babylonians killed King Zedekiah and his sons, and carried the Jews off into captivity. Jesse was the father of David. When the Davidic sons were killed, it looked as though Jesse's family tree was cut down; all that remained was a stump.

Yet Isaiah saw that the kingdom would not be defeated. A Messiah would appear, symbolized by a branch that grows forth from Jesse's tree and restore the kingdom. Jesus, the true Son of David, fulfills this. As the "morning star" He brings about the dawn of the new age.[14]

The Spirit and the Bride

Rev. 22:17. The Spirit and the Bride say, "Come." And let him who hears say, "Come." And let him who is thirsty come, let him who desires take the water of life without price.

22:17. Notice the close connection between the Spirit and the Bride. In this, there is a profound lesson concerning the relationship of the Spirit, Mary, and the Church.

Unveiling the Third Person

The Holy Spirit is that interpersonal bond of love between the Father and the Son. The Spirit unites the First and Second Persons of the Trinity in Himself. In Him, the Father gives all He is to the

Son, and the Son responds by pouring His life back to the Father. Their love is not given away in a moment. Rather, there is an eternal dynamic of life-giving love—an eternal act of giving. That action and that bond of love *is* the Holy Spirit.

Now, what I am about to propose may seem strange. Rest assured, I am simply following saints like the early Fathers Ephrem and Methodius, modern saints like Edith Stein, and respected theologians such as Pope Benedict XVI, Matthias Scheeben, Yves Congar, and Scott Hahn.[15] Although it is true that God is totally spiritual, having no body and thus no gender, the Spirit is often spoken of in bridal/maternal terms. Of course, the Spirit is not "feminine," or a "she," since God is spiritual. Neither is the Father male. But there is something in human fatherhood *and motherhood* that nevertheless reflects the Divine Persons.[16]

Eve-n Deeper Analogies

When God creates mankind, He creates man as an "image" of Himself. The author of Genesis stresses that man bears God's image in being male *and* female: "So God created man in his own image, in the image of God he created him; male and female he created them" (Gen. 1:27). The creation of Adam, who is called the son of God (Lk. 3:38), mirrors the way that God is Father and Son in the Trinity. But what of Eve? She is also part of God's creation of mankind. In what way is God's image found in man being male *and* female?

Some early heretics said that the Holy Spirit couldn't be God because He is not God's Son. Only sons (and daughters), they said, could share in nature. Since the Spirit proceeds from the Father in a way different from the Son, He could not truly share in the divine nature.

Well, Saint Gregory of Nazianzus had an answer for them. Eve isn't Adam's son, but she shares in the same human nature as Adam. She is not created the same way Adam was, but she is just as human! So it is possible for the Spirit to proceed from the Father in a way different than the Son and still share the divine nature.[17] Moreover, Saint Methodius went on and explained that Eve is created by God and comes from the side of Adam, just as the Spirit proceeds from the Father and the Son. Just as Eve was made from the rib of Adam, Saint Methodius said that the Holy Spirit is the rib of the Word.[18]

Scheeben goes on to show that just as a human mother is the bond of love between a father and son, the Spirit is the bond of love between the Father and Son. A human father begets his son "in the mother," as the Father begets the Son in the Spirit.[19] Scheeben and others, therefore, have noted that the role of the Spirit is often described in bridal and maternal terms.

The Comforter

Consider some of the ways the New Testament descriptions of the Spirit also seem to imply maternal roles.

—Through the Spirit we are born in baptismal water—as human mothers bear their children (Jn. 3:5–6).
—The Spirit is "fruitful" (Gal. 5:22–23).
—The Spirit is spoken of in terms of caring for children (Rom. 8:1–17).

These are only a few. Many other examples could be cited.[20]

Jesus Himself seems to imply a certain maternity of the Holy Spirit, when He says that He will not leave the Church "orphans" as He goes away to be with the Father (Jn. 14:18).[21] An orphan is someone without a father or a mother. Yet Jesus says that the Church will not be left as orphans once He goes to the Father because the Spirit will be with them.

We could also look at the Old Testament where the Spirit is spoken of as "Wisdom" (Wis. 9:17). In this, the Holy Spirit is described in maternal terms in relation to God's faithful ones: "Wisdom exalts her sons and gives help to those who seek her" (Sir. 4:11). In addition, Wisdom is portrayed as a bride, "I desired to take her as my bride, and I became enamored of her beauty" (Wis. 8:2).

Gentle Woman, Peaceful Dove

Saint Maximillian Kolbe described Mary as a kind of human replica of the Spirit. He called the Spirit the true and uncreated "Immaculate Conception," of which Mary is an image.[22] This is because, just as the Father and the Son pour themselves out to each other in the Spirit, so too the Father continues to beget the Son in Mary. When Jesus becomes man, the Trinity's life of love goes on as Jesus continues to offer Himself to the Father through His humanity.

Keep in mind that this offering doesn't simply take place on the Cross. From the moment of His virginal conception Jesus begins to sanctify humanity by offering Himself in His own human nature. This takes place from the moment of His conception, as He dwells in Mary. Jesus offers Himself to the Father in Mary, just as He does through the Spirit. Mary becomes the bond of love between the Father and the Son in human history. Through His overshadowing of her, the Spirit replicates His own Person and work in the Blessed Mother as a kind of human icon of Himself.[23]

Saint Maximilian Kolbe went on to say that the Spirit is so closely united to Mary that He fully dwells in her. He even cautiously calls her the "quasi-incarnation" of the Spirit, although, when he says this, he is clear that he is speaking of "incarnation" in a way different from the way we speak of Jesus as the Incarnate Word.[24] The Spirit was never made flesh like the Son was. Yet the Spirit dwells in the person of Mary as in a temple.

The difference may be stated like this: the Son is not present *in* Jesus—the Son *is* Jesus. The Spirit, however, is *not* Mary. To say so would be heresy and wrong-headedness. But in a very special way, we can say that the Spirit is present *in* the person of Mary.[25]

Holy Mother Church

Mary is the archetype for the Church. This means that by looking at Mary we can come to a better understanding of the Spirit's presence in the Church. Just as the Spirit is powerfully present in the person of Mary, so also is He united with the Church. In the Church, the Son's self-offering to the Father is continued in the lives of the faithful.

This, as we have seen, is the authentic faith of the New Testament. Paul states, "I rejoice in my sufferings for your sake, and in my flesh I complete what is lacking in Christ's afflictions for the sake of His body, that is, the Church" (Col. 1:24). Likewise, in Galatians he says, "I have been crucified with Christ; it is no longer I who live, but Christ who lives in me" (Gal. 2:20).

The Church, then, is taken up into that act of the Trinity's life-giving love. Just as the Son offered Himself to the Father through the Spirit in Mary, the Church, in a similar way, is united to the Spirit as the Son pours out His life to the Father in the Church. Jesus' sacrifice is re-presented through us. In other words, as Christ offers Himself through the suffering of believers, the believer is taken up into the life-giving love of the Trinity.

This can be seen from the words of the third Eucharistic Prayer: "May He make us an everlasting gift to you." What is the gift shared by the Father and Son? It is the Spirit. But what is striking about this prayer is that the Church herself is called the "everlasting gift," shared by the Father and Son. The Church, then, is truly taken into the life of God and is permeated by the Spirit. When the Son pours out His life, He gives over His Spirit. Similarly, Christ presents Himself to the Father through the Spirit in the Church.

Offer It Up

This is helpful for us all. The next time some suffering seems too great, or the next time something is too hard for us to "offer up," we should remember that in refusing to learn life-giving love, we prohibit the Father and the Son from loving each other through us in the Spirit. We refuse to be the temple of their love. What a privilege we turn down!

As the Spirit and Bride say, "Come," those believers who hear the call respond as they receive the Spirit and become a member of Christ's Bride (the Church). John tells us that believers therefore speak in unison with the Spirit and the Bride, uttering the same words, "Come" (Rev. 22:17). Grace cannot be contained. As the believer receives God's life of self-giving love, he then turns to others to share it with them. We see this in Mary—the Visitation follows the Annunciation.

Warning to the Reader

Rev. 22:18–19. 18 I warn every one who hears the words of the prophecy of this book: if any one adds to them, God will add to him the plagues described in this book, 19 and if any one takes away from the words of the book of this prophecy, God will take away his share in the tree of life and in the holy city, which are described in this book.

22:18–19. The warning at the close of the book is very similar to Moses' admonitions throughout Deuteronomy. Moses states: "You shall not add to the words which I command you, nor take from it; that you may keep the commandments of the LORD your God which I command you" (Deut. 4:2). Likewise, at the end of Deuteronomy we read what will happen to those who do not heed Moses' words, "The LORD would not pardon him, but rather the anger of the LORD and his jealousy would smoke against that man, and the curses written in this book would settle upon him, and the LORD would blot out his name from under heaven" (Deut. 29:20).

The Book of Deuteronomy is basically Moses' last sermon. This sermon was given as Israel stood on the plains of Moab, preparing to enter into the Promised Land. Now, as Christians stand at the edge of eternity and prepare to enter into the true Promised Land in heaven, Jesus gives a stern warning as Moses did—you're not there yet; do not fall away before you have entered your reward.

Coming Soon

Rev. 22:20–21. 20 He who testifies to these things says, "Surely I am coming soon." Amen. Come, Lord Jesus!

21 The grace of the Lord Jesus be with all the saints. Amen.

22:20–21. The promise that Jesus is coming soon is strengthened by an oath formula, "Amen." Jesus' coming is assuredly imminent. He is coming in the year 70, with the judgment on Jerusalem. He is also coming soon in the next celebration of the Eucharist. In fact, the very word "Amen" is a liturgical utterance. His coming in the Eucharist makes that coming present to us today.

Moreover, those who follow the Lord have nothing to fear when Jesus comes. Rather, they rejoice at His coming. Because of this the Church voices Her prayer: "Come, Lord Jesus." The book then ends with a prayer for the endurance of God's people—"grace be with all the saints." For it is through God's grace that the Church will learn life-giving love and thus more earnestly pray for the Lord's swift return.

Applying the Lessons of Revelation 21–22 Today

Revelation 21–22 teaches us that the Church is not simply a human reality, but a divine, heavenly reality as well. In a sense, this is related to the two natures of Christ Himself. Jesus is truly God and truly man. Analogously, the Church is truly human but also truly divine, since she shares in the divine life of the Trinity.

This is important for us to realize, especially in our day. Oftentimes, people think of the Church in strictly human terms. They talk about one pope as "conservative" and another as "liberal." They seem to think that the Church's teachings can be changed as easily as the rules for Major League baseball. With this type of thinking, people fail to see the Church's true supernatural identity.

The Church's primary mission is not to amass great wealth or importance. Her primary goal is union with God. Because of this, the Church is often more effective when she is persecuted. Indeed, wherever Christianity is illegal, the faith often flourishes! From all of this, then, we must learn that being a Catholic is more than wearing crosses, having positions at parishes, or going to social get-togethers. While all of these things are important, they are secondary. Our primary purpose is to live our life in self-giving love through the Spirit, who brings us into God's own life—even while we are still here on earth.

* * *

Multiple Choice

1. The prophet Isaiah used the imagery of the "new creation" to describe the _________.
(a) restoration of the kingdom
(b) destruction of Medo-Persia
(c) the celebration of the Passover
(d) the defeat of Babylon

2. To enter into a covenant one must _________.
(a) be sincere
(b) swear an oath
(c) sign a contract
(d) promise not to eat meat

3. The Latin word for "oath" is the word from which we get the term _________.
(a) salvation
(b) redemption
(c) sacrament
(d) vow

4. Covenants make those who enter into them _________.
(a) masters and slaves
(b) members of the same family
(c) good friends
(d) untrustworthy allies

5. The holy city is shaped as a cube, as the _______________ was.
(a) holy of holies
(b) the old Jerusalem

(c) the Upper Room
(d) other Babylon

Answers) 1. a; 2. b; 3. c; 4. b; 5. a.

* * *

Discussion/Study Questions

1. How is the river of life a symbol of the Holy Spirit? (See pages 267–268)

____

____

____

____

2. How is the Holy Spirit both bridal and maternal? How does this help us understand the connection between the "Spirit" and the "Bride"? The relationship of Mary to the Spirit? The Spirit and the Church? Mary and the Church? (See pages 273–277)

____

____

____

____

3. What does John's vision of the Bride of the Lamb teach us about the Church? (See page 258)

____

____

____

____

HINDSIGHT IS TWENTY-TWENTY

Getting the Big Picture

You've finally made it through the entire Book of Revelation. (Unless you simply skimmed the whole book and wanted to find out how it ends.) So now what? Don't worry. It's not important that you remember the historical and scriptural background for every verse in the book. What is important is getting the big picture.

Salvation History: God Rears His Children

As we have seen, the Book of Revelation teaches us one thing above all others. It wants us to see the true nature of the Church as a kingdom of priests—a family of life-giving lovers. In this, the book brings us into the mystery of God Himself.

This was God's goal from all eternity. In fact, the Book of Revelation comes last because it serves as the climax for the whole Bible—for all salvation history. Through it all, God acts as a Father, teaching us how to love Him. Salvation history, then, works as a certain pedagogy, for God's dealings with man represent nothing less than His raising us as His children.[1] Just as human parents discover, this involves a little love, a little discipline, a little child psychology, and a lot of patience.

The "Cliffs Notes" of Genesis

The first book of the Bible is Genesis. There God creates man for covenant relationship with Him; God wants to be our Father. Adam is called to realize this by loving God more than his own life. He fails. Man breaks the covenant relationship.

Later, Abraham comes along and begins man's long trip back home. He learns self-giving love by obediently taking his son Isaac to Mount Moriah to offer him as a sacrifice. This is true life-giving love, since by offering his beloved son, Abraham offered the love of his life. Abraham would have much rather sacrificed himself!

Because of his obedience, Abraham's descendants are blessed. Through them, God promises that all the nations will be blessed (cf. Gen. 22:18). Abraham's son Isaac has a son named Jacob, whose twelve sons become the twelve tribes of Israel. Through this nation God will bless all people.

Israel's Bull-headedness

Unfortunately, there's a snag in the plan. After entering into a covenant with God on Mount Sinai, Israel sins by worshipping the golden calf. This means Israel isn't quite ready to evangelize the nations. They themselves need to be rehabilitated before they can reconcile the nations. As a result, God gives Israel a "lower law," contained in the Levitical Law code and, later, in the Book of Deuteronomy.

Why does God command animal sacrifice? God tells Israel to sacrifice bulls and calves because that is what they were worshipping. Remember, it was a golden *calf.* God is like a Father teaching His children. "You're really sorry for worshipping a calf instead of me? Really? Well, show me. Prove it. Give me the calf." Because of this, Saint Paul calls the Law a "custodian," or "pedagogue"—a child's tutor (Gal. 3:24).[2]

Now, this wasn't the best law. Ezekiel even says that the Deuteronomic covenant was a "law that was not good:" "I gave them statutes that were not good and ordinances by which they could not have life" (Ezek. 20:25). These laws were simply meant to rehabilitate Israel so they would be strong enough to evangelize the nations.

What do we mean by "strong enough"? How difficult could it be to evangelize the nations? Evidently, more difficult than Israel realized. God's children go out to the nations, but instead of changing them, they start worshipping the other nations' gods! So God has to quarantine them. He has to be really strict. He has to make sure that they learn not to be influenced by the nations.

Therefore, God gives them these laws to keep them from imitating the nations.[3] They can't even wear "mixed fibers" because that is what the nations do (Deut. 22:11).

Is God crazy? No, He's a good Father (actually, He's the best). Television isn't always bad, but if children abuse it, parents might take it away from them. Friends aren't bad, but if the neighbor's kids start having a bad influence on your children, then your children ought not play with them. So too with God—He works with His children to lead them in right paths.

Jesse's Boy

Then the time came for God to start reaching out again, through Israel, to the nations. This happened in David. In many ways, David fulfills the Law of Deuteronomy, especially in "achieving rest" from God's enemies and preparing the way for the building of a temple (cf. 2 Sam. 7:1; Deut. 12:10–11; 17:14–15).[4] When David's son, Solomon, begins to reign, the temple is built, and the nations start streaming to Jerusalem to learn from him.

Unfortunately, that was short-lived. With a few notable exceptions, the Davidic kings turn from God and desire to have an earthly kingdom, just like the nations. Instead of setting their minds on spreading God's covenant, they seek to increase their earthly wealth and power. Israel was therefore taken off into exile. Only the southern tribes returned.

Living in the Past

Finally, Jesus comes and restores the kingdom. Furthermore, by offering Himself in life-giving love and bearing the covenant curses, Jesus makes the Levitical Law obsolete. It's no longer necessary.[5] He makes it possible for us to live as sons of God, giving us grace to enable us to become life-giving lovers. The training wheels are ready to come off. But some people aren't willing to let them go.

Some still preferred the earthly temple to the true Temple. Some still wanted to keep the Levitical system. By the time AD 70 came along, people were rallying to stay and fight for the earthly temple.

From AD 30 to 70 there was a certain kind of spiritual wandering, much like that of the Israelites in the desert. Christians had to decide whether they wanted "Egypt" or the heavenly Promised Land. The old had been made obsolete, and they couldn't have both. It was time to decide. The question was: How strong is your faith? Do you stay and fight with your Jewish relatives and friends, or do you flee to the mountains with the other Christians, as Jesus instructed (cf. Mt. 24:16; Lk. 21:21). Earthly or heavenly, which will it be? There's no in-between.

The Choice Is Yours

This is the same lesson God wants to teach us today. This earthly life is temporary and penultimate. It must be offered up in love. Only in learning this will we enter into our true heavenly homeland.

Yet, like those Jews who rejected Jesus and clung to the earthly city, we also can forfeit our heavenly reward by becoming attached to this life and its goods. The temple was glorious. The city was ancient. It was truly spectacular. But when "the good" becomes the enemy of "the best" it all becomes corrupted, thereby becoming evil.

The year 70 is part of salvation history. It's part of God's pedagogy—the education of His children. It teaches us to look behind the earthly realities and see that what really counts is the heavenly ones.

The Father Knows Best

The entire Bible, therefore, is connected. It recounts God the Father's saving plan to bring us to our true goal—heavenly life with Him. The New Testament doesn't use the Old Testament as a kind of "proof text"—it's part of the same story. "Saint Augustine said that the New Testament is concealed in the Old, and the Old is revealed in the New. For all history was the world's preparation for the moment when the Word was made flesh."[6]

In fact, as we've read through the Book of Revelation, we've seen how everything is connected. Jesus comes as the Son of David to restore the kingdom. He brings about the New Exodus, ending the Exile. In this restoration of the kingdom of Israel, He is like Moses. He is also like the son of man in the Book of Daniel, since the Son of Man received the kingdom and gives it to the saints. The prophets' words are fulfilled and history comes together as God fulfills His plan.

This knowledge should lead us to a deeper love of Scripture. By examining the first Exodus, where Israel was led out of slavery, through the wilderness to the Promised Land, we come to better understand our life on earth. We see we are pilgrims in this world, just passing through, headed toward the true Promised Land. By meditating on the second Exodus, we come to understand that we are in exile, and away from home. So we pray, "Pray for us, O Holy Mother of God, and after this our exile, show unto us the fruit of thy womb, Jesus."

By contemplating the way God reveals His plan for us in Scripture, we will come to a deeper appreciation of who God is as Father, and how He deals with us as His children. Furthermore, this will help us to understand our present sufferings. Once we see that God is a Trinity of life-giving Lovers, we will understand more clearly why His Son gave His life and why He asks us to do the same.

Finally, in studying Revelation, we learn that we prepare for Christ's Second Coming as we receive His coming in the Mass. Through Him, with Him, and in Him, we offer ourselves in communion with Christ, entering into the Trinity's life of love, praying, "May He make us an everlasting gift to You, and enable us to share in the inheritance of the saints" (Eucharistic Prayer III).

NOTES

Introduction

[1] Cf. *Catechism*, nos. 112–14; Second Vatican Council, Dogmatic Constitution on Divine Revelation *Dei Verbum* (November 18, 1965), no. 12.

Chapter 1

[1] Scholars are divided on the issue of authorship of Revelation. The argument which I develop in this chapter has both a long history of acceptance in the Church and is based on sound scholarship, as I will demonstrate. However, in this brief summary it is impossible to fully explore the various arguments on authorship and their possible validity.

[2] Eusebius, *The History of the Church*, bk. 3, chap. 39, no. 4, trans. G. A. Williamson (Harmondsworth, Middlesex, England: Penguin Books Ltd., 1965), emphasis added.

[3] Even if Papias wrote about a different John (whose existence we must recognize as possible, as Saint Jerome did, though Saint Jerome believed that John the Apostle wrote the Apocalypse [see Saint Jerome, *Against Jovinianus,* bk. 1, chap. 26, available from http://www.ccel.org]), Papias *never* says that this second John wrote Revelation.

[4] For a full discussion of these matters, see Donald Guthrie, *New Testament Introduction,* 3rd ed., rev. (Downers Grove, IL: Inter-Varsity Press, 1970), 887–89, 932–48; and Warren Dicharry, *Paul and John* (Collegeville, MN: Liturgical Press, 1992), 207–8.

[5] Saint Dionysius of Alexandria, in Eusebius, *The History of the Church*, bk. 7, chap. 25.

[6] "[T]here was a certain man with us, whose name was John, one of the apostles of Christ, who prophesied by a revelation that was made to him." Saint Justin, *Dialogue with Trypho*, chap. LXXXI, available from http://www.newadvent.org.

Speaking of Revelation 1, Saint Irenaeus writes: "When John could not endure the sight . . . the Word revived him. Christ reminded him that it was He upon whose bosom he had leaned at supper." *Against Heresies,* bk. 4, chap. 20, no. 11, available from http://www.ccel.org.

"And although here upon earth a spiritual man is not honored with the chief seat, he will sit down on the twenty-four thrones, judging the people, as John says in the Apocalypse." Clement of Alexandria, *Stromata* (or *Miscellanies*), bk. 6, chap. 13, available from http://www.newadvent.org.

"The King of the Romans, as tradition teaches, condemned John, who bore testimony, on account of the word of truth, to the isle of Patmos. John, moreover, teaches us things respecting his testimony [i.e., martyrdom], without saying who condemned him when he utters these things in the Apocalypse. He seems also to have seen the Apocalypse . . . in the island." Origen, *Commentary on Matthew*, 16:6, as quoted in Kenneth Gentry, *The Beast of Revelation* (Tyler, TX: Institute for Christian Economics, 1994), 156–57.

"Now the Apostle John, in the Apocalypse, describes a sword which proceeded from the mouth of God as 'a doubly sharp, two-edged one.'" Tertullian, *The Five Books Against Marcion,* bk. 3, chap. 14, available from http://www.ccel.org.

"For he sees, when in the isle Patmos, a revelation of awful mysteries, which he recounts freely, and makes known to others. Tell me, blessed John, apostle and disciple of the Lord, what didst thou see and hear concerning Babylon?" Saint Hippolytus, *Treatise on Christ and Antichrist,* no. 36, available from http://www.ccel.org.

Epiphanius of Salamis speaks about John and the "prophetic word according to the Apocalypse being disclosed." As quoted in Gentry, *The Beast of Revelation,* 145.

Saint Jerome writes that John was an "Apostle, because he wrote to the churches as a master; an Evangelist, because he composed a Gospel . . . a prophet, for he saw in the island of Patmos . . . an Apocalypse." *Against Jovinianus,* bk. 1, chap. 26, available from http://www.ccel.org.

[7] See Eusebius, *Ecclesiastical History,* bk. 3, chap. 1; the Arabic canons of Nicea; Gregory of Nazianzen, Oration XXIII; Jerome, *Lives of Illustrious Men,* chap. IX, XVII, XVIII, available from http://www.ccel.org; Tertullian, *Prescriptions Against Heretics,* chap. 32 in *Ante-Nicene Fathers,* vol. 3, ed. Alexander Roberts and James Donaldson (Peabody, MA: Hendrickson, 1994), 258.

[8] Some scholars assert that the author simply wanted his readers to think he was an apostle, even though he was not. Those who offer this view have little or no external evidence to support it; it is based on conjecture.

Other scholars have noted that documents written pseudepigraphically (under a false name) identify their author not just by his name, but also by his title, to underscore his authority. Hence, if someone pretending to be John wrote the Book of Revelation, he would have written that he was "John the Apostle," not simply "John" (Rev. 1:1). For a scholarly rejection of this position, see R. H. Charles *A Critical and Exegetical Commentary of the Revelation of Saint John: With Introduction Notes and Indices,* vol. 1 (Edinburgh: T & T Clark, 1920; reprint 1984), xxxviiiff., and G. K. Beale, *The Book of Revelation* (Grand Rapids, MI.: William B. Eerdmanns, 1999), 34.

Furthermore, contrary to popular opinion, writing a book under an apostolic pseudonym was not an accepted practice of the early Church. Although several books that claimed apostolic authorship were circulated, these books were discarded whenever the truth of their authorship was discovered. When one bishop, for example, out of love for Paul, wrote a pseudepigraphical *3 Corinthians,* the Asian bishops deposed him. In fact, several pseudepigraphical works were discarded not because of doctrinal objections, but because they were judged to be not truly apostolic. For further discussion, see E. Earle Ellis, "Pseudonymity and Canonicity of New Testament Documents," in *Worship, Theology, and Ministry in the Early Church: Essays in Honour of Ralph P. Martin,* ed. M. J. Wilkins and T. Paige (Sheffield: JSOT, 1992), 212–24.

[9] For further discussion of the similarities between the two books, see Warren Austin Gage, *St. John's Vision of the Heavenly City* (Ann Arbor, MI: UMI Dissertation Services, 2001). See also Guthrie, *New Testament Introduction,* 939; Beale, *The Book of Revelation,* (Grand Rapids, MI: William B. Eerdmanns, 1999), 35; S. S. Smalley, "John's Revelation and John's Community," *Bulletin of the John Rylands University Library* 69 (1987): 549–71; C. G. Ozanne, "The Language of the Apocalypse," *Tyndale House Bulletin* 16 (1965): 3–9; Scott Hahn, *The Lamb's Supper* (New York: Doubleday, 1999), 74; Andre Feuillet, *The Apocalypse* (Staten Island, NY: Alba House, 1964), 104–5.

[10] Those who take the later "Domitian" view begin by pointing to the testimony of St. Irenaeus, who appears to say that John wrote the Apocalypse in the 90s. It must be noted however that Irenaeus' words aren't exactly clear and some scholars doubt that he actually meant to date Revelation to 90s. See, for example, Kenneth Gentry, *Before Jerusalem Fell* (Atlanta, GA: American Vision, 1998), 41-67. Nevertheless, *even if* it were clear that Irenaeus meant to say that John wrote Revelation in the 90s, we would still have good grounds to be suspicious of his claim since Irenaeus was a notoriously poor historian. For example, Irenaeus insisted that Christ died at the age of 50—a view *no one* accepts as reliable. So, while a great theologian, Ireneaus' historical claims may be misleading. Though it is true that many early Fathers held to a 90s date for Revelation, those who did so based their opinion on Irenaeus' words and therefore are only as reliable as he was. See Milton Terry, *Biblical Hermeneutics* (Eugene, OR: Wipf and Stock Publishers, 1999), 135: "When we scrutinize the character and extent of this evidence, it seems equally clear that no very great stress can safely be laid upon it. For it all turns upon the single testimony of Irenaeus." Even late date advocates are aware of the fact that the testimony of the later Fathers is dependent on Irenaeus' statement. David Aune, for example, explains that subsequent patristic testimony is "dependent on Irenaeus." David Aune, Word *Biblical Commentary: Revelation 1-5* (Dallas, TX: Word Books, 1997), lviii.

[11] Gentry, *The Beast of Revelation*, 146.

[12] Clement of Alexandria, *Who Is the Rich Man That Shall Be Saved?* in *The Beast of Revelation,* 157.

[13] See Leonard L. Thompson who, though taking a Domitianic date, admits: "Most modern commentators no longer accept a Domitianic persecution of Christians." *The Book of Revelation: Apocalypse and Empire* (New York: Oxford University Press, 1990), 16; see also Leon Hardy Canfield, *The Early Persecutions of the Christians* (New York: Columbia University Press, 1913), 162, who states that if Revelation does refer to a persecution under Domitian, "it is the only source for such a persecution." Also see Beale, 12; Leon Morris, *Revelation* (Grand Rapids, MI: Inter-Varsity Press, reprinted 2000), 33.

[14] Pliny, *Natural History,* bk. 7 chap. 45; bk. 22, chap. 92, in Gentry, *Before Jerusalem Fell,* 69–70.

[15] Philostratus, *Life of Apollonius,* bk. 4, chap. 38, in Gentry, *Before Jerusalem Fell,* 70.

[16] Tacitus, *Histories,* in Gentry, *Before Jerusalem Fell,* 70.

[17] Suetonius, *De Vita Caesarum Nero*, no. 5, trans. J. C. Rolfe, available from http://www.fordham.edu/halsall/ancient/suet-nero-rolfe.html.

[18] Angus, "Nero" in *The International Standard Bible Encyclopedia,* James Orr, ed., (Grand Rapids, MI: Eerdmans, 1956), 3:2134.

[19] Suetonius, *De Vita Caesarum Nero,* no. 28–29.

[20] Eusebius, *Ecclesiastical History,* bk. 2, chap. 25. Clement of Alexandria, *Stomata,* bk. 7, chap. 17, available from http://www.newadvent.org; Jerome, *Letter LXVIII to Castrutius,* no. 1, available from http://www.newadvent.org.

[21] Tacitus, *Annals,* XV, 44, available from http://classics.mit.edu.

[22] Suetonius, *De Vita Caesarum Nero,* no. 49.

[23] Adapted from Gentry, *Before Jerusalem Fell*, 158. Among the ancient writers whom Gentry cites to support this enumeration are Flavius Josephus, *Antiquities of the Jews*, bk. 18, chap. 2, no. 2, and chap. 6, no. 10; Suetonius, *The Lives of the Twelve Caesars*; Theophilus of Antioch, *Theophilus to Autolycus*, bk. 3, chap. 27. For a full discussion of the evidence, see *Before Jerusalem Fell*, 152–59.

[24] Henry Barclay Swete, *The Apocalypse of St. John* (Reprinted: Eugene, OR.: *Wipf and Stock*, 1998), 176; Moses Stuart, *Commentary on the Apocalypse*, vol. 2 (Andover: Allen, Morrill, and Wardwell, 1845), 457; F. J. Hort, *The Apocalypse of St. John: I–III* (London: MacMillan, 1908), p. xxxi; Gentry, *Before Jerusalem Fell*, 199.

Chapter 2

[1] Scott Hahn and Curtis Mitch, *Ignatius Catholic Study Bible: The Gospel of Matthew* (San Francisco, CA: Ignatius Press, 2000), 62.

[2] Second Vatican Council, Dogmatic Constitution on Divine Revelation *Dei Verbum* (November 18, 1965), no. 19.

[3] Pius XII, Encyclical on Promoting Biblical Studies *Divino Afflante Spiritu* (September 30, 1943), 23.

[4] "It is interesting to note that even the word 'economy' has a familial meaning. It comes from the Greek words *oikos* (home) and *nomos* (law). Creation's economy is the law of God's household. It's how He fathers His family throughout salvation history." Scott Hahn, *First Comes Love* (New York: Doubleday, 2002), 41.

[5] "The fact is that the Temple and the world, God's localization and his ubiquity, are not *generally* perceived in the Hebrew Bible as standing in tension. On the contrary, the Temple is the epitome of the world, a concentrated form of its essence, a miniature of the cosmos. . . . [T]he temple is not a place in the world, but the world in essence. It is the theology of creation rendered in architecture and glyptic craftsmanship. In the Temple, God relates simultaneously to the entire cosmos, for the Temple . . . is a microcosm of which the world itself is the macrocosm." Jon D. Levenson, *Sinai and Zion: An Entry into the Jewish Bible* (Minneapolis: Winston Press, 1985), 138–39. See also Meredith Kline, *Images of the Spirit* (Eugene, OR: Wipf and Stock Publishers, 1998), 35, 37: "The earth-cosmos was made after the archetypal pattern of the Glory-Spirit referred to in Genesis 1:2 and accordingly is viewed in Scripture as a cosmic royal residence or temple. . . . The history of the exodus, culminating in the building of the tabernacle, is so recounted as to bring out its nature as a redemptive reenactment of creation."

[6] While Matthew's and Mark's account may refer to the flight to Pella, the great Italian scholar Eugenio Corsini believes that Luke's account focuses on something different: "What Jesus commands and advises is not a flight from a besieged Jerusalem, but the abandoning of Judaism and its cult. The break with Judaism, so long avoided despite his many difficult encounters with it, now becomes inevitable for Jesus, as he looks forward to the final breach caused by his being slain by them." *The Apocalypse: The Perennial Revelation of Jesus Christ* (Wilmington, DE: Michael Glazier, 1983), 57–58.

[7] When the Romans launched fiery missiles over the walls of the city, the watchmen shouted, "The son cometh." Josephus, *The Wars of the Jews*, bk. 5, chap. 6, no. 3, in *The Works of Josephus*, trans. William Whiston (Peabody, MA: Hendrickson, 1998).

[8] Pius XI, *To the Directors of the Belgium Catholic Radio Agency* (1938), as quoted in *New Catholic Encyclopedia*, s.v. "anti-Semitism."

[9] Second Vatican Council, Declaration on the Relation of the Church to Non-Christian Religions *Nostra Aetate* (October 28, 1965), no. 4.

Chapter 3

[1] N. T. Wright, a well-respected biblical scholar, argues that there is ample historical evidence to convince even critical exegetes that Jesus foretold the destruction of Jerusalem in AD 70. See *Jesus and the Victory of God* (Minneapolis, MN: Fortress Press, 1996), 320–68.

[2] For the most comprehensive Catholic treatment on the rapture, I strongly recommend David Currie, *Rapture: The End Time Error That Leaves the Bible Behind* (Manchester, MA: Sophia Press, 2003).

[3] "Two structural features of the Apocalypse predispose us toward finding in this strange document at least allusory references to eucharistic meals. . . . [M]ost of John's visions have to do with scenes of worship in the heavenly sanctuary. Numerous hymns are sung (a phenomena otherwise unattested in the apocalyptic literature known to us), and full homage is paid not only to God the Creator but also to the Lamb enthroned. . . . [Passages like Revelation 3:20] strongly suggest that eucharistic liturgies on earth formed a basic part of John's consciousness and that of his readers." John Koenig, *The Feast of the World's Redemption: Eucharistic Origins and Christian Mission* (Harrisburg, PA: Trinity Press International, 2000), 167–68.

[4] Joseph Cardinal Ratzinger (later Pope Benedict XVI), *The Spirit of the Liturgy* (San Francisco: Ignatius Press, 2000), 185–86.

[5] Hahn, *Lamb's Supper*, 119–20.

[6] Ibid.,120–21.

[7] Joseph Cardinal Ratzinger, *Eschatology: Death and Eternal Life*, trans. Michael Waldstein (Washington, DC: Catholic University Press, 1988), 203. Also see Francois-Xavier Durwell, "Eucharist and Parousia: The Fundamental Basis of the Interpretation of the Real Presence," *Lumen* 26 (1970): 296. He writes, "And so when [Jesus] comes to us, his advent is parousiac. When he avails himself of matter of worldly creation, bread and wine, for his coming, he is acting through his eschatological power, power which he wields as being the culmination and fullness of the world, a cosmic power which he possesses as being the cosmic plentitude."

[8] Cf. Hahn, *The Lamb's Supper*, 35.

[9] Second Vatican Council, The Constitution on the Sacred Liturgy *Sacrosanctum Concilium* (December 4, 1963), no. 8.

[10] "When this arrangement of the assembly was first adopted is unknown. But it must have been well within the first century, for not only is it the absolutely universal later traditional arrangement, but it is clearly reflected in the symbolism of the heavenly 'assembly' of the church triumphant—the real 'assembly' of which all earthly churches are only symbols and foreshadowings—in the visions of the Revelation of S. John." Gregory Dix, *The Shape of the Liturgy* (London: Dacre Press, 1945), 28.

[11] Ibid.

[12] Joseph Cardinal Ratzinger, *The Spirit of the Liturgy* (San Francisco: Ignatius Press, 2000), 185–86.

Chapter 4

[1] See Saint Augustine, Tractate CXXII, chap. 21, no. 8, available from http://www.newadvent.org. The "seven spirits" may also be linked with the sevenfold gifts of the Spirit in Isaiah 11. See Saint Ambrose, *On The Holy Spirit to the Emperor Gratian*, bk. 1, chap. 16, in *Nicene and Post-Nicene Fathers*, vol. 10, 2nd ser., eds. Philip Schaff and Henry Wace (Peabody, MA: Hendrickson, 1994), 114: "And let it not trouble you that either here it is said 'rivers,' or elsewhere 'seven Spirits,' for by the sanctification of these seven gifts of the Spirit, as Isaiah said, is signified the fullness of all virtue; the Spirit of wisdom and understanding, the Spirit of counsel and strength, the Spirit of knowledge and godliness, and the Spirit of the fear of God." Also see modern commentators such as G. B. Caird, *The Revelation of St. John* (London: A & C Black, 1966; repr., Peabody, MA: Hendrickson Publishers, 1999), 15; T. F. Glasson, *The Revelation of John* (Cambridge: Cambridge University Press, 1965), 17; J. Massyngberde Ford, *The Anchor Bible: Revelation* (New York: Doubleday, 1975), 377.

[2] For a full discussion, see Scott Hahn, *Kinship by Covenant: A Biblical Theological Study of Covenant Types and Texts in the Old and New Testaments* (Ann Arbor: UMI Dissertation Services, 1995), 212–304; Michael Barber, *Singing in the Reign: The Psalms and the Liturgy of God's Kingdom* (Steubenville, OH: Emmaus Road Publishing, 2001), 42.

[3] For a fuller discussion on Adam's calling as the "son of God" see my *Singing in the Reign,* 40.

[4] Hahn, *First Comes Love,* 73.

[5] For further reflection, see Hahn, *First Comes Love.*

[6] Dexter E. Callender, *Adam in Myth and History: Ancient Israelite Perspectives on the Primal Human* (Winona Lake, IN: Eisenbrauns, 2000), 50–54; Austin Gage, *The Gospel of Genesis: Studies in Protology and Eschatology* (Winona Lake, IN: Carpenter Books, 1984), 57.

[7] The phrase "coming in the clouds" is also an allusion to Daniel 7:13. We will look at this passage in greater depth when we come to Rev. 1:12–18. Suffice it to say for now, Daniel 7 speaks of one "like a son of man," from whom the saints receive the kingdom. This passage fits nicely then with what John just said in Revelation 1:6, that is, that Christ has made the Church "a *kingdom* of priests."

[8] For a discussion on the Glory-cloud as a manifestation of the Holy Spirit, see Meredith Kline, *Images of the Spirit* (Eugene, OR: Wipf and Stock, 1998), 15: "There is indeed a considerable amount of biblical data that identify the Glory-cloud as peculiarly a manifestation of the Spirit of God. Here we will cite only a few passages where the functions performed by the Glory-cloud are attributed to the Spirit—Nehemiah 9:19, 20; Isaiah 63:11–14; and Haggai 2:5—and mention the correspondence of the work of the Holy Spirit at Pentecost to the functioning of the Glory-cloud at the exodus and at the erection of the tabernacle."

[9] For a great treatment of the "kingdom" in Acts, see Stephen Pimentel, *Witnesses of the Messiah: On Acts of the Apostles 1–15* (Steubenville, OH: Emmaus Road, 2002).

[10] For a fuller treatment of the importance of the Davidic Covenant see Barber, *Singing in the Reign*, 39–57.

[11] Also see Jer. 4:19, 21; 6:1, 17; 42:14; Ezek. 33:3–6; Hos. 8:1; Joel 2:1.

[12] Also see Lev. 23:24; 25:9; Num. 29:1; 2 Chron. 5:12–13; 7:6; 29:27–28; Ps. 150:3.

[13] See Aune, *Revelation 1–5*, 87.

[14] Robert Briggs, *Jewish Temple Imagery in the Book of Revelation* (New York: Peter Lang, 1999), 55–66. Also see Leonard Thompson, *The Book of Revelation: Apocalypse and Empire* (New York: Oxford University Press, 1990), 70.

[15] Some have seen "one like a son of man" as a reference to the divinity of Christ—in other words, Christ is not just a son of man, but more than that. We must be careful, however, that we don't put too much emphasis on this because it could lead to a heretical view that Christ was not both truly God and man.

[16] Some scholars object to the identification of Christ's garments as priestly noting that the word that occurs here, *podárás*, is not the word that is most frequently used to describe the high priest's attire, *chitôn*. However, this neglects the fact that *podárás* is sometimes used to describe the priestly attire of the priest as well (cf. Ex. 25:7, 28:4, 35:9; Wis. 18:24; Sir. 27:8; 45:8). Moreover, given the surrounding temple imagery of the lampstands, it is harder to believe that John is using some other image of Jesus (e.g., that as a god such as Apollo) than it is to simply recognize a cultic allusion here.

[17] Josephus, *Antiquities of the Jews*, bk. 3, chap. 7, nos. 1–2. Also see Sir. 45:6–12 and Wis. 18:24.

[18] Beale, *The Book of Revelation*, 208.

[19] For an in-depth study of the relationship between the lampstands and the stars, see Beale, *The Book of Revelation*, 211.

There may also be a secondary sense in which the seven stars refer to the seven-star cluster called the Pleiades, which forms part of the constellation of Taurus. This cluster is mentioned in Job 9:5–9; 38:31–33 and Amos 5:8. During the spring the sun is with Taurus, and thus the Pleiades may function as an Easter symbol of resurrection and rebirth. David Chilton, *Days of Vengeance: An Exposition of the Book of Revelation* (Tyler, TX: Dominion Press, 1987), 75.

[20] Chilton, *Days of Vengeance*, 76.

[21] That is from the version of the Septuagint found in what is called Codex B. See Beale, *The Book of Revelation*, 212. Beale points out the connection between the victorious warrior in Daniel and Judges, and Christ as He appears in Revelation 1:16.

[22] "*Midr. Rab.* Gen. 12:6; *Midr. Rab.* Lev. 28:1; *Midr. Rab.* Num. 13:12; *Midr.* Ps 11:6 and 49:1; *Tannah Debe Eliyyahu* 16; *Pesikta de Rab Kahana* 8; *Pesikta Rabbati* 18.1 and 48.3; and *Sifre* Deut. 10 and 47 apply Judg. 5:31 to God's renewal of the faces of the righteous in the world to come (*Midr.* Ps. 11:6 and *Sifre* Deut. 10 and 47 combine Judg. 5:31 with Dan. 12:3)." Beale, *The Book of Revelation*, 213.

[23] This is also found in the Theodotian LXX Dan 4:34; 6:27; 12:7. See Beale, *The Book of Revelation*, 103.

[24] See James Charlesworth, ed., *The Old Testament Pseudepigrapha*, vol. 1 (New York: Doubleday, 1998), 14.

[25] See Caird, *The Revelation of St. John*, 26.

[26] See Beale, *The Book of Revelation*, 217; Aune, *Revelation 1–5*, 108; Leon Morris, *Revelation* (Grand Rapids, MI: Intervarsity Press, reprinted 2000), 56. Furthermore, angels are frequently associated with stars (cf. Judg. 5:20; Job 38:7; Is. 14:14; Jude 13; Rev. 8:10–12; 9:1; 12:4).

[27] Beale, *The Book of Revelation*, 218.

Chapter 5

[1] Canon Muratorianus, no. 3, trans. Roberts-Donaldson, *Ante-Nicene Fathers*, vol. 5, www.earlychristianwritings.com.

[2] Adapted from P. S. Minear, *I Saw A New Earth: An Introduction to the Visions of the Apocalypse* (Washington, OR: Corpus Press, 1969), 59–61. Also see Gage, *St. John's Vision*, 23.

[3] Beale, *The Book of Revelation,* 229; Morris, *Revelation,* 58.

[4] L. M. McDonald, "Ephesus," in *Dictionary of the Background of the New Testament*, eds. Craig Evans and Stanley Porter (Downers Grove, IL: Intervarsity Press, 2000), 319.

"Ephesus was also the center of the imperial cult, boasting six imperial temples, one honoring Roma and Julius Caesar, two honoring Augustus, one honoring Domitian, and two honoring Hadrian." Aune, *Revelation*, 154. Also see S. R. Price, *Rituals and Power: The Roman Imperial Cult in Asia Minor* (Cambridge: Cambridge University Press, 1984), 254–56.

[5] R. H. Charles, *The Revelation of St. John*, vol. 1, 48; J. Massyngberde Ford, *The Anchor Bible: Revelation*, 389; Beale, *The Book of Revelation*, 233.

[6] William Hendriksen, *More Than Conquerors: An Interpretation of the Book of Revelation* (Grand Rapids, MI: Baker Book House, 1962), 61.

[7] This was mentioned by the Council of Ephesus. Also see Aune, *Revelation,* 140–41.

[8] Chilton, *Days of Vengeance,* 97.

[9] Cf. Irenaeus, *Against Heresies*, bk. 1, chap. 26, no. 3; bk. 3, chap. 11, no. 1, http://www.ccel.org; Hippolytus, *Heresies,* bk. 7, chap. 24, http://www.newadvent.org.

[10] Beale, *The Book of Revelation*, 235.

[11] Aphrahat, *Demonstration* VI, no. 6, http://www.ccel.org.

[12] See *The Martyrdom of Polycarp*, chap. 12, in *ANF*, vol. 1, 41; Charles, *The Revelation of St. John*, 56–58.

[13] The interpretation given above is the meaning understood by most commentators and is supported by passages such as Romans 2:29: "He is a Jew who is one inwardly, and real circumcision is a matter of the heart, spiritual and not literal." The members of Qumran, who opposed the corrupt Jewish leadership in Jerusalem, referred to them as "a congregation of Belial" (1 QH 2:22). Other scholars see the reference to "a synagogue of Satan" as a description of certain Jewish synagogues that worshipped pagan gods and combined elements of mystical religions into their own beliefs. See Ford, *Revelation*, 393. However, this interpretation is not well attested and it is not known for certain that such synagogues existed in Smyrna.

[14] This interpretation receives support from an analysis of the Greek text: "The juxtaposition of aorist and future verbs here is significant. The aorist subjunctive is used because the aorist summarizes the meaning that the Smyrnaean Christians will derive from the whole persecution experience, i.e., *testing*, while in the future indicative the future tense focuses simply on the element of anticipation: it will be limited to 'ten' days." Aune, *Revelation,* 166.

[15] Pliny, *Natural History*, 5.126

[16] Aune, *Revelation*, 194.

[17] See Charles, *The Revelation of St. John*, 61–62; Richard C. Trench, *Commentary on the Epistles to the Seven Churches in Asia Minor* (London: Macmill, 1883; repr. Eugene, OR: Wipf and Stock Publishers, 1997), 116.

[18] Aune, *Revelation*, 194.

[19] Beale, *The Book of Revelation*, 246.

[20] Indeed, Revelation 12 describes Satan as "the ancient serpent" (12:9).

[21] See Trench, *Commentary on the Epistles to the Seven Churches* , 82–83; Chilton, *Days of Vengeance,* 107.

[22] Hendriksen, *More Than Conquerors,* 60.

[23] Saint Paul describes the manna in connection with the Church's Eucharistic celebration (cf. 1 Cor. 10:1–4, 16–21). Likewise, the Fathers like Ephrem spoke of the Eucharist in terms of "manna." Ephrem writes, "Earthly creatures consumed the heavenly Manna—and they became dust on the earth, because of their sins. The spiritual Bread of the Eucharist makes light and causes to fly." *Unleavened Bread* 27:8–12, as quoted in Sebastian Brock, *The Luminous Eye: The Spiritual World Vision of Saint Ephrem the Syrian* (Kalamazoo, MI: Cistercian Publications, 1985), 101.

[24] Cf. Chilton, *Days of Vengeance,* 110; also see Beale, *The Book of Revelation*, 253, who points to *Midr.* Ps. 78:4 and *B. Yoma* 75a.

[25] There are problems, though, with seeing the stone in connection with the stones worn by the high priest, since they were onyx, which is black. Nonetheless, it is possible that John is combining imagery of the "bdellium" with the "onyx." See Chilton, *Days of Vengeance,* 110.

[26] This idea is also found in the non-biblical book, *The Testament of Levi*, no. 8, in which Levi prophecies to his children that "a new name shall be called over Him because He shall arise as king over Judah, and shall establish a new priesthood, after the fashion of the Gentiles, to all the Gentiles," http://www.ccel.org.

[27] Swete, *The Apocalypse of St. John*, 40.

[28] "Refusing to partake of idol-meats, and especially refusal to attend the heathen feasts, meant withdrawal from a great part of the whole social life of that time. For one thing, the trades had their tutelary deities, which would be worshipped at the feasts. Refusal to join in these feasts often meant that a man would lose his job, his trade; he would become an outcast. Hence, some people began to argue that, after all, one might attend the feasts and partake of meats offered to idols, and perhaps even offer incense to the gods of the heathen, provided that he constantly bear in mind—a kind of mental reser-

vation—that an idol is nothing! Others might carry this line of reasoning even farther and say, 'How can you condemn and defeat Satan unless you have become thoroughly acquainted with him?'" Hendriksen, *More Than Conquerors*, 67.

[29] Chilton, *Days of Vengeance*, 114.

[30] In regard to Catholic apologetics, it is important that Jesus says that He will give to us in accord with our "works," not simply our "faith." This poses a problem for traditional Protestantism, which holds that we are saved by our faith alone.

[31] David Aune, "Religion, Greco-Roman," in *Dictionary of New Testament Background*, 924–25.

[32] The "bonds" that are burst (Ps. 2:3), are an image for covenant relationship. See Dennis J. McCarthy, *Treaty and Covenant* (Rome: Biblical Institute Press, 1981), 75.

[33] J. A. Harrill, "Asia Minor," in *Dictionary of New Testament Background*, 132.

[34] See Jean Daniélou, *The Bible and the Liturgy* (Notre Dame, IN: University of Notre Dame Press, 1956), 49. Daniélou examines the early Church's Baptismal rite, saying: "After the rite of Baptism itself, there is still one final ceremony: the clothing with the white garment. 'After Baptism,' says St. Ambrose, 'you have received white garments, that they may be the sign that you have taken off the clothing of sin and that you have been clad in the pure garments of innocence (De Myst. 34).'"

[35] Swete, *The Apocalypse of St. John*, 52.

[36] Beale, *The Book of Revelation*, 286; Charles, *The Revelation of St. John*, 85; Robert L. Thomas, *Revelation 1–7: An Exegetical Commentary* (Chicago, IL: Moody Press, 1992), 280.

[37] For more on the "key," see the commentary on Rev. 20:1–3 in chapter 13.

[38] For a full discussion on Matthew 16:16–19 and the papacy, see Stephen K. Ray, *Upon This Rock: St. Peter and the Primacy of Rome in Scripture and the Early Church* (San Francisco: Ignatius Press, 1999). Scott Butler, et al. *Jesus, Peter and the Keys: A Scriptural Handbook on the Papacy* (Santa Barbara, CA: Queenship Publishing, Co. 1996).

[39] *The Demurrer against the Heretics*, in William Jurgens, *Faith of the Early Fathers*, vol. 1 (Collegeville, MN: Liturgical Press, 1970), 122.

[40] *Against Heresies*, bk. 3, chap. 3, no. 3, http://www.ccel.org.

[41] Chilton, *Days of Vengeance*, 134; Thomas, *Revelation 1–7*, 305; Morris, *Revelation*, 81–82.

[42] "One of the famous cities of Asia, Laodicea, was that same year overthrown by an earthquake, and, without any relief from us, recovered itself by its own resources." *Annals*, bk. 14, chap. 27, in *Tacitus: The Annals and the Histories*, (Chicago; Encyclopedia Britannica, 1990).

[43] See Gen. 9:22–23; Lev. 18:6–23; 20:10–21; Is. 57:8; Lam. 1:8; Ezek. 16:36; 22:10–11; 23:28–30; Hos. 2:9–13.

[44] Morris, *Revelation*, 83; Ford, *The Anchor Bible: Revelation*, 419; Beale, *The Book of Revelation*, 306; Aune, *Revelation 1–5*, 260.

[45] Chilton, *Days of Vengeance*, 138.

Chapter 6

[1] Beale, *The Book of Revelation*, 314–15, adaptations indicated in italics.

[2] Chilton, *The Days of Vengeance*, 21.

[3] Noah is portrayed as a new Adam through a number of parallels, which include: (1) he is told "Be fruitful and multiply, and fill the earth," as Adam was (Gen. 1:28; 9:1); (2) he is given dominion over the animals as Adam was (Gen. 1:28; 9:2); (3) he is told that he is given the plants to eat (Gen. 1:29; 9:3); (4) as Adam is placed in a garden, Noah found himself in a vineyard (Gen. 2:15; 9:20); (5) both Adam and Noah fell through the consumption of the fruit of their garden / vineyard (Gen. 3:6–7; 9:20–21); both find themselves naked (Gen. 3:7; 9:21–23). Similarly, the flood account is described much like creation: the flood flows from the "deep", from which creation came forth (Gen. 1:2; 7:11); the number seven is prominent in both stories (Gen. 2:2; 7:2, 10; 8:4, 10, 12). See Scott Hahn, *A Father Who Keeps His Promises* (Ann Arbor, MI: Servant Press, 1998), 84–5.

[4] There is one possible exception, Is. 24:23: "[F]or the LORD of hosts will reign on Mount Zion and in Jerusalem and before his elders he will manifest his glory." It must be pointed out, though, that even here it is not entirely clear that these elders are angels. J. Fekkes, for example, has argued that these are not angels. See *Isaiah and Prophetic Traditions in the Book of Revelation: Visionary Antecedents and Their Development* (Sheffield: Sheffield Press, 1994), 141–43.

[5] See Beale, 189: "It is not too speculative to understand these 'lamps' (=spirits) from John's metaphorical perspective as burning on 'the seven golden lampstands' (i.e., the churches 1:12ff). Therefore, the Spirit is what empowers the church to be effective as a burning lamp of witness in the world."

[6] Andrea Spatafora explains: "While it is not stated explicitly that Moses was to build a sanctuary according to a model that existed in heaven, the text, seems to suggest that the Israelites understood the tabernacle, and accordingly the temple, to be patterned on a heavenly model." *From the "Temple of God" to God as the Temple: A Biblical Study of the Temple in the Book of Revelation* (Rome: Editrice Pontificia Universita Gregoriana, 1997), 25.

[7] Aune, *Revelation 1–4*, 300; Josè Marìa Casciaro, et al, eds. *Navarre Bible: Revelation* (Dublin, Ireland: Four Courts Press, 1992), 62.

[8] See Ex. 25:22; 2 Sam. 22:11; 2 Sam. 6:2; 2 Kings 19:15; 1 Chron. 28:18; Ps. 18:10; 80:1; 99:1; Is. 37:16; Ezek. 10:4, 18.

[9] While the Eagle is not present in modern-day Zodiacs, there does appear to be some evidence that it replaced the sign of the Scorpio in the ancient times. The reason for this may have been the association of scorpions with evil. See Chilton, *The Days of Vengeance*, 158.

[10] Ernest Martin, *The Birth of Christ Recalculated* (Pasadena, CA: Foundation for Biblical Research, 1980), 167ff.; J. A. Thompson, "Numbers," in *The New Bible Commentary*, eds. D. Guthrie and J. A. Motyer (Grand Rapids, MI: William B. Eerdmans, 1970), 173.

[11] See Beale, 331.

[12] Targums are ancient translations and paraphrases of biblical passages. They were very widely used, especially in places where Hebrew was not known. For more on the cherubim see *Targ.* Ezek. 1:14.

[13] The saints in heaven seem to offer their prayers of praise directly to God. The incense then symbolizes the prayers of Christians on earth. A number of scholars recognize this. "Earth also enters into heavenly worship in indirect ways. The twenty-four elders and the four living creatures offer bowls of incense, "which are the prayers of the saints (5:8), presumably the saints on earth as well as in heaven." Thompson, *The Book of Revelation,* 70. Also, Beale, *The Book of Revelation,* 357: "The saints' prayers are to be identified with those of 6:9–11 and 8:4ff., which call for divine vindication of martyred believers and which are both directly linked to judgment of the ungodly." See also, Swete, *The Apocalypse of St. John,* 79.

[14] "The LXX addition to Daniel 3 (vv 52ff.) combines five elements that also appear in Rev. 4:11a and its context: (1) praise is directed to 'you'; (2) heavenly beings and the whole creation are exhorted to sing praises to God; (3) God is portrayed as sitting on a throne over the 'abyss,' and cherubim are portrayed as sitting in the temple; (4) there are repeated expressions of eternity; and (5) praise of God is directly associated with creation and redemption. This may provide a hint that John was familiar with a Jewish-Christian liturgical tradition influenced by Daniel." Beale, *The Book of Revelation,* 336–7.

[15] "Another major difference between contracts and covenants may be discovered in their very distinctive forms of exchange. A contract is the exchange of property in the form of goods and services ('That is mine and this is yours'); whereas a covenant calls for the exchange of persons ('I am yours and you are mine')." Hahn, *A Father Who Keeps His Promises,* 26.

[16] Hahn, *A Father Who Keeps His Promises,* 26.

[17] "We have, then, an idea of father-son relationship which is essentially that of the covenant. And there is no doubt that covenants, even treaties, were thought of as establishing a kind of quasi-familial unity. In the technical vocabulary of these documents a superior partner was called 'father', his inferior 'son', and equal partners were 'brothers'." D. J. McCarthy, *Old Testament Covenant: A Survey of Current Opinions* (Richmond: John Knox Press, 1972), 33. Likewise, McCarthy states, ""It becomes increasingly clear that treaty relationships were felt to be somehow familial. A treaty created 'brotherhood' and made 'fathers' and 'sons,'" 66.

[18] Pope John Paul II, *Puebla: A Pilgrimage of Faith* (Boston: Daughters of St. Paul, 1979), 86.

[19] "The 'book' in ch. 5 should be understood as a covenantal promise of inheritance." Beale, *The Book of Revelation,* 340. The scroll also recalls the one seen by Ezekiel, written on both sides, it is God's proclamation of judgment (Ezek. 2:9–10).

[20] See Barber, *Singing in the Reign,* 39–57.

[21] It may also be possible to connect this imagery to Daniel 7, where the fourth beast is described with horns and eyes. The little horn in Daniel's vision, which is described as having "eyes like the eyes of a man," may be connected to the seven eyes of the Lamb. G. K. Beale points out that by the use of parody of the beast in Daniel 7, Christ shows that He is the one who truly has authority and power. *The Book of Revelation,* 354.

[22] See Barber, *Singing in the Reign,* 118–24.

[23] For a full discussion on the "New Exodus" see Barber, *Singing in the Reign,* 60–66.

[24] Chilton, *The Days of Vengeance*, 182. Also see Andre Feuillet's comments on J. A. T. Robinson's views on the parallels in *The Apocalypse* (Staten Island, New York: Alba House, 1964), 60.

[25] Josephus, *The Wars of the Jews*, bk. 6, chap. 5, no. 3. In no way am I saying John used Josephus as a source, or the other way around. I'm simply pointing out the striking similarities between the two.

[26] See *The Wars of the Jews*, bk. 2, chaps. 13–22.

[27] See accounts cited in Gentry, *Before Jerusalem Fell*, 311.

[28] Morris, *Revelation*, 103; Swete, *The Apocalypse of St. John*, 86.

[29] Special credit for this interpretation goes to Curtis Mitch, co-author of the Ignatius Study Bible series. For a description of the feasts see B. D. Chilton, "Festivals and Holy Days: Jewish," in *Dictionary of New Testament Background*, eds. Craig A. Evans, and Stanley E. Porter (Downers Grove, IL: Intervarsity Press, 2000), 373–74. This judgment may also be an allusion to Titus's order that prohibited soldiers sacking Jerusalem to destroy vineyards.

Another possible interpretation sees "oil and wine" as symbols for God's blessing of the righteous, as in Ps. 104:15, thus implying that the righteous shall be unharmed by this rider.

[30] Josephus, *The Wars of the Jews*, bk. 5, chap. 10, no. 2.

[31] Scott Hahn and Curtis Mitch, *Ignatius Study Bible: The Gospel of Luke* (San Francisco, CA: Ignatius Press, 2001), notes on Lk. 23:28–31 and 23:31, p. 66.

Chapter 7

[1] *Jesus and the Victory of God* (Minneapolis, MN: Fortress Press, 1996), 248.

[2] The meaning of the "trees" here is not clear. However, it is most probably a symbol for the righteous, as trees often are in Scripture (Ps. 1:3; 92:12–14; Is. 61:3; Jer. 17:5–8). In this way the angels hold back the winds from harming the righteous until they can be sealed, as John describes in the next two verses.

[3] See Tertullian, *Against Marcion*, bk. 3, chap. 22, in *ANF*, vol. 3, Alexander Roberts and James Donaldson, eds. (Peabody, MA: Hendrickson, 1994), 340–41.

[4] Shepherd of Hermas, *Similitudes Ninth*, chap. 16, in *ANF*, vol. 2, Alexander Roberts and James Donaldson, eds., 49.

[5] Tertullian, *An Answer to the Jews*, chap. 9, in *ANF*, vol. 3, 160. Also see Ambrose, *On The Holy Spirit*, bk. 1, chap. 6, no. 78, in *NP-NF*, 2nd series, vol. 10, eds. Philip Schaff and Henry Wace (Peabody, MA: Hendrickson, 1994), 103: "Do we live in the water or in the Spirit? Are we sealed in the water or in the Spirit?"

[6] *Testament of Simeon Concerning Envy*, no. 7, trans. Roberts and Donaldson, http://www.earlychristianwritings.com/text/patriarchs.html.

[7] 2 Baruch 78:7, trans. R. H. Charles, in *Apocrypha and Pseudepigraphia of the Old Testament in English* (Oxford: Clarendon Press, 1913).

[8] That "all Israel" refers to the salvation of all the tribes, see 2 Sam. 2:8; 5:3, 5; 19:11; 1 Chron. 21:5. Also see *Testament of Benjamin*, no. 10. For the understanding that the

northern tribes would be subsumed into the Gentiles, see *Book of Jubilees*, 16:17: "All his [Abraham's] other sons would be Gentiles and would be reckoned with Gentiles, although one of Isaac's sons would become a holy offspring, not to be reckoned with Gentiles." Also see *Testament of Moses*, 4:8-9: "Now, the two tribes will remain steadfast in their former faith, sorrowful and sighing because they will not be able to offer sacrifices to the Lord of their fathers. But the ten tribes will grow and spread out among the nations during the time of their captivity." Citations from James H. Charlesworth, ed. *The Old Testament Pseudepigrapha.* Two Volumes. New York: Doubleday, 1983/1985.

[9] Cited by Oskar Skarsaune, "The Mission to the Jews—A Closed Chapter?" in J. Adna and H. Kvalbein, eds., *The Mission of the Early Church to Jews and Gentiles* (Tubingen: JCB Mohr, 2000), 70; citing Hennecke-Schneemelcher-Wilson I, 212. Also see Shepherd of Hermas, *Similitude Ninth*, 1–4 .

A note is necessary here. The list of the twelve tribes in Revelation 7 differs from the list of the twelve tribes in the Old Testament. For example, the tribe of Dan is not mentioned here. Why Dan is not present is not clear. The early Church speculated that it was because Dan was associated with the serpent and thus it was labeled as an evil tribe (Gen. 49:17; see also *Testament of Dan.* 5; Irenaeus, *Against Heresies*, bk. 5, chap. 30, no. 2; Hippolytus, *On the Antichrist*, nos. 14–15; *Midr. Rab.* Num. 2.7; *Midr. Rab.* Num. 13:8. Another possibility is that this list shows "all Israel" is saved, but not simply on the basis of the tribal affiliations. In the end, God saves "all Israel," not because of their race, but because of grace (Rom. 11:5).

[10] Cf. Thomas Aquinas, *Summa Theologiae*, III, q. 84, art. 2.

Chapter 8

[1] Chilton, *Days of Vengeance*, 229–30; Briggs, *Jewish Temple Imagery in the Book of Revelation*, 74–85. Others have attempted to explain the "half hour of silence" in other ways. Yet, given that the verses immediately following describe the rite itself, it seems that the view presented here makes the most sense.

[2] The apocryphal book, 1 Enoch, does list the seven archangels: Uriel, Raphael, Raguel, Michael, Saraqaeul, Gabriel and Remiel (1 Enoch 20:2–8).

[3] In fact, the RSV–CE translation of 8:3 may not be the best translation possible. One scholar explains that the incense is the prayers of the saints. Robert Mounce, *The Book of Revelation* (Grand Rapids, MI: William B. Eerdmans, 1998), 174.

[4] See Aune, *Revelation, 6–16*, 515; Mounce, *The Book of Revelation*, 174.

[5] Chilton, *Days of Vengeance*, 232.

[6] Aune, *Revelation, 6–16*, 494; Beale, *The Book of Revelation*, 455.

[7] Hahn, *Lamb's Supper*, 96. Gage, *St. John's Vision*, x.

[8] Gage, *St. John's Vision*, x.

[9] "Possibly also in the background are the seven trumpets blown by the Levites, which formed part of the music for the temple liturgy (1 Chron. 15:24 [note the association with the ark of God]; Neh. 12:41). These were blown each of the seven days of the week (cf. the context of 1 Chron. 15:24–16:7, 37; Neh. 12:41–47). These trumpets were to be a 'reminder' of Israel's needs 'before . . . God' and were to remind the Israelites to thank God for the way in which he had graciously remembered them in past times (e.g., 1 Chron. 16:4; Num. 10:10; Psalm 150)." Beale, *The Book of Revelation*, 471–72. Also see Caird, *The Revelation of St. John*, 109–11.

[10] "The first four trumpets apparently refer to the series of disasters that devastated Israel in the Last Days, and primarily the events leading up to the outbreak of the war." Chilton, *Days of Vengeance,* 236. See also Steve Gregg, ed., *Revelation: Four Views: A Parallel Commentary* (Nashville, TN: Thomas Nelson Publishers, 1997), 148.

[11] Josephus, *The Wars of the Jews,* bk. 6, chap. 1, no. 1.

[12] Chilton, *Days of Vengeance,* 238: "God is now speaking of *Jerusalem* in the same language He once used to speak of *Babylon,* a fact that will become central to the imagery of this book."

[13] N. T. Wright, *Jesus and the Victory of God,* 334–35, commenting on the Markan parallel. See also Gregg, *Revelation: Four Views,* 154.

[14] Josephus, *The Wars of the Jews,* bk. 6, chap. 5, no. 1.

[15] Ibid., bk. 3, chap. 10, no. 9.

[16] Also see 1 Enoch 88:1–3 where a fallen angel is referred to as a "star that had fallen from heaven . . . into an abyss." Also the Testament of Solomon 20:14–17 explains that demons appear as "stars . . . falling from heaven . . . dropped like flashes of lightning to the earth" (cf. Lk. 10:17–20).

[17] LXX Job 41:22, he makes the deep ["*abusson*"] boil.

[18] Donald Guthrie, et al, eds., *The New Bible Commentary: Revised.* 3rd Ed. (Carmel, NY: Guideposts, 1970), 1292; Beale, *The Book of Revelation,* 497; Aune, *Revelation, 6–16,* 530; Mounce, *The Book of Revelation* 188; Chilton, *Days of Vengeance,* 244.

[19] See Aune, *Revelation, 6–16,* 530; Morris, *Revelation,* 126.

[20] Josephus, *The Wars of the Jews,* bk. 2, chap. 14, no. 9–chap. 19, no. 9. Also see Chilton, *Days of Vengeance,* 244–45.

[21] For example, see Job 3:1–26; 6:8–9; 7:15–16; Jer. 8:3; 20:14–18; Jon. 4:3, 8; Lk. 23:27–30. See Beale, *The Book of Revelation,* 498.

[22] Others have sought to explain the appearance of the locusts in terms of an ancient description of actual locusts. However, the Old Testament allusions seem pretty clear.

[23] Josephus, *The Wars of the Jews,* bk. 4, chap. 9, no. 10.

[24] See Suetonius, *Augustus,* 70; http://www.fordham.edu/halsall/ancient/suet-augustus-rolfe.html; also see Morris, *Revelation,* 131; Beale, *The Book of Revelation,* 504.

[25] Swete, *The Apocalypse of St. John,* 118.

[26] Cf. LXX, Gen. 24:60; Lev. 26:8; Num. 10:35[36]; Deut. 32:30; 33:2, 17; 1 Kings [Sam.] 18:7–8; 21:12[11]; Ps. 3:7[6]; Song 5:10; Sir. 47:6; Mic. 6:7; Dan. 7:10.

[27] Gregg, *Revelation: Four Views,* 186.

[28] Josephus, *The Wars of the Jews,* bk. 7, chap. 1, no. 3.

[29] The word is the same in both places in the Greek, "*ischyron.*"

[30] Beale, *The Book of Revelation,* 527, format changed from original.

[31] Scott Hahn, *Kinship By Covenant: A Biblical Theological Study of Covenant Types and Texts in the Old and New Testaments* (Ann Arbor: University Microfilms, 1995), 36.

[32] J. Stuart Russell, *The Parousia: The New Testament Doctrine of Our Lord's Second Coming* (Grand Rapids, MI: Baker Books, 1983), 453.

[33] Chilton, *Days of Vengeance*, 274.

[34] Beale has another interpretation, analogous to this: "[T]he lamps on the lampstand in Zech. 4:2–5 are interpreted as representing God's presence or Spirit, which was to empower Israel (= the lampstand, v 6) to finish rebuilding the temple, despite resistance (cf. vv 4:6–9).

"So now the new Israel, the church, as God's spiritual temple on earth, is to draw its power from the Spirit, the divine presence, before God's throne in its drive to stand against the world. This continues the theme from 11:1–3 of God's establishment of his presence among his end-time community as his sanctuary." Many other things can be stated here. Lamps "bear" light, just as these two witness will "bear" testimony to God (cf. the description of the law in Ps. 119:105; Prov. 6:23). *The Book of Revelation*, 576–77.

[35] Also see Philo, *Life of Moses*, 2.282–84 and *Psikta Rabbati* 4 where Moses and Elijah are compared given their ability to call down fire from heaven.

[36] "The two witnesses seem rather to be allegorical personages; they clearly suggest Moses and Elias; they are the incarnation of the ceaseless witness rendered in the Church to Christ by the Law (Moses) and the Prophets (Elias)." Andrè Feuillet, *The Apocalypse* (Staten Island, NY: Alba House, 1964), 61.

There is also another tradition, which saw the two tablets of the Law as a symbol for God's two witnesses, Moses and Elijah. *Midr. Rab.* Deut. 3:16–17, records the Lord's promise to Moses: "So too in the time to come when I [God] bring Elijah, the prophet, to them, the two of you will come together."

[37] Scott Hahn and Curtis Mitch, *Matthew* (San Francisco, CA: Ignatius Press, 2000), 47.

[38] This passage gave rise to a tradition, especially circulated among the Samaritans, of a coming "prophet like unto Moses." This is referred to in John 19. Other biblical references include Mal. 3:1–5; 4:1–6; Sir. 48:4, 10; Mt. 11:10–14; 27:47, 49; Mk. 9:11–13; 15:35–36; Lk. 1:15-17; Jn. 1:21; 6:14; 7:40; Acts 3:22–23. For a lengthy list of extra-biblical references see Beale, *The Book of Revelation*, 585.

[39] Matthew presents John as dressed as Elijah, who also wore "a garment of haircloth, with a belt of leather about his loins" (Matt. 3:4; 2 Kings 1:8). Matthew's Mosaic / Jesus parallels are numerous. Hahn and Mitch note several of them: "(1) The lives of both Jesus and Moses are threatened in their infancy by an imperial edict to kill Hebrew male children (Ex. 1:15–16 [Mt. 2:16]); (2) both were saved from the decree by the intervention of a family member ([Mt.] 2:13; Ex. 2:1–10); (3) both found protection for a time within Egypt ([Mt.] 2:14–15; Ex. 2:5–10); (4) both were called back to their respective birthplaces after a time of flight and exile ([Mt.] 2:20; Ex. 4:19); (5) both spent 40 days and nights fasting alone in the wilderness ([Mt.] 4:2; Ex. 34:28); (6) both were commissioned by God to promulgate his covenant Law ([Mt.] chaps 5–7; Deut. 5:1–21)." Hahn and Mitch, *Matthew*, 21.

[40] See, for example, 1 Kings 21:27; 2 Kings 6:30–31; 2 Kings 19:1–2; 1 Chron. 21:16; Neh 9:1–2; Is. 58:5; Jer. 4:8; Dan. 9:3ff; Joel 1:13; Jon. 3:5–8; Mt. 11:21; Lk. 10:13

[41] One scholar even says these two witnesses may be understood as Peter and Paul. See Beale, *The Book of Revelation*, 583.

[42] Psalm 79 has many parallels with this passage. "The following motifs are common to both passages: (1) the presence of 'the nations' in Jerusalem, (2) the murder of the servants of God, and (3) the slain servants of God lying unburied. Ps. 79:1–3 may actually have influenced the formulation of the narrative of the two witnesses or one witness used by the author." Aune, *Revelation, 6–16*, 622.

[43] Many modern scholars argue that "where their Lord was crucified" does not necessarily indicate Jerusalem. However, as Aune points out, "Rev. 11:1–2 clearly sets the scene in *Jerusalem*, and nothing in 11:3–13 suggests a change in scene." Aune, *Revelation, 6–16*, 620. The deaths of these "prophets" are further support for a Jerusalem location. "The murder of the two witnesses in Jerusalem reflects the traditional view that prophets must die in Jerusalem, a tradition made explicit in Luke 13:33, where Jesus links his own mission to Jerusalem: 'it is impossible for a prophet to be killed outside of Jerusalem.'" Aune, *Revelation, 6–16*, 620.

[44] See Philo, *On the Birth of Abel and the Sacrifices Offered by Him and by His Brother Cain*, 3:8; Josephus, *Antiquities of the Jews*, 4.8.48; *Midr. Rab.* Deut. 9.5; *Sifre* Deut. Piska 357; *Assumption of Moses* 10:11–13.

[45] Still another interpretation of this passage holds that the 7,000 are, in fact, the righteous remnant, who, like the righteous witnesses, are killed. Caird, *The Revelation of St. John*, 140. It is also possible that John was referring to the actual population number of Jerusalem. Josephus writes that the population of Jerusalem in the first century was about 70,000 (cf. Beale, *The Book of Revelation*, 603). A "tenth" of this would be 7,000. It is possible, then, that John might have had this in mind.

Chapter 9

[1] "However, according to the primary intention of the sacred author, if the birth of the baby represents the advent of the Messiah, the woman obviously personifies the people of God, whether biblical Israel or the Church. The Marian interpretation is not opposed to the ecclesial meaning of the text, since Mary is a 'figure of the Church' ("Lumen Gentium," 63; see St. Ambrose, Expos. Lk, II, 7)." Pope John Paul II, Wednesday Audience, March 14, 2001.

[2] Adapted from Tim Gray, "Mary, the God-bearing Ark," in *Catholic for a Reason II: Scripture and the Mystery of the Mother of God*, Leon Suprenant, ed., (Steubenville, OH: Emmaus Road Publishing, 2000), 76.

[3] Scott Hahn, *Hail, Holy Queen: The Mother of God in the Word of God*, (New York: Doubleday, 2001), 60–61: "Whatever made the ark holy made Mary even holier. If the first ark contained the Word of God in stone, Mary's body contained the Word of God enfleshed. If the first ark contained miraculous bread from heaven, Mary's body contained the very Bread of Life that conquers death forever. If the first ark contained the rod of the long-ago ancestral priest, Mary's body contained the divine person of the eternal priest, Jesus Christ."

[4] Saint Methodius, *Oration Concerning Simeon and Anna on the Day That They Met in the Temple*, no. 5 in *ANF*, vol. 6, Roberts and Donaldson, eds., 386.

[5] Ephraim the Syrian, *Nineteen Hymns on the Nativity of Christ in the Flesh*, Hymn 11, in *NP-NF*, 2nd series, vol. 13, Philip Schaff and Henry Wace, eds., 246. See also Hymn 3.

[6] Saint John Damascene, *Oration on the Glorious Dormition of the Most Holy Mother of God the Ever-Virgin Mary,* 2.

[7] The New Testament applies this prophecy to Mary exclusively.

[8] "The woman is not Mary, nor Israel, nor the church but less and more than all of these." Eugene Boring, *Revelation* (Louisville, KY: John Knox Press, 1989), 152.

[9] "What John probably intended was a personification of the ideal community of God's people, first in its Jewish form, in which Mary gave birth to Jesus the Messiah, and then in its Christian form, in which it was persecuted by a political power as evil as the dragon (12:6)." Bruce Metzger, *Breaking the Code: Understanding the Book of Revelation* (Nashville, TN: Abingdon Press, 1993), 74.

[10] The *Catechism* explains, "By her complete adherence to the Father's will, to his Son's redemptive work, and to every prompting of the Holy Spirit, the Virgin Mary is the Church's model of faith and charity. Thus she is a 'preeminent and ...wholly unique member of the Church'; indeed, she is the 'exemplary realization' *(typos)* of the Church" (no. 967).

[11] Andre Feuillet, *Jesus and His Mother: The Role of the Virgin Mary in Salvation History and the Place of Woman in the Church* (Still River, MS: St. Bede's Publications, 1984), 17.

[12] Hahn, *Hail, Holy Queen,* 33–34.

[13] Saint Justin Martyr, *Dialogue with Trypho,* chap. 100 in *ANC,* vol. 1, 249.

[14] Saint Jerome, *Letter to Eustochium,* in *NP-NF,* 2nd series, vol. 6, 30.

[15] See 2 Chron. 12:13; 13:2; 15:16; 20:31; 22:2; 24:1; 25:1; 26:3; 27:1; 29:1.

[16] This is demonstrated in the New Testament, which frequently alludes to this Psalm in reference to Jesus (e.g., Acts 4:25–26; 13:33; Heb. 1:5; 2 Pet. 1:17; Rev. 2:26). Rabbinic tradition also understood this Psalm in messianic terms. *Midr. Rab.* Ps. 2:2: "In the time to come, Gog and Magog will set themselves against the Lord and his Messiah, only to fall down. David, foreseeing this said: 'Why do the nations rage?'" Cited in David C. Mitchell, *The Message of the Psalter: An Eschatological Programme in the Book of Psalms* (Sheffield: Sheffield Academic Press, 1997), 31–32.

[17] For more evidence for the multiple heads of Leviathan, see Aune, *Revelation 6–16,* 684ff., who mentions Rabbinic tradition and Ugaritic literature.

[18] It may also be an allusion to Daniel 8:10, where Daniel foresees the destruction of Jerusalem in terms of a ram's horn, which "grew great, even to the host of heaven; and some of the host of the stars it cast down to the ground and trampled upon them."

[19] See Aune, *Revelation 6–16,* 685.

[20] "Chapter 12 can be characterized as a flashback, telling of the birth of the Messiah and the attempt of King Herod to kill Jesus soon after he was born. However, instead of telling this as a historical narrative in a straightforward manner as Matthew does (Matt. 2), John presents a heavenly tableau of characters that are portrayed with sensational Near Eastern imagery." Metzger, *Breaking the Code,* 72.

Although John is probably not alluding to it, it is interesting to note that Herod also minted coins, which described him as king, with a depiction of a "diadem." Aune, *Revelation 6–16,* 685.

[21] Cited in David W. Bercot, ed., *A Dictionary of Early Christian Beliefs. A Reference Guide to More than 700 Topics Discussed by the Early Church Fathers* (Peabody: Hendrickson Publishers, 1998), 593.

[22] Augustine, *City of God*, bk. 11, chap. 13. See also Adela Yarbro Collins, *The Apocalypse* (Wilmington, DE: Michael Glazier, 1982), 86.

[23] In his monumental work on the theology of the angels, *The Mission of the Holy Angels in the Economy of Salvation,* Father William Wagner writes: "The Incarnation was the stumbling block. The fallen angels virtually willed supernatural beatitude, and might have accepted it as a grace direct from God, but rebelled against the plan of the instrumentality of Christ, in virtue of which should have been conferred on them the untold grace of glory, a state so beyond the excellence of nature. They rejected the humiliation of subordination beneath Christ. . . . The divine economy in Christ constituted an inversion of the order of nature. From the lesser, from the depths of humanity—he was made a little less than the angels (cf. Heb 2, 7)—should come the glory and beatitude of the angels." William Wagner, O.S.C., *The Mission of the Holy Angels in the Economy of Salvation* (Austria: Confraternity of the Guardian Angel, 1984), 209.

[24] See Wright, *Jesus & The Victory of God*, 401.

[25] Caird, *The Revelation of St. John*, 154. In fact, as Caird explains, the word "satan" is used of human opponents in courtroom settings (Ps. 109:6, "accuser" = "satan"). Also see Beale, *The Book of Revelation*, 661, who cites extra-biblical sources, which depict a heavenly courtroom where Michael, presented as the defender of God's people, defeats Satan, the prosecuting attorney (cf. *Test. Levi* 5:6; *Test. Dan.* 6:1–6; *Mirdr. Rab.* Ex. 18:5).

[26] Pius XII, Encyclical on the Sacred Liturgy *Mediator Dei* (November 20, 1947), 93.

[27] "Heaven" is plural in the Greek. This is the only place in the whole apocalypse where the word "heaven" appears in the plural. This echoes certain Old Testament passages, especially in Isaiah, where "rejoicing" occurs in "the heavens" at the redemptive work of God. John uses the same word in Greek as is used in the Septuagint for "heavens" (LXX Deut. 32:43; Ps. 95:11; Is. 44:23; 45:23; 49:13). Beale, *The Book of Revelation*, 666.

[28] Indeed, there may be yet another way in which the passage could be understood: that is, in terms of the angelic fall at the dawn of creation, after which the devil came to tempt the "woman" in the garden out of envy (Wis. 2:23–24).

[29] See, for example, Jonah 2:2–3: "[O]ut of the belly of Sheol I cried, and thou didst hear my voice. For thou didst cast me into the deep, into the heart of the seas, and the flood was round about me; all thy waves and thy billows passed over me." Also see Thomas Fawcett, *Hebrew Myth and Christian Gospel* (London: SCM Press, 1973), 84–88.

[30] Though her children are still within the striking distance of the dragon, she is not. Even though the Assumption is not specifically mentioned here, God's special protection of the woman may hint at it. Nonetheless, it must be pointed out that this passage has never been cited by the Church as evidence for the Assumption.

Chapter 10

[1] Hahn, *Lamb's Supper*, 84.

[2] Gentry, *Before Jerusalem Fell*, 310: "[I]t will be necessary to recall that John allows some shifting in his imagery of the Beast: the seven-headed Beast is here conceived generically as the Roman Empire, there specifically as one particular emperor. It is impossible to lock down the beast imagery to either one referent or the other. At some places the beast has seven-heads that are seven kings collectively considered (Rev. 13:1; Rev. 17:3, 9–10). Thus, he is generically portrayed as a kingdom with seven kings that arise in chronological succession (cf. Rev. 17:10–11). But then again, in the very same contexts, the beast is spoken of as an individual (Rev. 13:18), as but one head among the seven (Rev. 17:11). This feature, as frustrating as it may be, is recognized by many commentators."

[3] See Thompson, *The Book of Revelation*, 16. Also see Leon Hardy Canfield, *The Early Persecutions of the Christians* (New York: Columbia University Press, 1913), 162. Also see Beale, *The Book of Revelation*, 12; Morris, *Revelation*, 33.

[4] Gentry, *Before Jerusalem Fell*, 158.

[5] Charles, *Revelation*, vol. 1, cxliii: "*while he writes in Greek, he thinks in Hebrew*" (italics in original).

[6] Gentry, *The Beast of Revelation*, 34–36.

[7] Henderson, *The Five Roman Emperors* (Cambridge: Cambridge University Press, 1927), 1: "Upon the death of Nero on June 9, AD 68, the first line of Roman Emperors, that of the 'Julio-Claudian' House, became extinct. Whatever the demerit of its Princes may have been, their continuity of descent at least preserved the Roman Empire from the horrors of civil war."

[8] For Nero's death by a sword, see Suetonius, *Nero*, 49. Suetonius also wrote: "The race of the Caesars ended with Nero." In fact, he tells of "many portents" that foretold this as a coming tragedy. Suetonius, *Galba* 1.

[9] Tacitus writes of this time: "I am entering of the history of a period rich in disasters, frightful in its wars, torn by civil strife, and even in peace full of horrors." *Histories*, bk. 1, no. 2, in *Tacitus: The Annals and the Histories* (Chicago: Encyclopedia Britannica, 1990).

[10] Josephus, *The Wars of the Jews*, bk. 4, chap. 9, no. 2.

[11] Tacitus, *Histories*, bk. 1, no. 11.

[12] "To all appearances it was Nero's downfall, ending the only dynasty that had ruled as Roman emperors, which opened the way for revolt and civil war. . . . [It] is entirely understandable that John should find in Nero's suicide an appropriate *symbol* for the mortal blow to the empire that occurred at the end of his reign, especially as the image of a fatal wound with a sword could also hint at an act of divine judgment." Richard Bauckham, *The Climax of Prophecy* (Edinburgh, Scotland: T & T Clark, 1993), 444.

[13] Beale points out that this prophecy reflects "the suicide of Nero in 68 A. D. followed by a year of civil war, in which the future of the Roman state was in question." *The Book of Revelation*, 689.

Most commentators take this passage as a reference to a certain revival of the Nero myth, which foretold that Nero would return from the grave. However, the idea that Nero was revived from the dead was a much later development. The idea was that Nero had simply never died at all! This is totally inconsistent with the image presented here.

If anything, the "resurrection" of Nero may be understood in terms of later Emperors who called themselves "Nero." See Guthrie, *Introduction,* 953–54; D. A. Carson, et al. ed.. *An Introduction to the New Testament* (Grand Rapids, MI: Zondervan Publishing House, 1992), 475.

[14] See Aune, *Revelation 6–16,* 726; Hahn, *Lamb's Supper,* 80–83; Caird, *The Revelation of St. John,* 164.

[15] "For John 'the current embodiment of the chaos monster is Rome, but he sees Rome as the residual legatee of all the Pagan Empires of the past,' and the evil spirit inspiring Rome as potentially able to dominate other world empires after Rome. The dragon and the beast include world empires of the past and the present and potentially the future." Beale, *The Book of Revelation,* 685, citing Caird, *Language and Imagery* (Philadelphia, PA: Westminster, 1980), 229. Also see Hahn, *Lamb's Supper,* 82.

[16] Chilton, *Days of Vengeance,* 333.

[17] Some have taken both beasts to be symbolic of Rome. Yet, this doesn't take into account the later developments of the two figures. The relationship of the two beasts is also portrayed as "the beast and the false prophet" (16:13; 19:20; 20:10) and the "harlot who rides the beast" (cf. chapter 17). In the latter vision, the beast turns on the harlot, devouring her and burning her with fire (17:16). One is hard pressed to explain how both images symbolize Rome.

[18] Hahn, *Lamb's Supper,* 83.

[19] Bauckham, *Climax of Prophecy,* 398, 409–10.

[20] Of course, this is not to say Nero destroyed Jerusalem. It simply means "Nero" stands for the wickedness of all the Roman emperors symbolized by the beast. This follows John's method closely, which also uses the name "Nero" as the name for the kingdom of seven kings/heads. In relation to this see chapter 12, commentary on Rev. 17:9–11.

[21] This is the only time in Revelation where a song is mentioned, but not quoted. It may be noteworthy that John does not give us the words of this song. He may not know the words because he has not yet died and entered the heavenly glory himself; he has only seen it in a vision. See Aune, *Revelation 6–16,* 808–9.

[22] See Chilton, *Days of Vengeance,* 359–60.

[23] See also Lk. 18:28–29 and 1 Cor. 7.

[24] Revelation 14:5 also evokes Zeph. 3:13, where God's restored remnant from Israel stands on Mount Zion: "Those who are left in Israel . . . shall do no wrong, and utter no lies, nor shall there be found in their mouth a deceitful tongue."

[25] Given its place in the Psalter, the Psalm also paints a picture of an Israel restored in the New Exodus, which further ties it to this passage. See Barber, *Singing in the Reign,* 127. While I don't believe this text was in John's mind as he wrote Rev. 14, I do believe it reflects the same hope, which he understood had been fulfilled.

[26] The angels of chapters 8 and 14 may also be compared to the one who announces the final judgment in chapter 19. This angel also speaks in a "loud voice," calling to the birds who fly "in midheaven" (19:7). Furthermore, given the close correspondence to the angel in chapter 8, there might be a connection between that angel's threefold "woe" and the three angels who appear here. Beale, *The Book of Revelation,* 748–49.

[27] God also promised Daniel "rest" in the age to come (Dan. 12:12). Furthermore, "rest" was a term used by God to describe the reward of the Promised Land (cf. Ps. 95:11). The attainment of it by the saints paints a picture of them as those restored in the New Exodus.

[28] Saint Josemaría Escríva, *The Way, The Furrow, The Forge* (New York: Scepter, 1939), 180.

[29] Also see Is. 63 where God's day of wrath is compared to stamping out the wine presses.

[30] Josephus, *The Wars of the Jews*, bk. 6, chap. 5, no. 1.

[31] Ford, *Revelation*, 250; Chilton, *Days of Vengeance*, 376; Swete, *The Apocalypse of St. John*, 189; Beale, *The Book of Revelation*, 782; G. R. Beasely-Murray, *The Book of Revelation* (London: Marshal Morgan, 1974), 230.

[32] Perhaps the imagery of the sea of glass on fire is meant to paint a picture of a new Red Sea. See Beale, *The Book of Revelation*, 791–92, for discussion on the connection between the Red Sea and the sea of glass in extra-biblical sources.

[33] The wording may also come from Ps. 98:1–2, which was understood as a Mosaic Psalm: "O Sing to the Lord a new song, for he has done marvelous things. His right hand has made known his victory, he has revealed his vindication in the sight of the nations." In connection with this, see the commentary on 5:8 where we also explained how the new song of Moses appears in the Psalter to describe the victory of the restoration of Israel.

[34] The Greek word here, *phialai,* which may be translated "bowl" or "cup," is used interchangeably by John with the word *potárion* (cf. Rev. 16:19). The two words are also used synonymously in LXX Prov. 23:31. That *phialai* may be translated "cup," see H. G. Liddel, et al., *A Greek-English Lexicon.* (Oxford: Clarendon, 1968); J. H. Moulton and G. Milligan. *The Vocabulary of the Greek Testament Illustrated from the Papyri and Other Non-Literary Sources,* (Grand Rapids, MI: Eerdmans, 1930).

[35] Hahn, *Lamb Supper's*, 107; Chilton, *Days of Vengeance*, 389.

[36] Caird, *The Revelation of St. John*, 200. See commentary on Rev. 1:12–13, "Investments of a Priest."

[37] Though the word in 14:10 is *potárion*, and not *phialai*, the link is still possible because the words can be used interchangeably and in association with each other. See note 34 above.

[38] In fact, this is the only place where "smoke" and "temple" appear together in the whole Old Testament. See Fekkes, *Isaiah and Prophetic Traditions in the Book of Revelation*, 200.

Chapter 11

[1] Chilton, *Days of Vengeance*, 396.

[2] Ford, *The Anchor Bible: Revelation*, 269: "Thus the chapter is but a graphic elaboration of the statement in 11:8 that the city is allegorically called Sodom and Egypt, Egypt because of the plagues and Sodom because of its destruction."

[3] Gregg, *Revelation: Four Views*, 372; Chilton, *Days of Vengeance*, 405–6.

[4] Josephus, *The Wars of the Jews*, bk. 5, chap. 11, no. 2.

[5] Josephus, *The Wars of the Jews*, bk. 6, chap. 2, no. 2

[6] Josephus, *The Wars of the Jews*, bk. 6, chap. 1, no. 1.

[7] Chilton, *Days of Vengeance*, 408; Philip Carrington, *The Meaning of Revelation* (London: SPCK, 1931), 265. Furthermore, the ancient historian Herodotus writes that Babylon was destroyed by a surprise attack coming from the east (cf. Herodotus, *History*, 1.191; Beale, *The Book of Revelation*, 827; Morris, *Revelation*, 191; Chilton, *Days of Vengeance*, 407). Thus, the New Babylon is taken as the old one was.

[8] Is. 11:14–16; Is. 44:26–28; Jer. 50:37–39; Jer. 51:35–37; Zech. 10:10–12

[9] Josephus, *The Wars of the Jews*, bk. 6, chap. 4, no. 6.

[10] Josephus, *The Wars of the Jews*, bk. 6, chap. 3, no. 4.

[11] Josephus, *The Wars of the Jews*, bk. 6, chap. 6, no. 2.

[12] Other scholars have speculated that another meaning might be found in later Jewish tradition, which described the customary punishment Levitical priests received for falling asleep on duty. Carrington explains: "There was an officer on duty at the Temple whose business it was to walk round and see that those who were on watch kept awake; if he found them asleep he beat them; if he found them a second time, he burned their clothes." Carrington, 265f. However, whether this accurately describes the practice of the Levites in the first century or not is unclear.

[13] See Ford, *Revelation*, 274; Gregg, *Revelation: Four Views*, 382; Chilton, *Days of Vengeance*, 411; Beale, *The Book of Revelation*, 840; Adela Yarbro Collins, "The Apocalypse (Revelation)," *The New Jerome Biblical Commentary*, eds. Raymond Brown, J. Fitzmeyer, and R. Murphy (Englewood Cliffs, NJ: Prentice Hall, 1968), 1011.

[14] Day further strengthens the case that Zech. 12 is the source for "Armageddon," by pointing out that it is the only place in the Hebrew Bible where Megiddo is referred to as *megiddon* rather than *megiddo*. Though the term *megiddon* appears in several places in the Greek Old Testament, this fact is significant because John asserts that "Armageddon" is derived from a Hebrew word (i.e., "at the place which is called in Hebrew…"). See J. Day, "Origin of Armageddon: Revelation 6:16 as an Interpretation of Zechariah 12:11," *Crossing the Boundaries: Essays in Biblical Interpretation in Honour of Michael D. Goulder*, Stanley Porter, et al., eds. (Leiden: Brill, 1994), 315–26.

[15] Josephus, *The Wars of the Jews*, bk. 6, chap. 9, no. 4.

[16] Cf. Josephus, *The Wars of the Jews*, bk. 5, chap. 5, no. 1–5. See Chilton, *Days of Vengeance*, 415–16; Carrington, *The Meaning of Revelation*, 266; Ford, *Revelation*, 274; Gregg, *Revelation: Four Views*, 392.

[17] See Aune, *Revelation 6–16*, 901.

[18] Morris, *Revelation*, 195.

[19] The Greek word used here, *talentiaia*, means "talent." See Beale, *The Book of Revelation*, 845; Morris, *Revelation*, 195; also see footnote in the *New American Bible,* "literally 'weighing a talent.'"

[20] Josephus, *The Wars of the Jews*, bk. 5, chap. 7, no. 3, in *The Works of Josephus*, trans. William Whiston (Peabody, MA: Hendrickson, 1998, 13th printing). See translator's note *a*.

[21] For a detailed explanation of this, see John Saward, "Love's Second Name," *The Canadian Catholic Review,* March (1990): 87–97.

Chapter 12

[1] Russell, *The Parousia*, 485.

[2] The Book of Revelation can be divided into seven sections, with a prologue and an epilogue. Prologue (1:1–8); 1. The Vision to the Seven Churches (1–3); 2. Seven Seals (4–7); 3. Seven Trumpets (8–11); 4. Seven Chalices (15–16); 5. The Judgment of the Harlot (17–19); 6. The Millennium (20); 7. The New Jerusalem (19–22); Epilogue (22:8–21). See Russell, *The Parousia*, 377.

[3] C. Deutsch, "Transformation of Symbols: The New Jerusalem in Revelation 21:3–22:5" in *ZNW* 78 (1987): 106–26.

[4] Many scholars see the reference to Babylon as a reference to Rome. While it is true that many first century sources referred to Rome as "Babylon" (e.g., 1 Pet. 5:13), that does not necessarily force the conclusion that all references to "Babylon" must be understood that way. However, as we have shown, it is more likely a reference to Jerusalem, for it is the place where the Lord and the prophets have died (cf. 11:8, 17; 18:24).

[5] See H. W. Hoehner, "Herodian Dynasty" in *The Dictionary of New Testament Background*, eds. Craig Evans and Stanley Porter, (Downers Grove, IL: Intervarsity Press, 2000), 485–94.

[6] Also see LXX Jer. 28:13: "[Babylon] dwelling on many waters."

[7] Virtually every commentator recognizes that this beast is the same as the one in 13:1. See Robert L. Thomas, *Revelation 8-22: An Exegetical Commentary* (Chicago, IL: Moody Press, 1995), p.285; Hendriksen, *More Than Conquerors*, 166; Caird, *The Revelation of St. John,* 213; Beale, *The Book of Revelation,* 853; Swete, *Apocalypse of St. John*, 211; Mounce, *The Book of Revelation*, 310, to name a few.

[8] Beale, *The Book of Revelation*, 862.

[9] Ford, *Revelation*, 288.

[10] "The chalice which the prostitute holds in her hand is, therefore, like the one that Jesus drinks, a symbol of a blood which is shed in sacrifice. The difference is that the blood poured out by the prostitute is not her own and it is not poured out for a good and holy cause. On the contrary, it is poured out in violence, in the search for authority and domination." Corsini, *The Apocalypse,* 338.

[11] In Revelation 12:10, the saints cheer, "Now the kingdom of our God and the authority of His Christ have come", once Satan is defeated, showing us the connection between the fall of the city, the defeat of Satan, and the establishment of the kingdom on earth.

[12] See Aune, *Revelation 17-22*, 950; Beale, *The Book of Revelation*, 875. Also see the Sibylline Oracles 1:328–29.

[13] See Gentry, *Before Jerusalem Fell*, 208.

[14] Ibid., 316.

[15] Aune, *Revelation 17-22*, 950-51.

[16] The harlot of Revelation 17 also has much in common with the woman Jezebel, whom Christ uses as an example of someone who leads God's people astray. (1) Jezebel "adorned" herself, as the harlot is arrayed in jewels and scarlet (2 Kings 9:30; Rev. 17:4); (2) Both are queens (cf. 2 Kings 10:13; Rev. 18:7); (3) Both are guilty of idolatry, which is associated with "fornication" (2 Kings 9:22; cf. 2 Chron. 21:13; Rev. 17:1-2, 5; (4) Both deceive through sorceries (2 Kings 9:22; Rev. 17:2); (5) Both persecute and kill prophets and the innocent (1 Kings 18:4; 19:2; Rev. 17:6; 18:24); (6) Both are opposed by a faithful remnant (1 Kings 18:17–18; 19:18; 2 Kings 9:22; Rev. 17:14); (7) God avenges the blood each has shed by killing them (2 Kings 9:7; Rev. 19:2); (8) The followers of both are judged (1 Kings 18:40; 2 Kings 10:19; Rev. 18:9–11); (9) both of their bodies are eaten by scavengers (2 Kings 9:36–37; Rev. 19:17–18). Adapted from Beale, *The Book of Revelation,* 884, citing the work of H. Okayama.

[17] "None is depicted as loving the city for herself, but only for what they could get out of her. She might seduce and enrich people but there was nothing lovely in her." Morris, *Revelation,* 212.

[18] There is a connection between Tyre and the temple in Jerusalem, since Hiram of Tyre was the man contracted by Solomon to build the temple (1 Kings 5:1ff).

[19] Josephus, *The Wars of the Jews*, bk. 6, chap. 8, no. 3.

[20] In the Synoptic Gospels, Christ's statement echoes Jer. 51:63, which spoke of a small stone being cast into the Euphrates in connection with the judgment of Babylon. However, He changed Jeremiah's "small stone," to a "millstone." That John does the same thing indicates his awareness of Jesus' statement. See Beale, *The Book of Revelation*, 919.

[21] David C. Mitchell, *The Message of the Psalter*, 244, 266; Daniel S. Mynatt, "The Poetry and Literature of the Psalms," in *An Introduction to Wisdom Literature and the Psalms: Festschrift Marvin E. Tate*, eds. Wayne Balard and W. Dennis Tucker, Jr. (Macon, GA: Mercer University Press, 2000), 59; Jerome F. D. Creach, *Yahweh as Refuge and the Editing of the Hebrew Psalter* (Sheffield, England: Sheffield Academic Press, 1996), 100. For a discussion of the structural links between these psalms see Gerald Wilson, "Evidence of Editorial Divisions in the Hebrew Psalter," *Vetus Testamentum* 3 (1984): 336–52.

[22] James D. Nogalski, "From Psalm to Psalms," in *An Introduction to Wisdom Literature and the Psalms: Festschrift Marvin E. Tate*, 51; Scott Hahn, "Shaking Out the Psalter, Part 1" in *Scripture Matters* (Envoy 4:1[2001]).

[23] Barber, *Singing in the Reign*, 91–92.

[24] Cf. for references to Ps. 109 see Mt. 27:39; Mk. 15:29; Ps. 110 is alluded to in Mt. 22:64; Mk. 14:62; Mk. 16:19; Lk. 22:69; Acts 2:34; 1 Cor. 15:25; Eph. 1:20; Col. 3:1; Heb. 1:3; Heb. 1:13; Heb. 10:12–13; Heb. 12:2).

[25] For a full treatment on the organizational movement in the Psalms see Barber, *Singing In The Reign*, 86ff.

[26] Joachim Jeremias, *The Eucharistic Words of Jesus* (London: SCM Press, 1960), 55, 86; Scott Hahn, *A Father Who Keeps His Promises* (Grand Rapids, MI: Servant Publications, 1998), 229.

[27] See Jeremias, *The Eucharistic Words of Jesus,* 123, 206.

[28] Massey H. Shepherd, *The Paschal Liturgy and the Apocalypse* (London: Lutterworth Press, 1960), 78.

[29] Also see *Targ.* Zech. 3:1–5, where the high priest is said to be clothed with "righteousness," as is the Bride in Rev. 19.

[30] That the garments represent priestly attire is confirmed once one looks at the Isaiah passage quoted in context, which explicitly describes Israel as being made "priests of the Lord" (Is. 61:6). Furthermore, the Targum to Is. 61:10 reads: "As bridegroom serving as a priest with a crown." See Beale, *The Book of Revelation,* 938.

[31] Matthias Scheeben writes: "Man is to attach himself to his divine bridegroom by faith; and the bridegroom seals His union with man in baptism, as with a wedding ring. But both faith and baptism are mere preliminaries for the coming together of man and the God-man in one flesh by a real Communion of flesh and blood in the Eucharist, and hence for the perfect fructifying of man with the energizing grace of his head. By entering the Church every soul becomes a real bride of God's Son, so truly that the Son of God is able, in the Apostle's words, not only to compare His love and union with the Church and her members with the unity achieved in matrimony but can even propose it as the ideal and model of the latter." *The Mysteries of Christianity* (St. Louis, MO: B. Herder Book Co., 1946), 543–44.

[32] Hurtmut Gese, *Essays on Biblical Theology,* (Minneapolis, MN: Augsbury Publishing House, 1981), 132: "In these psalms we do not have the expression of an enlightened critique of sacrifice, but rather the total involvement of the person in the essence of sacrifice, as that involvement grew out of a deeply rooted spiritual understanding of the thank offering."

[33] See Tim Gray, "From Jewish Passover to Christian Eucharist: The Todah Sacrifice as Backdrop for the Last Supper," Scott Hahn and Regis J. Flaherty, eds., *Catholic for a Reason III: Scripture and the Mystery of the Mass* (Steubenville, OH: Emmaus Road, 2004), 65–76.

[34] After showing the similarities between the Passover and the Todah, Gray concludes: "The Passover is Israel's corporate *todah.*" Ibid., 21.

[35] Likewise, Jesus comes down on a "white cloud" in chapter 14, to cast His sickle of judgment.

[36] The Targum to Ps. 45:7 reads: "Your beauty, King Messiah, surpasses that of the sons of men." See David C. Mitchell, *The Message of the Psalter: An Eschatological Programme in the Book of Psalms* (Sheffield: Sheffield Academic Press, 1997), 248.

[37] Some ancient copies of Revelation add that the "new name" is written on Christ's forehead. Furthermore, the close relationship between the diadems and the inscription lends credence to this view. See Beale, *The Book of Revelation,* 955.

[38] Scott Hahn and Mark Shea. *@Home With the Word: A Complete Study of Revelation* (available through e3mil.com), 16; 3.

[39] This is especially clear when one examines the original Greek text. See Beale, *The Book of Revelation,* 967; Aune, *Revelation 17–22,* 1064–65; Corsini, *The Apocalypse,* 356ff.

[40] Pope Paul VI explains: "In order that the oblation by which the faithful offer the divine Victim in this Sacrifice to the Heavenly Father may have its full effect, it is necessary that the people add something else, namely the offering of themselves as victim." *Mediator Dei,* 98.

Chapter 13

[1] Merrill Simon, *Jerry Falwell and the Jews* (New York: Jonathon David Publishers, 1984), 47.

[2] My interpretation of the Millennium as referring to the Davidic covenant takes its cue from Scott Hahn, who explains this interpretation in Scott Hahn's series of lectures, The End: The Book of Revelation, available through Saint Joseph Communications, P.O. Box 1911, Suite 83, Tehachapi, CA, CA 93581 / Phone: (800) 526-2151.

[3] For a fuller discussion see David Currie, *Rapture: The End-Times Error That Leaves the Bible Behind* (Manchester, NH: Sophia Press, 2003), 348-356.

[4] Also see Job 33:22–30; Ps. 16:10; 30:3; 69:15; 88:6–7; Prov. 1:12; Is. 14:15; 38:18; Ezek. 26:20; Jon. 2:2–7.

[5] See Ben F. Meyer, *Five Speeches that Changed the World* (Collegeville, MN: Liturgical Press, 1994), 89. Zev Vilnay, *Legends of Jerusalem: The Sacred Land,* vol. 1 (Philadelphia, PA: The Jewish Publication Society of America, 1973), 78ff.

[6] Vilnay, *Legends of Jerusalem,* 18.

[7] As quoted in Vilnay, *Legends of Jerusalem,* 80.

[8] See Meyer, *Five Speeches,* 89–90.

[9] See footnote *r* in RSV-CE for this translation. See also my *Singing in the Reign,* 75; and Hahn, *A Father Who Keeps His Promises,* 213.

[10] Vilnay, *Legends of Jerusalem,* 41. Indeed, one of the gates leading to the temple area is still known today as the Gate of the Chain in Arabic, and extends to a square known as the Market of the Chain. Ibid., 41ff.

[11] See, for example, Josephus, *Antiquities,* bk. 8, chap. 5.

[12] Corsini, *The Apocalypse,* 364: "For John, the angels represent the mediators of the Old Economy and thus, if he insists here that it is one angel who binds Satan, then the event is somehow to be connected with that economy."

[13] Josephus, *The Wars of the Jews,* bk. 5, chap. 10, no. 5.

[14] Corsini notes that John never says that the saints will "rise" with Christ, but simply that they "have life." This would further indicate that John is not envisioning a bodily resurrection here. See Corsini, *The Apocalypse,* 379. As Elijah was taken up body and soul, the souls of the rest of the Old Testament saints were taken up to await Christ, who would usher them into the final heavenly glory.

[15] This is found in the Targums and Rabbinic writings. See Swete, *The Apocalypse of St. John,* 264; Beale, *The Book of Revelation,* 1025; Aune, *Revelation 17–22,* 1094–95.

[16] For a great discussion on the history of the modern calendar and its meaning, see N. T. Wright, *The Millennium Myth: Hope for a Postmodern World* (Louisville, KY: John Knox Press, 1999).

Chapter 14

[1] Also see Jer. 31:32 and various Rabbinic sources cited by Beale, *The Book of Revelation,* 944.

[2] The Hebrew and Greek words used here, *asah* and *poieo,* may be translated either "do" or "make." The word *poieo* is used in Revelation 21:5.

[3] That Jesus was referring to Baptism is clear from the fact that after this discourse He immediately goes out with His disciples who baptize—the only place in the Gospels where He does so.

[4] G. K. Chesterton, *The Everlasting Man* (New York: Dodd, Mead, 1926), 321.

[5] Paula Fredricksen, *Jesus of Nazareth: King of the Jews* (New York: Vintage Books, 1999), 98.

[6] As in Ezekiel's vision, the measuring probably denotes God's "protected" area. In Rev. 11:1–2 John is told not to measure the "outer court" since that will be given over to be trampled on. See also Zech. 1:16 and 2:5.

[7] See Morris, *Revelation,* 244.

[8] Thomas, *Revelation 8–22,* 468; Aune, *Revelation 17–22,* 1162; Swete, *The Apocalypse of St. John,* 286.

[9] One could also look to Is. 54:11–12 where the foundations of the restored Jerusalem are said to be made of precious stones.

[10] Notice that the measurement of the wall is 144 cubits, echoing the 144,000 of Rev. 7. The righteous remnant of the twelve tribes now enters into God's presence in the heavenly Jerusalem.

[11] Scott Hahn and Curtis Mitch, *Ignatius Catholic Study Bible: The Gospel of John* (San Francisco: Ignatius Press, 2003), note on John 7:38–39.

[12] B. D. Chilton, "Festivals and Holy Days: Jewish," 374; Bruno Barnhart, *The Good Wine: Reading John from the Center* (Mahwah, NJ: Paulist Press, 1993), 91.

[13] Jehovah Witnesses attempt to explain this verse away by saying that some scholars doubt that this verse was actually penned by John, since some of the most ancient manuscripts omit it. And yet, they themselves include this verse in their own Bible, the *New World Translation.*

[14] There may also be an allusion here to Is. 60:1–3: "Arise, shine: for your light has come, and the glory of the Lord has risen upon you."

[15] In fact, Bishop Fabian Bruskewitz of Lincoln, Nebraska wrote a defense of the orthodoxy of Scott Hahn's treatment of the subject, saying, that his research "stands in a long line that begins with the very texts of the Sacred Scriptures as they have been interpreted by saints and doctors of the Church, and by the Church's living tradition and liturgy—not to mention by some of the finest orthodox theologians of our generation." "In Defense of a Theologian Who Keeps His Promises," *National Catholic Register* 78 (2002): 9.

[16] "By calling God 'Father,' the language of faith indicates two main things: that God is the first origin of everything and transcendent authority; and that he is at the same time goodness and loving care for all his children. God's parental tenderness can also be

expressed by the image of motherhood [cf. Sam. 7:14; Ps. 68:6], which emphasizes God's immanence, the intimacy between Creator and creature. The language of faith thus draws on the human experience of parents, who are in a way the first representatives of God for man. But this experience also tells us that human parents are fallible and can disfigure the face of fatherhood and motherhood. We ought therefore to recall that God transcends the human distinction between the sexes. He is neither man nor woman: he is God. He also transcends human fatherhood and motherhood, although he is their origin and standard [cf. Ps. 27:10; Eph. 3:14; Is. 49:15]: no one is father as God is Father" (*Catechism*, no. 239).

[17] Gregory of Nazianzus, *Oratio theologica* V, no. 11, in *ANF*, vol. 7, eds. Schaff and Wace, 321.

[18] *Banquet of the Ten Virgins,* Discourse 3, Chap. 8, in *ANF*, vol. 6, eds. Roberts and Donaldson, 320.

[19] Scheeben, *Mysteries of Christianity*, 187–88.

[20] See Hahn, *First Comes Love,* chapter 10, 126–45.

[21] I have here quoted from the *New American Bible.* The RSV translates this word "desolate." The Greek word is *orphanos.*

[22] H. M. Manteau-Bonamy, *Immaculate Conception and the Holy Spirit: The Marian Teachings of Father Kolbe* (Kenosha, WI: Prow Books, 1977), 17.

[23] Scheeben writes that Mary is united to the Spirit in that, through the Spirit, she is "the bond of love between the Father and His Son become man, just as [the Holy Spirit] is between the Father and the Son in the Godhead." *Mysteries of Christianity*, 188. Therefore, in the Incarnation Mary participates in the Spirit's role as the bond of the Father and Son. The Spirit makes Mary the bond of the Father and Son in the Incarnation as He is the bond between Them in eternity.

[24] Manteau-Bonamy, *Immaculate Conception and the Holy Spirit*, 5217.

[25] Ibid., 41–45.

Chapter 15

[1] The early Fathers saw God's dealings with man in salvation history in terms of "divine accommodation," wherein God stoops down to speak to His children in order to raise them up to be with Him. Jewish scholar, Stephen D. Benin, explains, "From Irenaeus to Eusebius, accommodation would become a tool of Christian historical investigation focusing on the development of the divine *oikonomia.* The pedagogical aspects of accommodation were introduced into Christian exegesis by Origen, who employed accommodation dazzlingly in his remarkable oeuvre painting poignant word pictures of the Lord speaking 'baby-talk' with humanity in order to reveal his grand design." *The Footprints of God: Divine Accommodation in Jewish and Christian Thought* (Albany, NY: State University of New York Press, 1993), xvii. Benin quotes Origen's *Contra Celsum*: "Just as when we are talking to very small children we do not assume as the object of our instruction any strong understanding in them, but say what we have to say accommodating it to the small understanding of those whom we have before us, and even do what seems to us useful for the education and upbringing of children, realizing that they are children: so the Word of God seems to have disposed the things which were written, adapting the suitable parts of his message to the capacity of his hearers and to their ultimate profit." Benin, 12.

[2] "To use Saint Paul's human analogy: in the time of Abraham, the Father by a covenant makes the infant Israel his heir and promises him an inheritance; as the infant grows up, he becomes wayward; the Father, while reaffirming his intention that the boy shall enter into his inheritance, puts him under tutors who are to enforce a code of strict rules. These rules are not meant to render the covenant ineffectual. On the contrary, they are meant to help the child to grow up so as to be worthy of his inheritance." John Bligh, *Galatians* (London: St. Paul Publications, 1970), 301.

[3] The Syriac Father, Saint Aphrahat, wrote, "When the Holy One saw . . . that they were not purified from the leaven of the Egyptians, but remained in that very opinion of paganism, then he commanded Moses to distinguish foods for them. He made unclean for them those very things . . . which had been clean for them to eat in the land of Egypt, and he commanded them to eat those very things which they had worshipped in the land of Egypt and of which they had [formerly] not eaten. On account of their evil impulse, he commanded that they even bring as an offering before him that thing which they had worshipped. They should eat the flesh of sheep and oxen, which they had not wanted to eat because they were sacrifices." As quoted in Jacob Neusner, *Aphrahat and Judaism: The Christian-Jewish Argument in Fourth-Century Iran* (Leiden: E. J. Brill, 1971), 53.

[4] See Barber, *Singing in the Reign*, 55.

[5] This is Saint Paul's point in renouncing the "works of the law" (Rom. 3:28). By saying we are saved by "faith, apart from works of law," Paul doesn't say we are saved apart from "good works," instead, he says that we are saved apart from the ceremonial ritual works added to the Law because of sin. Saint Thomas Aquinas wrote, "The moral [laws], although they were contained in the Law, could not, strictly speaking, be called 'works of the law,' for man is induced to them by natural instinct and by the natural law. But the ceremonial works are properly called the 'works of the Law.' . . . [W]ith respect to being made just by the works of the Law, a man does not seem to be justified by them, because the sacraments of the Old Law did not confer grace." *Commentary on Saint Paul's Epistle to the Galatians* (Albany, NY: Magi Books, Inc., 1966), 54.

[6] Hahn, *Hail, Holy Queen,* 21.

BIBLIOGRAPHY

The following is a list of some of the works cited. Many of the most important and influential commentaries are listed. Other important theological and historical works relevant to Revelation are given here as well. However, an exhaustive list of the sources used to study the Book of Revelation could never truly be given. Indeed, there were many books consulted in this project that are not listed here.

Aquinas, Saint Thomas. *Commentary on Saint Paul's Epistle to the Galatians.* Albany, NY: Magi Books, 1966.

Aune, David. *Word Biblical Commentary: Revelation.* 3 vols. Dallas, TX: Word Books, 1997

———. "Religion, Greco-Roman." In *Dictionary of New Testament Background.* Edited by Craig Evans and Stanley Porter. Downers Grove, IL: Intervarsity Press, 2000.

Barber, Michael. *Singing in the Reign: The Psalms and the Liturgy of God's Kingdom.* Steubenville, OH: Emmaus Road, 2001.

Barnhart, Bruno. *The Good Wine: Reading John from the Center.* Mahwah, NJ: Paulist Press, 1993.

Bauckham, Richard. *The Climax of Prophecy.* Edinburgh, Scotland: T & T Clark, 1993.

Beale, G. K. *The Book of Revelation.* Grand Rapids, MI: William B. Eerdmanns, 1999.

Benin, Stephen D. *The Footprints of God: Divine Accommodation in Jewish and Christian Thought.* Albany, NY: State University of New York Press, 1993.

Bercot, David, ed. *Dictionary of Early Christian Beliefs.* Peabody, MA: Hendrickson, 1988

Bligh, John. *Galatians.* London: St. Paul Publications, 1970
Briggs, Robert. *Jewish Temple Imagery in the Book of Revelation.* New York: Peter Lang, 1999.
Brock, Sebastian. *The Luminous Eye: The Spiritual World Vision of Saint Ephrem the Syrian.* Kalamazoo, MI: Cistercian Publications, 1985.
Caird, G. B. *A Commentary on the Revelation of St. John the Divine.* London: A & C Black, 1966. Repr., Peabody, MA: Henderickson Publishers, 1999.
———. *Language and Imagery.* Philadelphia, PA: Westminster, 1980.
Carrington, Philip. *The Meaning of Revelation.* London: SPCK, 1931.
Carson, D. A., et al., eds. *An Introduction to the New Testament.* Grand Rapids, MI: Zondervan, 1992.
Casciaro, Jose Maria, et al., eds. *Navarre Bible: Revelation.* Dublin, Ireland: Four Courts Press, 1992.
Charles, R. H. *A Critical and Exegetical Commentary of the Revelation of St. John.* Edinburgh: T & T Clark, 1920. Reprinted 1985.
Charlesworth, James, ed. *The Old Testament Pseudepigrapha.* 2 vols. New York: Doubleday, 1998.
Chase, S. H. "The Date of the Apocalypse." *Journal of Theological Studies* 8 (1907): 431.
Chilton, B. D. "Festivals and Holy Days: Jewish." in *Dictionary of New Testament Background.* Edited by Craig A. Evans and Stanley E. Porter. Downers Grove, IL: Intervarsity Press, 2000.
Chilton, David. *The Days of Vengeance: An Exposition of the Book of Revelation.* Tyler, TX: Dominion Press, 1987.
Collins, Adela Yarbro. *The Apocalypse.* Wilmington, DE: Michael Glazier, 1979.
———. "The Apocalypse (Revelation)." in *The New Jerome Biblical Commentary.* Edited by Raymond Brown, J. Fitzmeyer, and R. Murphy. Englewood Cliffs, NJ: Prentice Hall, 1968.
Corsini, Eugenio. *The Apocalypse: The Perennial Revelation of*

Jesus Christ. Translated and edited by Francis J. Moloney. Wilmington, DE: Michael Glazier, 1983.

Danièlou, Jean. *The Bible and the Liturgy.* Notre Dame, IN: University of Notre Dame Press, 1956.

Day, J. "Origin of Armageddon: Revelation 6:16 as an Interpretation of Zechariah 12:11." in *Crossing the Boundaries: Essays in Biblical Interpretation in Honour of Michael D. Goulder.* Edited by Stanley Porter, et al. Leiden: Brill, 1994.

Dicharry, Warren. *Paul and John.* Collegeville, MN: Liturgical Press, 1992.

Dix, Gregory. *The Shape of the Liturgy.* London: Dacre Press, 1945.

Durwell, Francois-Xavier. "Eucharist and Parousia: The Fundamental Basis of the Interpretation of the Real Presence." *Lumen* 26 (1970): 273–315.

Ellis, E. Earle. "Pseudonymity and Canonicty of New Testament Documents." in *Worship, Theology and Ministry in the Early Church: Essays in Honour of Ralph P. Martin.* Edited by M. J. Wilkins and T. Paige. Sheffield: JSOT, 1992.

Escríva, Saint Josemaría. *The Way.* Manila: Sinag-Tala Publishers, 1982.

Fawcett, Thomas. *Hebrew Myth and Christian Gospel.* London: SCM Press, 1973.

Fekkes, J. *Isaiah and Prophetic Traditions in the Book of Revelation: Visionary Antecedents and Their Development.* Sheffield: Sheffield Press, 1994.

Ford, J. Massyngberde. *The Anchor Bible: Revelation.* New York: Doubleday, 1975.

Fredricksen, Paula. *Jesus of Nazareth: King of the Jews.* New York: Vintage Books, 1999.

Fueillet, Andrè. *The Apocalypse.* Translated by Thomas E. Crane. Staten Island, NY: Alba House, 1965.

———. *Jesus and His Mother: The Role of the Virgin Mary in Salvation History and the Place of Woman in the Church.* Translated by Leonard Maluf. Still River, MA: St. Bede's Publications, 1984.

Gentry, Kenneth. *Before Jerusalem Fell.* Atlanta, GA: American Vision, 1998

———. *The Beast of Revelation.* Tyler, TX: Institute for Christian Economics, 1994

Glasson, T. F. *The Revelation of John.* Cambridge: Cambridge University Press, 1965.

Gray, Tim. "Mary, the God-bearing Ark." in *Catholic for a Reason II.* Edited by Leon Suprenant. Steubenville, OH: Emmaus Road, 2000.

Gregg, Steve, ed. *Revelation: Four Views: A Parallel Commentary.* Nashville, TN: Thomas Nelson, 1997.

Guthrie, Donald. *New Testament Introduction.* Downers Grove, IL: Inter-Varsity Press, 1970.

Guthrie, Donald, et al, eds. *The New Bible Commentary.* 3rd ed. Revised. Carmel, NY: Guideposts, 1970.

Hahn, Scott. *A Father Who Keeps His Promises: God's Covenant Love in Scripture.* Ann Arbor, MI: Charis, 1998.

———. *First Comes Love.* New York: Doubleday, 2002.

———. *Hail, Holy Queen: The Mother of God in the Word of God.* New York: Doubleday, 2001.

———. *Kinship by Covenant: A Biblical Theological Study of Covenant Types and Texts in the Old and New Testaments.* Ann Arbor: University Microfilms, 1995.

———. *The Lamb's Supper.* New York: Doubleday, 1999.

———. "The Mystery of the Family of God." in *Catholic for a Reason.* Edited by Scott Hahn and Leon Suprenant. Steubenville, OH: Emmaus Road, 1998.

———. "Shaking Out the Psalter." *Scripture Matters,* 4:1 in *Envoy* (2001).

Hahn, Scott and Curtis Mitch. *Ignatius Study Bible: The Gospel of Luke.* San Francisco: Ignatius Press, 2001.

———. *Ignatius Catholic Study Bible: The Gospel of Matthew.* San Francisco: Ignatius Press, 2000.

Harrill, J. A. "Asia Minor." in *Dictionary of New Testament Background.* Edited by Craig Evans and Stanley Porter. Downers Grove, IL: Intervarsity Press, 2000.

Henderson, B. W. *The Five Roman Emperors.* Cambridge: Cambridge University Press, 1927.

Hendriksen, William. *More Than Conquerors: An Interpretation of the Book of Revelation.* Grand Rapids, MI: Baker Book House, 1962.

Hoehner, H. W. "Herodian Dynasty." *The Dictionary of New Testament Background.* Edited by Craig Evans and Stanley Porter. Downers Grove, IL: Intervarsity Press, 2000.

Horsely, G. H. R. and S. R. Llewelyn. *New Documents Illustrating Early Christianity,* vol. 1. North Ryde: Ancient History Documentary Research Centre, 1981.

Hort, F. J. *The Apocalypse of St. John: I–III.* London: MacMillan, 1908.

Jeremias, Joachim. *The Eucharistic Words of Jesus.* London: SCM Press, 1966.

Jurgens, William. *Faith of the Early Fathers,* vol. 1. Collegeville, MN: Liturgical Press, 1970.

Kittel, Gerhard. *Theological Dictionary of the New Testament.* 10 vols. Grand Rapids, MI: William B. Eerdmans, 1964.

Kline, Meredith. *Images of the Spirit.* Eugene, OR: Wipf and Stock Publishers, 1998.

Koenig, John. *The Feast of the World's Redemption: Eucharistic Origins and Christian Mission.* Harrisburg, PA: Trinity Press International, 2000.

Levenson, Jon D. *Sinai and Zion: An Entry into the Jewish Bible.* Minneapolis: Winston Press, 1985.

Liddel, H. G., et al. *A Greek-English Lexicon.* Oxford: Clarendon, 1968.

Manteau-Bonamy, H. M. *Immaculate Conception and the Holy Spirit: The Marian Teachings of Father Kolbe.* Kenosha, WI: Prow Books, 1977.

Martin, Ernest, *The Birth of Christ Recalculated.* Pasadena, CA: Foundation for Biblical Research, 1980.

McCarthy, Dennis J. *Treaty and Covenant.* Rome: Biblical Institute Press, 1981.

McCarthy, D. J. *Old Testament Covenant: A Survey of Current Opinions.* Richmond, VA: John Knox Press, 1972.

McDonald, L. M. "Ephesus." in *Dictionary of the Background of the New Testament.* Edited by Craig Evans and Stanley Porter. Downers Grove, IL: Intervarsity Press, 2000.

Merrill, Simon. *Jerry Falwell and the Jews.* New York: Jonathon David, 1984.

Metzger, Bruce. *Breaking the Code: Understanding the Book of Revelation.* Nashville, TN: Abingdon Press, 1993.

Meyer, Ben F. *Five Speeches That Changed the World.* Collegeville, MN: Liturgical Press, 1994.

Minear, Paul S. *I Saw a New Earth: An Introduction to the Visions of the Apocalypse.* Washington, DC: Corpus Press, 1968.

Mitchell, David C. *The Message of the Psalter: An Eschatological Programme in the Book of Psalms.* Sheffield: Sheffield Academic Press, 1997.

Moulton, J. H., and G. Milligan. *The Vocabulary of the Greek Testament Illustrated from the Papyri and Other Non-Literary Sources.* Grand Rapids, MI: William B. Eerdmans, 1930.

Mounce, Robert. *The Book of Revelation.* Grand Rapids, MI: William B. Eerdmans, 1998.

Neusner, J. *Aphrahat and Judaism: The Christian-Jewish Argument in Fourth-Century Iran.* Leiden, Netherlands: E. J. Brill, 1971.

Nogalski, James D. "From Psalm to Psalms to Psalter." *An Introduction to Wisdom Literature and the Psalms: Festschrift Marvin E. Tate.* Edited by Wayne Balard and W. Dennis Tucker, Jr. Macon, GA: Mercer University Press, 2000.

Orr, James, ed., *The International Standard Bible Encyclopedia.* Grand Rapids, MI: Eerdmans, 1956.

Oskar Skarsaune, "The Mission to the Jews—A Closed Chapter?" *The Mission of the Early Church to Jews and Gentiles.* Edited by J. Adna and H. Kvalbein. Tubingen: JCB Mohr, 2000.

Ozanne, C. G. "The Language of the Apocalypse." *Tyndale House Bulletin* 16 (1965): 3–9.

Price, S. R., *Rituals and Power: The Roman Imperial Cult in Asia Minor.* Cambridge: Cambridge University Press, 1984.

Ratzinger, Joseph Cardinal. *The Spirit of the Liturgy.* San Francisco: Ignatius Press, 2000.

———. *Eschatology: Death and Eternal Life.* Washington, DC: Catholic University Press, 1988.

Ray, Stephen K. *Upon This Rock: St. Peter and the Primacy of Rome in Scripture and the Early Church.* San Francisco: Ignatius Press, 1999.

Russell, J. Stuart. *The Parousia: The New Testament Doctrine of Our Lord's Second Coming.* Grand Rapids, MI: Baker Books, 1983.

Saward, John. "Love's Second Name." *The Canadian Catholic Review.* March (1990): 87–97.

Scheeben, Matthias. *The Mysteries of Christianity.* St. Louis, MO: B. Herder Book, 1946.

Shepherd, Massey H. *The Paschal Liturgy and the Apocalypse.* London: Lutterworth Press, 1960.

Smalley, S. S. "John's Revelation and John's Community." *Bulletin of the John Rylands University Library* 69 (1987): 549–71.

Spatafora, Andrea. *From the "Temple of God" to God as the Temple: A Biblical Study of the Temple in the Book of Revelation.* Rome: Editrice Pontificia Universita Gregoriana, 1997.

Stuart, Moses. *Commentary on the Apocalypse,* vol. 2. Andover, MA: Allen, Morrill, and Wardwell, 1845.

Swete, Henry Barclay. *The Apocalypse of St. John.* Eugene, OR: *Wipf and Stock,* 1998.

Terry, Milton. *Biblical Hermeneutics.* Grand Rapids, MI: Zondervan, 1974

Thomas, Robert L. *Revelation 1–7: An Exegetical Commentary.* Chicago: Moody Press, 1992.

———. *Revelation 8–22: An Exegetical Commentary.* Chicago: Moody Press, 1995.

Thompson, J. A. "Numbers." *The New Bible Commentary.* Edited by D. Guthrie and J. A. Motyer. Grand Rapids, MI: William B. Eerdmans, 1970.

Thompson, Leonard. *The Book of Revelation: Apocalypse and Empire.* New York: Oxford University Press, 1990.

Trench, Richard. *Commentary on the Epistles to the Seven Churches in Asia Minor.* Eugene, OR: Wipf and Stock Publishers, 1997.

Vilnay, Zev. *Legends of Jerusalem: The Sacred Land,* vol. 1. Philadelphia, PA: Jewish Publication Society of America, 1973.

Wagner, William, O.S.C. *The Mission of the Holy Angels in the Economy of Salvation.* Austria: Confraternity of the Guardian Angel, 1984.

Walton, John, et al., eds. *The IVP Bible Background Commentary: Old Testament.* Downers Grove, IL: Intervarsity Press, 2000.

Wright, N. T. *Jesus and the Victory of God.* Minneapolis, MN: Fortress Press, 1996.

———. *The Millennium Myth: Hope for a Postmodern World.* Louisville, KY: John Knox Press, 1999.

Bible Studies from Emmaus Road Publishing

▪ The Kingdom Series ▪

The Kingdom studies explore the teaching and mission of Jesus Christ as revealed in the New Testament and carried on by His Church.

> *"Accessible and compelling! Seldom does a biblical commentary combine clarity and theological insight as well as this one. Highly recommended."*
>
> **—Scott Hahn**

149 pages, $9.95 + s/h

160 pages, $9.95 + s/h

Tim Gray
Mission of the Messiah
On the Gospel of Luke
A compelling study of the Gospel of Luke presenting the messianic mission of Jesus as the fulfillment of Old Testament prophecy.

Edward Sri
Mystery of the Kingdom
On the Gospel of Matthew
Discover why our Lord places the kingdom of heaven at the center of His teaching. Sri's accessible style and provocative study questions make this book ideal for group or individual study.

Stephen Pimentel
Witnesses of the Messiah
On Acts of the Apostles 1–15
Stephen Pimentel brings Luke's vision of the early Church to life, showing how God's actions in salvation history find their fulfillment in the Body of Christ.

Stephen Pimentel
Envoy of the Messiah
On Acts of the Apostles 16–27
Stephen Pimentel completes the journey begun in *Witnesses of the Messiah.*

141 pages, $9.95 + s/h

86 pages $8.95 + s/h

(800) 398-5470
www.emmausroad.org